ENGLAND'S OTHER CATHEDRALS

ENGLAND'S OTHER CATHEDRALS

PAUL JEFFERY

For my wife Margy, with love

Also by Paul Jeffery

The Collegiate Churches of England and Wales (Robert Hale, 2004)

Paul Jeffery should not be confused with the author of the same name who lived from 1927 to 1997.

First published 2012

The History Press
The Mill, Brimscombe Port
Stroud, Gloucestershire, GL5 2QG
www.thehistorypress.co.uk

British Library Cataloguing in Publication Data.
A catalogue record for this book is available from the British Library.

ISBN 978 0 7524 5347 7

Typesetting and origination by The History Press
Printed in the EU by Gutenberg Press Limited
Manufacturing managed by Jellyfish Print Solutions Ltd

CONTENTS

	Preface	6
	Introduction	8
1.	Lost Pre-Conquest Sees	16
2.	Lost Cathedrals of the Later Middle Ages	48
3.	New Cathedrals Proposed under Henry VIII	66
4.	Lost Predecessor Cathedrals	95
5.	Post-Reformation Anglican Cathedrals	119
6.	Cathedrals of Other Denominations	153
7.	Churches with Cathedral Nicknames	197
8.	Other Churches of Cathedral Stature	212
	Glossary	245
	Select Bibliography	249
	Index	252

PREFACE

The great cathedrals of England are our finest and best-loved buildings.

They are the background to this book. Its genesis came in part from my appreciating the broader meaning and significance possessed by the word 'cathedral' and the concept that it represents. As well as being used for those great churches, the word has come to be applied figuratively to almost anything exceptionally large and fine: St Pancras Station in London is the 'Cathedral of the Railway Age'; the $8 billion Large Hadron Collider completed at Geneva in 2008–9 has been called a 'cathedral of science'; and the symphonies of Anton Bruckner are sometimes described as cathedrals in sound. Moreover, cathedrals have inspired many forms of secular art: Constable and Turner both produced famous paintings of Salisbury Cathedral. Novels, too, have been written on the theme of a medieval cathedral construction project. The Whipsnade Tree Cathedral, planted in the 1930s, has trees, hedges and shrubs around grassy avenues in the shape of a cathedral and its cloisters.

With this came the realisation that around or related to the great cathedrals as we know them today, there are, or were, many more similarly remarkable churches. Some have, or had, true cathedral status, others not. We might call them 'churches with cathedral connections'. They share many of the qualities of the great cathedrals: in varied ways they have much of the cathedrals' splendour, excitement and fascination. They reveal much interesting history, and are a large and enthralling subject. England's great cathedrals as generally considered may be numbered as twenty-six; discussed in this book are well over a hundred 'other cathedrals'.

One such group is of cathedrals that with the march of history have lost their cathedral status. Some ceased in the Anglo-Saxon era; others ended in the later medieval centuries. A few began but were never completed. Another fascinating category comprises the churches that were identified to become new cathedrals under Henry VIII, but in the event did not or, after a brief existence, ceased.

Many of the existing great cathedrals had predecessors. It is well known that the present St Paul's in London replaced a medieval cathedral; but even that had yet earlier ancestors, back into Anglo-Saxon times. So did many others.

The great cathedrals are all ancient (if we allow this of the seventeenth-century St Paul's); but many relatively modern cathedrals also exist. Unlike the ancient cathedrals, they belong to multiple denominations: Anglican, Roman Catholic, and others too. A few are famous, notably Coventry's, which came out of the destruction of war, and the two at Liverpool. But most are little known.

Two further groups have, instead of a historical connection to the true cathedrals, a different type of relationship. One is of churches that use the 'cathedral' name informally, while those of the other are defined by their cathedral-worthy size and splendour.

So addressed in this book are eight groups of 'other cathedrals'. They are a very diverse set. In part this diversity applies to their size and character, but all groups contain churches that are large and splendid, and most include some that are fully comparable with the great cathedrals. They are varied in date too, ranging from the seventh century to the twenty-first. Most widely varied of all is their condition today. Among them are many, from all periods, that stand gloriously complete, while others, though themselves destroyed, have been replaced by a splendid successor. Yet others are mutilated or are roofless ruins: some of these are still fine and beautiful but others are only sad relics. Then there are those that are now no more than sites – empty or covered by later structures – though even these may have been fascinatingly illuminated by archaeology. A few have nothing more than their history, with even where they once stood being unknown.

Visiting these churches and sites all round the country has been a rewarding task. Equally fascinating has been the research into their background and history. Many people have helped me. First among these is Dr Charles Knighton, to whom I offer my warmest thanks for his assistance concerning the Henry VIII cathedral schemes. Others to whom I am particularly grateful are Lucy Beckett, Anthony Cornwell, Professor J.J. Scarisbrick, Dr Joanna Story and Professor Barbara Yorke. I also thank Derek Adlam, Keith Barker, James Bettley, Professor Martin Biddle, Professor Christopher Brooke, Richard Buckley, Dr John Crook, Philip Dearcy, the Revd Michael Dolan, Toria Forsyth-Moser, Bill Jerman, the Very Revd Peter Judd, Phil McGahan, Cath Moloney, Canon Barry Naylor, Fr Vassilios Papavassiliou, Dr Arthur Percival, Konstanze Rahn, Professor Warwick Rodwell, Graham Scobie, Gill Shrimpton, Tessa Smart, Mrs Barbara Solomon, Mrs Margaret Sparks, Peter Stretton, Jane Sumpter, Tim Tatton-Brown, Sally Thompson and Maureen Tooze. I express my appreciation of the services offered, without charge, by those excellent institutions, our libraries, particularly the Martial Rose Library of the University of Winchester, the Hartley Library of Southampton University, the Minster Library at York and the Public Record Office in Kew. Last but not least, I thank my wife for her encouragement and help. Photographs were taken by me except where otherwise indicated.

INTRODUCTION

Cathedrals are supreme works of art and architecture. Arguably, England's ancient cathedrals are the country's greatest treasures. Architectural historian Alec Clifton-Taylor called them 'the master-works of English architecture'. Although created hundreds of years ago, their artistic achievement has hardly been matched by any creations of our age.

Cathedrals are also prodigies of engineering. Even by the standards of today's buildings they are very large. Some are notably tall: the spire of Salisbury Cathedral was the country's tallest building as recently as the 1960s. Cathedrals are also exceptional in the size of their continuous enclosed spaces. Although size is a technical rather than an artistic achievement, it is an essential component of their inspirational character, especially powerful when we consider the elementary technology available to their makers. We feel the cathedrals were made as the greatest and most beautiful things that their creators could conceive; they are often said to have been built to the glory of God, and in many ways this must be true.

Moreover, cathedrals are frequently of outstanding historical importance. Some go back to the early years of Christianity in England. They may be connected with major historical events and with figures prominent in the country's history. Within them are to be found tombs of many great men and women of the past.

A measure of the importance of the cathedrals in our national culture is the number of visitors they receive. York and Canterbury have the highest numbers, each with over 2 million annually. Altogether, the cathedrals receive perhaps 15 million a year. As attractions, they rank high among the most popular.

The central value of a cathedral – its reason for existence – is religious. Cathedrals are the most spectacular physical manifestation of Christianity. A cathedral has a specific function: it contains a 'cathedra', the throne of a bishop, and it is this that gives it its name. A bishop has ecclesiastical jurisdiction over an area or territory known as a diocese. A few cathedrals, such as Canterbury, have the additional dignity of being the seat of an archbishop, who presides over a larger area known as a province.

The religious aspect stands beside their art, their engineering and their history as an essential part of their importance. Some who visit them are Christians visiting for religious reasons; but most probably are not. Yet for a large proportion of visitors the fact that cathedrals are religious buildings is part of their value. They inspire awe, reverence and wonderment. All the great cathedrals and many of the 'other cathedrals' are the property of a Church, which is responsible for their care and maintenance and for which they are working buildings. They are not museums.

Although the word 'cathedral' is now generally used for a bishop's church at any stage of history, it would not have been recognised in Anglo-Saxon and Norman times. It appeared in the late thirteenth century, although only as an adjective: the term 'cathedral church' is still used today. Use as a noun began only in the sixteenth century. Even in the late medieval years and beyond, a building containing a bishop's throne was usually referred to simply as a church. It is only relatively recently that such a church has come almost always to be called a cathedral.

WHICH ARE THE GREAT CATHEDRALS?

What might be called the 'canon' of the English cathedrals has as its basis the cathedrals of the medieval centuries. From 1133 to 1539, there were nineteen cathedrals in England. Two then ceased. The remaining seventeen (of which St Paul's in London has since been completely rebuilt) are:

Canterbury
Carlisle
Chichester
Durham
Ely
Exeter
Hereford
Lichfield
Lincoln
London
Norwich
Rochester
Salisbury
Wells
Winchester
Worcester
York

Seven further cathedrals were created under Henry VIII in 1540–2 and 1546. All were previously monastic churches. Five are still cathedrals, and are always considered part of the canon. They are:

Bristol
Chester
Gloucester
Oxford
Peterborough

Between 1836 and 1927, twenty more dioceses were created. For most of these, an existing church was promoted to be the cathedral. This had usually been built as a parish church, but six had belonged to a medieval religious house: two monastic and four collegiate. Both monastic churches are large and of cathedral character, as are two of the collegiate churches. Many authorities[1] include these four among the great cathedrals. They might be called the 'extended canon'. They are:

Ripon
St Albans
Southwark
Southwell

This completes the canon. Addressed in this book are the cathedrals, interpreted widely, that are <u>not</u> part of the canon.

It has already been suggested that many of these 'other cathedrals' – some relatively modern, but others medieval – are or were of comparable size and splendour to the cathedrals of the canon. It might be asked whether any can match the very greatest of the cathedrals. Are any here the equal of (say) Canterbury, Durham, Lincoln, Wells or York? Of the cathedrals built in the past two centuries, probably not. Physically the greatest of these is Liverpool, which indeed is larger than any cathedral of the canon: but it would be rash to assert that it is their equal as a work of art, and it certainly cannot match them in historical value. When it comes to the medieval churches addressed here, however, the answer is probably yes. It can with good justification be claimed for Bury St Edmunds and Glastonbury, although both are now ruins. Also of this stature, though completely destroyed, is Old St Paul's in London. Happily, one further church of this quality still stands complete: this is Westminster Abbey.

Many of the churches that appear in this book belonged to medieval religious houses, going, in some cases, back to early Anglo-Saxon years. Aspects of the history of religious houses in medieval England form the background to much of what is discussed later.

After a short Christian period in late Roman times, which was subsequently snuffed out, it was not until the seventh century that Christianity came to most of England. The first religious houses soon appeared. Though often referred to as monasteries, these early religious houses were different from monasteries as they became later. They were Christian centres, usually involved in evangelisation and preaching, containing mixed communities. Typically some of their members, perhaps both men and women, lived lives of monastic character, while others did not. The communities of the early cathedrals were similar.

It was only from about the tenth century that monasteries took the form that continued through the Middle Ages, mostly having only either monks or nuns, who were enclosed and bound by the vows of poverty, obedience and chastity. Alongside them, but quite different, were colleges. These too were religious houses; they had nothing to do with education. Their communities were of priests. The priests received a pecuniary reward for their work, and they were not enclosed: they can be called canons or secular priests. The church of a college is known as a collegiate church.

After the Norman Conquest, a vast programme of construction and reconstruction began. At almost all the cathedrals, major monasteries and colleges, the church and other buildings were rebuilt, usually larger, in the Norman style. Many more monasteries were founded. Until this time, all monasteries were of the Benedictine order, but there now appeared a series of new orders. The Benedictine order nevertheless remained the largest and most important (as it still is today).

The Cluniac order was a reformed version of the Benedictine, originating at Cluny in Burgundy. Its first English houses were established about 1080. They never became numerous, but some were large. Cluniac architecture was characterised by its richness.

A very different type of reformed Benedictine rule was the Cistercian order, named from Cîteaux in Burgundy. Cistercians were also known as the white monks. Their first monastery in England was founded in 1128; they spread widely and became numerous. Their aim was to return to the simplicity of the early days of Benedictine monasticism. They often chose sites in wilderness areas, remote from towns and villages. Their ideals were expressed in their buildings, which though on a large scale had an austere purity of architecture. In time they relaxed their standards, and by the thirteenth century their architecture was scarcely distinguishable from that of any other order.

Another newcomer that appears frequently in these pages was the Augustinian order, also known as the black canons. This was an order not of monks, but of priests or canons who adopted a rule attributed to St Augustine of Hippo, and led a monastic life. Their first houses appeared in England at the end of the eleventh century. Some were existing colleges in which the secular canons adopted this rule, and so became regular canons. In this way, a college would change into an Augustinian monastery: a notable example is Waltham. Other houses were newly founded. They were usually situated in towns, and they became very numerous. Several of the cathedrals of the canon were once Augustinian monasteries.

A second order of regular canons was the Premonstratensian order, named from their mother-house at Prémontré in France. They were comparable to the Augustinians, but were relatively few.

Almost every monastery was either an abbey or a priory. An abbey, although belonging to an order, was a self-governing institution, whereas most priories were subject to a mother-house. As a generalisation, abbeys were larger and more important than priories. However, there were many exceptions. Cluniac houses were all priories. The Augustinians had a few abbeys, but most were priories; nevertheless, some of their priories had very great churches, several of which appear in this book. Among the Benedictine houses, all of the most important were abbeys. All Cistercian and Premonstratensian houses were abbeys. The head of an abbey was an abbot or abbess; that of a priory was a prior or prioress.

In 1530 there were still well over 600 monasteries in England, though this number was considerably lower than it had been two centuries earlier.[2] By this time, the esteem in which they were held by the lay population had declined, and it is clear that the life in some (though certainly not all) had become worldly and far from the ideals of their founders. So it was reasonable to consider that reform was needed; but it could not have been foreseen that monastic life was about to be extinguished altogether. The beginning of the end came with Henry VIII's break with Rome in the early 1530s, which enabled him to achieve his divorce from Catherine of Aragon. The Act of Supremacy of 1534 made him the supreme head of the Church in England. In 1535 came the *Valor Ecclesiasticus*, an assessment of the entire income of the Church. This was followed in March 1536[3] by an Act of Parliament whereby all smaller monasteries, that is those with fewer than twelve monks or nuns and an annual income of less than £200, were to be dissolved. This was presented as a reform, and probably was not intended to be the first stage of a greater dissolution. However, at least in part as a result of the northern rebellion known as the Pilgrimage of Grace, which began in autumn 1536 and was put down in 1537, the position rapidly changed. Beginning in January 1538, groups of commissioners travelled round the country visiting the greater monasteries and by pressure bringing about what was ostensibly their voluntary surrender. Legal support for this process was not obtained until 1539, when it was well advanced. In the few cases of resistance, the result was a charge of treason and the execution of the abbot and perhaps others. The dissolution was complete by March 1540.

Probably the principal motivation for the dissolution of the monasteries was the Crown's need for money. Money was required largely for military purposes: as in much of Henry's reign, war threatened at this period with both Scotland and France. The endowment properties of the dissolved monasteries were an immense source of wealth. In addition, their churches and buildings, bells, roofing lead and contents would bring in much further cash. Valuables connected with monuments and shrines, often including gold and silver, were another rich source.

However, at least from 1537 onwards, there was a second major motive that is important to our understanding of what happened to the dissolved monasteries. This was both political and ideological. With their historic loyalty to a supranational movement and ultimately to the pope, the monasteries in Henry's Church represented an *imperium in imperio*, an order within an order. Following the declaration of the royal supremacy, the members of the monasteries had been required to subscribe to it. Almost all did so; but this did not mean that their support was always wholehearted, and monasteries remained a potential source of opposition to the king. This was vividly illustrated by the Pilgrimage of Grace, in which some abbots and priors were involved, and moreover the rebels reinstated some suppressed houses. There was therefore reason not just for the dissolution of the monasteries but for their destruction such that they could not be restored.

Because of this, following the dissolution of a monastery, its church and perhaps its principal buildings were in some cases quickly demolished while still under Crown ownership. The purpose here was not primarily to recover the value of their materials; indeed, it involved considerable expense. Lewes Priory is a notable example, where detailed letters survive written by Giovanni Portinari, the leader of the team of twenty-five Italian engineers employed to do the job. He describes their progress as, over the course of a month in early 1538, they completely destroyed the huge church using gunpowder and undermining. To us, these letters may make painful reading; moreover it seems shocking that such a great building could so quickly be brought to naught. Yet, ironically, this and comparable reports elsewhere often represent our best documentary source of information about the lost building. Such radical demolition was only carried out in a few cases, no doubt because of its cost. However, the policy in the disposal of the monastic churches and buildings always leaned towards destruction rather than survival. Some monasteries were demolished in order to use their materials immediately for construction elsewhere. Much of the stone from Faversham Abbey went into the fortifications of Calais, while materials from Beaulieu and other south coast monasteries were used for the new coastal defence castles at Hurst and Calshot. In most cases, monastic sites were quickly sold or leased, but the demolition of specified buildings might be made a condition of the transaction. Sometimes when buildings were disposed of, the Crown retained ownership of the roofing lead, which the new owner was therefore required to remove immediately.

Once the church and the main buildings had been stripped of everything valuable, the remaining shell was often simply left, becoming a convenient quarry for the neighbourhood. Typically, the result of the dissolution of a monastery in a town was the complete disappearance of the church and cloister buildings, as at Abingdon and Colchester. Those far from centres of population, most famously Fountains, were more likely to survive as ruins. Quite often, even though the principal structures were soon destroyed, some ancillary buildings would remain in alternative uses.

In other cases, as at Vale Royal and Welbeck, a part of the monastery was converted into a mansion, with the parts not used being demolished. Often re-used in this way was the abbot's or prior's lodging, but sometimes part of the main cloister quadrangle or even the church itself would be made into a residence.

Certain circumstances could lead to different outcomes. In some monasteries, generally only Benedictine or Augustinian, the parish had the use of part of the church: typically the nave, or perhaps just an aisle. Accordingly, despite the destruction of the rest, this part would be preserved. It is this that led to the survival of the naves of Dunstable, Shrewsbury and others. In a few places, a local initiative might purchase much or all of the church for the use of the parish. This could be the philanthropic action of a wealthy individual or a fundraising effort among the townspeople. It was such moves that led to the largely complete survival of the churches of Dorchester, St Albans, Sherborne and Tewkesbury. However, these cases are the exceptions to an all too general story of destruction. The dissolution was an immense architectural and artistic disaster.

The position concerning colleges was different. Colleges had continued to grow in numbers through the Middle Ages, mainly because they were added to from about the thirteenth century onwards by new types, principally those with chantry or academic functions. Nevertheless, the colleges, too, were dissolved in a process begun under Henry VIII. This happened later than the dissolution of the monasteries, and was not completed until 1548 under Edward VI. The academic colleges were exempted. A major motivation for this dissolution was again the Crown's need for money. The process was mostly one of voluntary surrender, comparable to that of the greater monasteries. Remarkably, however, there was a major difference in the effect the process had. There was no political aspect here: the colleges had no overseas allegiance, and so posed no threat to the Crown. Nor was there an ideological problem: indeed, just a few colleges survived the dissolution or were re-founded afterwards, and these continued to function in the Church of England through subsequent centuries. There was therefore no pressure for the dissolved colleges to be physically destroyed. Moreover, most collegiate churches were used by a parish as well as by their college. As a consequence, they usually survived the dissolution of the college, with the parish taking the entire church into its own use with no question of having to purchase it. In striking contrast to the monastic churches, with the exception of Chester St John, all the collegiate churches that appear in this book still stand complete.

The English cathedrals in the Middle Ages were divided almost equally into two types. Some were served by secular canons, akin to those of a college: these were the secular cathedrals. The others were monastic, served by monks; the monastery was called a cathedral priory.

After the period of the Reformation, relatively little building activity concerning cathedrals or 'other cathedrals' took place through the following three centuries. The rebuilding of St Paul's Cathedral in London was the greatest exception. Matters changed dramatically in the nineteenth century, reflecting both a new vigour in the established Church, and the rapidly growing strength of other denominations. The Roman Catholic Church built churches, and then cathedrals. Rather later the Church of England, too, undertook much cathedral building. There was also widespread restoration of existing churches and cathedrals, often securing structures that had been long neglected, though sometimes involving regrettable destruction of ancient fabric. A feature for which we may feel gratitude was the re-creation of such lost limbs of major medieval churches as the naves of Bristol Cathedral and Hexham Priory and the eastern arm of Shrewsbury Abbey.

Most of what we know about churches or parts of churches that have been totally destroyed above ground often comes from archaeology. The achievements of modern archaeology are very impressive; it is remarkable how much detailed information can often be recovered by excavation even from sites where almost all foundation stonework has been robbed. The results are often shown in detailed phased plans, sometimes supplemented by evocative reconstruction drawings of the lost building. By contrast, as recently as the 1930s excavations were often crude. One problem sometimes affecting both recent and earlier archaeological investigations is the long delay, perhaps of decades, before full publication of the findings. Indeed, in some older cases, not only has publication never taken place, but the records have been lost; Leicester Abbey is an example. Modern archaeological examination of standing structures can also sometimes reveal important hitherto unknown information. On the other hand, the recent non-invasive techniques of resistivity survey and ground-penetrating radar are of more doubtful effectiveness.

Other information about lost buildings may come from old pictures or descriptions. While representations exist from the sixteenth century and earlier, it was not until the seventeenth century that the first reasonably reliable illustrations were produced. The cathedrals and major medieval churches have a large literature, in which the first substantial printed studies appeared in the seventeenth century.

The term 'great church' is sometimes used in this book, referring to the character as well as the size of major medieval churches. More will be said about this later.

Medieval churches were usually oriented close to east-west (though exceptions occur, usually caused by site constraints, notably at Rievaulx Abbey, which is almost south-north). In the cathedral construction of the nineteenth and twentieth centuries by the Church of England and the Roman Catholic Church, strict orientation was less usual. It was no longer seen as very important, and new sites in towns could rarely be chosen with freedom. Another interesting comparison concerns statuary. It is normal with medieval churches and cathedrals to see many internal and external image niches empty of statues. This is usually because of destruction by iconoclasts in the sixteenth and seventeenth centuries. Churches of the nineteenth and early twentieth centuries often appear similar. Here, however, the reason is usually financial stringency: provision of statuary was intended but often left until last, when funding or resolve then failed.

Dimensions of churches, especially lengths, are often mentioned in this book. Unless stated otherwise, lengths are measured externally. Sources often give lengths without specifying whether internal or external, yet the difference in a major church can be 30 feet or more, made up not only of the thickness of walls but of turrets and buttresses. Published plans and measurements are also sometimes disappointingly inaccurate. An effort has been made to ensure that figures quoted here are reliable; this has sometimes been assisted by the new internet availability of satellite views.

Architectural descriptions in this book use the well-known terms Early English, Decorated and Perpendicular for the styles and periods of medieval architecture, based on those devised in the early nineteenth century by Thomas Rickman. Geographical locations of places discussed are given as their traditional and, if different, their present ceremonial county. Unitary authorities and former metropolitan counties are not mentioned.

Some figures famous in Church history appear in this book. Among the Anglo-Saxons many, such as Augustine, Cedd, Chad, Dunstan, Felix and Wilfrid, were after their deaths elevated to sainthood. They are here, however, usually referred to in their lifetimes, and are not attributed as saints. This also applies to some who lived after the Norman Conquest, such as Wulfstan and Hugh.

Some towns or cities today have more than one cathedral or 'other cathedral'. In several places with two, for example Portsmouth or Shrewsbury, one is Anglican and one Roman Catholic. Birmingham has three, belonging to the Anglicans, Roman Catholics and Greek Orthodox. London has many. Particularly interesting is Leicester, which has a lost Anglo-Saxon cathedral, an unfulfilled Henry VIII cathedral, and finally an Anglican cathedral established in 1927. Chester is distinctive for having, as well as its existing cathedral created under Henry VIII, another church that served as cathedral in Norman times. Most remarkable, though, is Coventry. It has the one medieval English cathedral physically destroyed in the Reformation; the only cathedral wrecked beyond repair by Hitler's bombs; and what is arguably the finest and most moving cathedral created in the twentieth century.

Notes

1. Including Cannon (2007); Clifton-Taylor (1967); Cook (1957); Harvey (1974).
2. Knowles and Hadcock (1971), p.494.
3. Dates between 1 January and 25 March (Lady Day) before 1752 can be ambiguous, as years were often regarded as starting on the latter date. The modern form is intended in this book.

1

LOST
PRE-CONQUEST SEES

England had its first bishops at a very early stage: three were sent to the Council of Arles in 314, only two years after the recognition of Christianity in the Roman Empire under Emperor Constantine I. Of these bishops, Eborius came from York and Restitutus from London; the location represented by Adelphius is uncertain. Presumably each of these bishops was associated with a church building, so these were the first English cathedrals. However, nothing is known of them, and no evidence has been established for any continuity between these early bishops or cathedrals and their successors of three centuries later. A series of pagan invasions followed the final departure of Roman forces from Britain in 410, and whatever organised Christianity there had been was extinguished in most of the country.

Only in the far west, in Wales, Cornwall and Ireland, did Christianity survive, at least sufficiently to leave records or traces. From these areas, and especially from Ireland via Scotland, leaders in the sixth century began to spread Christianity back into England. Meanwhile, Augustine landed in Kent in 597, sent by Pope Gregory I on a mission to evangelise the Anglo-Saxons. Augustine established the diocese and cathedral of Canterbury, and became its first archbishop. The sees of Rochester and London both followed in 604. Progress, however, was erratic and slow through the first half-century and more. The new see of London ceased after little over a decade. York was established in 625 as the see for the great kingdom of Northumbria, but only lasted until 633, after which it was vacant for thirty years. Honorius, archbishop of Canterbury from perhaps 627 to 653, was the last survivor of those who came with Augustine on his mission. Under him, two further sees were founded: in East Anglia, Felix established Dommoc in about 631; for the West Saxons, Birinus began Dorchester (in what is now Oxfordshire) in 635. The latter see moved to Winchester about thirty years later. A diocese for Mercia was created in 655. Meanwhile, following the failure of the attempt at York, a monastery and see were established in 635 at Lindisfarne in the northern part of Northumbria by Aidan, who came from Iona in Scotland. This monastery was of the Irish Celtic form of Christianity. The Roman religious forms practised by those from the mission in the south and east differed from the Celtic practices of those who were evangelising the country in the north and west. The Synod of Whitby met in 664 with the aim of reconciling the two, and concluded in favour of the Roman practices, which had been argued for by Wilfrid, a prominent and sometimes controversial figure.

In 668, Pope Vitalian chose and consecrated the Syrian Theodore of Tarsus as the new archbishop of Canterbury. Theodore arrived in England in 669, at the age of 68. He found a confused and unsatisfactory situation. Few dioceses were firmly established, and several had no bishop. Despite his age, Theodore was a dynamic figure who in the course of an archiepiscopate lasting twenty-two years transformed the English Church. His changes included the creation of a series of new dioceses, several of the existing dioceses, such as Dommoc, Lichfield and York, being broken into smaller units. This was a time when England was still divided into multiple kingdoms, at times at war with each other. Some of the new dioceses related to the kingdoms or sub-kingdoms as they existed at the time. The diocese of Lindsey was created for the kingdom of that name. Those of Worcester and Hereford corresponded with the areas respectively of the Hwicce and Magonsaete, sub-kingdoms within Mercia. York was reduced to the area of Deira, the southern sub-kingdom of Northumbria.

Theodore died in 690. At the beginning of the eighth century two further dioceses were established, at Sherborne and Selsey. By this time, Christianity had been established through almost all of England, with a firm organisation and dioceses of manageable size. As they now existed the dioceses were Canterbury, Dommoc, Elmham, Hereford, Hexham, Leicester, Lichfield, Lindisfarne, Lindsey, London, Rochester, Selsey, Sherborne, Winchester, Worcester and York. This total of sixteen compares with the seventeen that existed between 1133 and 1540. Not all of these early sees continued into the latter period; but Canterbury, Hereford, Lichfield, London, Rochester, Winchester, Worcester and York did, and they still exist today.

This first maturity of the Church in England in the eighth century brought relative stability, and no more new dioceses were created in the next century and a half. A continuous sequence of bishops is recorded in almost all the dioceses. The only organisational changes concerned the division of England into provinces. When Pope Gregory told Augustine in 596 that he was sending him on his mission, he had advised that the country should be divided into two provinces, of London and York, each with twelve dioceses. In the event, Augustine established his initial archbishopric at Canterbury, and it was never transferred to London. Following the establishment of the see of York in 625, Pope Honorius I had agreed that it should be created as an archbishopric. However, its first bishop, Paulinus, had not yet been made archbishop when in 633 he fled from York. Even after York was re-established in the 660s, its becoming an archbishopric remained in abeyance until 735. In 787 Lichfield, too, became an archbishopric. This was due to King Offa of Mercia, and was an expression of the ascendency of Mercia among the English kingdoms at that time. This third province of England covered all of the Midlands, containing as well as the diocese of Lichfield those of Dommoc, Elmham, Hereford, Leicester, Lindsey and Worcester. After Offa's death, these dioceses were returned in 803 to the province of Canterbury, and Lichfield again became simply a bishopric.

This stability of the Church in the eighth century was not to last. The Anglo-Saxon history of England is in many ways divided into two parts by the pagan Viking or Danish raids and invasions that began in the late eighth century and were severe in their effects for more than a century. Much of the Christianity that had been established was weakened; monasteries and churches were pillaged or destroyed. Some of the sees, especially those in the east and in the Midlands, were at least temporarily extinguished. Those of Dommoc, Hexham, Leicester and Lindisfarne ceased and never resumed. Lindsey ceased, and though twice briefly re-established in the tenth century it ultimately disappeared. Elmham ceased for a time, but eventually recovered (possibly in a different location). By the mid-tenth century the worst was over, and the Church steadily regained its strength. This was also the period in which, under the leadership of Wessex, rapid progress was made towards the political unification of England.

During these years, some further sees were created. A revived see of Dorchester was established in replacement of Leicester. Chester-le-Street replaced Lindisfarne. However, even in the late tenth century Chester-le-Street came under threat of Viking raids and the see made its final move, to Durham. In Wessex in 909, the three new dioceses of Crediton, Ramsbury and Wells, each coinciding with a shire, were taken from the large diocese of Sherborne. Soon afterwards, Cornwall, in the far west, which had hitherto had a Celtic pattern of Christianity, became a further diocese within the English Church. In East Anglia, Hoxne appeared. Further changes followed in Wessex in the last years of the Anglo-Saxon era: Ramsbury ceased and its diocese was re-incorporated into that of Sherborne, and the sees of Devon and Cornwall were united and moved to Exeter.

The division of England into the two provinces of Canterbury and York, as it stood in 803, has not changed since. Pope Gregory had intended his proposed two provinces to be equal in size. However, between 1133 and 1541, the Province of York contained only the three dioceses of Carlisle, Durham and York, whereas the Province of Canterbury had fourteen. An attempt was made in the 1130s by the powerful bishop of Winchester, Henry of Blois, to divide the Province of Canterbury, with Winchester becoming an archdiocese; but this was unsuccessful. Pope Gregory had also planned that the two provinces should be equal in status, but in the event the creation of the province of York was the beginning of centuries of dispute over precedence. Only in the later medieval years was this finally settled, with the archbishops of Canterbury and York being known respectively as 'Primate of All England' and 'Primate of England', but with the former having pre-eminence.

The Norman Conquest introduced a policy that the seats of bishops should be in important towns: those in villages were to be moved. This brought several of the Anglo-Saxon sees to an end. Among these was Dorchester, which ceased for the second and final time.

So while many of the Anglo-Saxon sees have continued to this day, many others ended either during the Anglo-Saxon centuries or in the first years of the Norman era. This chapter looks at these lost Anglo-Saxon sees and their cathedrals. Most remain rewarding places to visit. Usually, the site continued in ecclesiastical use: although in the majority nothing now exists of the Anglo-Saxon cathedral itself, most have a representative today. As well as their historical significance, these successors are almost all interesting in themselves, and some are major buildings of very high aesthetic value. Dorchester, Hexham and Sherborne might be accounted the finest. Of the sixteen sites discussed in this chapter, about half continued as religious houses after their cathedral days, or were later re-founded as such. Five of these religious houses were monasteries, and at most of these the important later medieval church survives in use to this day. Only at Lindisfarne has the church of the monastery established in succession to the early cathedral-monastery fallen into ruin. Dorchester, Hexham, St Germans and Sherborne are all at least partly intact. Considering the generally very poor rate of survival of monastic churches through the period of the Reformation, this seems highly remarkable. Could local pride in past greatness have been a factor in their preservation? Such memories remained alive and important, as illustrated for example by the survival at Hexham of a late fifteenth-century reredos with impressive paintings of seven former bishops. The successor religious houses to the cathedrals of Chester-le-Street and Crediton were colleges, at both of which the large church built in later medieval times has survived intact. That of Crediton is particularly fine. In some other places, the successors were simply parish churches, as at Ramsbury, Selsey, and probably also Hoxne and Leicester.

In other cases, however, ecclesiastical use of the site either ceased altogether, or knowledge of it has been lost. Most of these former sees are problematical and have been a subject of much debate among historians of the last century and more. A notable case is Lindsey, still far from fully solved. The exact location of Leicester is not definitely known. In East Anglia, it is striking that every one of the possible Anglo-Saxon cathedral sites (Dommoc, Hoxne, North Elmham, Soham and South Elmham) remains a subject of uncertainty or controversy, at least to some degree.

Not all places mentioned in documentary sources as having been at some time the location of a bishop warrant treatment in this chapter. There can be several reasons for this. Some are uncertain: as with many aspects of Anglo-Saxon history, our understanding is often limited by inadequate documentary evidence. Other places were probably not actually sees. Certain places mentioned as having had a bishop were probably the location only of an episcopal residence. Some may have had a bishop's church, but only briefly: on the creation of a new diocese the see might temporarily be in one place for some months or years before moving to its permanent location. An example of this is the diocese of Crediton, where it may be that for the first few years the see was at Bishops Tawton. Such short-lived early locations for sees might be compared with the Anglican and Roman Catholic pro-cathedrals (provisional cathedrals) of the nineteenth and twentieth centuries (which appear in chapters five and six). However, that of Bradwell-on-Sea, which served only for about a decade and might be considered marginal, warrants full discussion because of its historical importance and also the remarkable survival of its very early church.

An interesting case not treated below is the beginning of the diocese of Mercia. The first bishop, Diuma, was appointed in or soon after 655. Only in 669 on the appointment of the fifth bishop, Chad, was the see fixed at Lichfield. It has been suggested that the bishops of the period 655–69 were peripatetic. It may be, however, that the see was at Repton (Derbyshire), the principal town of Mercia at this time. The bishops must often have been here. Repton's important early monastery may already have existed in these years; that its church served as cathedral is quite plausible, but positive evidence is lacking. Nevertheless, Repton is a place of especial interest. The present fine parish church is successor to the early monastic church, and retains some very remarkable Anglo-Saxon work. Each wall of the short, square chancel externally has two lesenes. Below it is a crypt: one descends a narrow stair to what is one of the most thrilling and atmospheric of places. Vaulted in three small bays each way, it has rough unmoulded round arches resting on four tapering columns decorated with a spiral moulding. Archaeological investigations in recent decades have concluded that the crypt is early eighth-century (so later than the time of the first bishops), with the vaulting and the chancel above added a century later.[1] On a new site immediately to the east, an Augustinian priory was founded in the mid-twelfth century; a few of its buildings remain as part of Repton School.

Soham (Cambridgeshire) also requires mention: some well-known sources state that an Anglo-Saxon cathedral was here. However, there is no adequate evidence for this. The first story relates to Felix's arrival in East Anglia about 631. He seems to have founded a monastery at Soham, which is said briefly to have served as the see before Felix went on to establish it at Dommoc. Even if true, this is not significant. Later, following the destruction of the monastery of Soham by the Danes in about 870, a new monastery seems to have been founded in about 900 by a layman called Lutting. This too is suggested as having been a cathedral. This was a time when the East Anglian sees of Elmham and Dommoc had both been extinguished; Soham lies further west where the troubles were perhaps less severe. So the proposal is plausible, but it lacks historical authority.

Anglo-Saxon cathedrals appear not only here but also in chapter four, which addresses those where the see has continued to the present day. Among those considered in this chapter, there are several in which some Anglo-Saxon structure still exists. Until the 1980s, the most important case was thought to be North Elmham, where it was believed that the ruins of a complete late Anglo-Saxon cathedral could be seen. However, this is now usually considered to be wrong. In compensation, though, at Sherborne, where it has long been known that a little above-ground Anglo-Saxon fabric remains in situ, it is now recognised that it is more extensive than was previously appreciated. It has also recently been shown that a little standing fabric still exists of the Anglo-Saxon cathedral of Dorchester. In a sense more spectacular, because most of it stands intact, is the very early church at Bradwell-on-Sea. But possibly the most exciting cathedral structures of early Anglo-Saxon date are to be seen below ground. These are the amazing crypts at Hexham and (as discussed in chapter four) Ripon.

By contrast, no above-ground Anglo-Saxon fabric remains at any of the still-existing cathedrals of Anglo-Saxon origin. On the other hand, as will be seen in chapter four, considerably more excavation of below-ground remains has taken place among them than of those considered in this chapter. There is nothing among the lost Anglo-Saxon sees comparable to what has been discovered particularly at Winchester, where the structural evolution of the cathedral through four Anglo-Saxon centuries has been elucidated in remarkable detail. However, significant archaeological investigations have taken place at Dorchester, North Elmham, Sherborne and South Elmham.

Although at least in their later years many Anglo-Saxon cathedrals were substantial structures of stone, it is thought probable that a few remained of timber throughout their lives. Considering that churches of stone were already being constructed in the seventh century (for example at Bradwell-on-Sea), this may seem surprising. However, masonry building often depended on the local availability of suitable materials (including sometimes stone or brick from nearby Roman remains). There must have been timber buildings of high status, both ecclesiastical and secular, but because none have survived we have little appreciation of their character.

Through the twentieth century, archaeologists gradually came to recognise a particular characteristic of some important early Anglo-Saxon religious sites. This is the development of a series of two or more church buildings, together perhaps with other features such as a tower, tomb or well, on an east-west axial alignment. Later, some of these structures might be linked to create a larger building. Among the lost pre-Conquest cathedrals such axially aligned churches may have existed at least at Lindisfarne. Further examples will appear later in this book, including several in chapter four.

As will be discussed in chapter two, two of the dioceses of the later Middle Ages had two cathedrals. This seems also to have happened in Anglo-Saxon times, though we know much less about it. The clearest case is Hoxne, which at least in its later years functioned as a joint see with Elmham. Another possible example occurred after the diocese of Ramsbury was reunited with that of Sherborne, when we hear of the bishop being referred to as of Sherborne and Ramsbury. This may not have meant much; around the time of the transfer of the diocese of Dorchester to Lincoln in 1072 we find the bishop using the title 'Bishop of Dorchester, Leicester and Lincoln'. A different situation is that of Lindsey in the ninth century, where it is suggested that the bishop was closely connected with not one but two churches, probably situated fairly close together.

The Church of England today has many suffragan bishoprics. The term 'suffragan' comes from Latin *suffragium*, meaning support or assistance: a suffragan bishop is an assistant to the bishop of a diocese. Although bishops in such a role had existed earlier, the term suffragan bishopric originated in an Act of 1534. Most of those existing today, however, are of relatively recent creation. All suffragan bishops hold the title 'Bishop of (place)'; however, they do not have a throne, and the church of that place is not a cathedral. The places chosen for suffragan bishoprics often have a church that has been important in Church history. Thus the titles of many lost Anglo-Saxon sees are now revived as those of suffragan bishoprics: there are suffragan bishops of Crediton, Dorchester, Dunwich, Ramsbury, St Germans and Sherborne. Another is of Repton.

Bradwell-on-Sea (Essex)   Plate 1

The diocese of London, established in 604, covered the Kingdom of Essex. However, this initial attempt at bringing Christianity to the East Saxons was not successful: Mellitus, the first bishop, was driven out in 616. A new attempt at the evangelisation of Essex was made in 653 when, at the request of King Sigiberht, Cedd was sent by sea from

Northumbria; in 654 he was consecrated bishop. Cedd was a Celtic missionary with a peripatetic style; he did not rule his diocese from London but set up his headquarters on the coast at the former Roman fort of Othona, at what is now Bradwell-on-Sea. Although now relatively remote, it was probably chosen for its excellent communications by water. Here, in or soon after 654, a church was built, with a monastery attached. As the bishop's church, this may be considered as being the cathedral of Essex at this time. Cedd also established churches at Tilbury and elsewhere. He attended the Synod of Whitby in 664, but soon afterwards died. In Essex an uncertain period followed, but in 675 with the arrival of Erkenwald as bishop the diocese was set on a secure basis, with its cathedral in London.

Bradwell is of unique interest because of the remarkable survival of Cedd's church, known as the chapel of St Peter-on-the-Wall. It is one of the earliest standing church buildings in England. After its initial importance it eventually declined to the status of chapel of ease to the medieval parish church 2 miles inland. In the seventeenth century it became a barn. In 1920 it was restored and re-consecrated. It stands in a lonely and wind-swept setting near the end of a peninsula, above salt marshes that are now a nature reserve. It is built across the west wall of the Roman fort, almost certainly on the foundations of the fort's west gate. Half of the fort has been lost to the sea, and the walls of the rest are no more than bumps in the grass. It is an evocative and much-visited place.

This is one of what are known as the Kentish group of seventh-century churches. What remains is the substantial and quite tall nave, a plain rectangle over 50 feet long. It is built of reused Roman materials, mostly small squared blocks of Kentish ragstone, well laid in regular courses; some tile is also used. An apsidal chancel, two small porticus near the east end, and a west porch later raised as a small tower, have all vanished. The marks or beginnings of their former attachment remain, and except for the porch their foundations are marked in the grass. There are also ragged remains of buttresses. Two large barn openings were filled in in the restoration. Each side has two windows, set quite high (one on the north is blocked); these and the west doorway have renewed wooden lintels but are otherwise basically original. Also authentic is the quite large, round-arched west window. The east wall shows the springing in tile of a former arcade opening to the chancel; opinions differ as to whether it was of three arches or of two. Considerable plaster remains on the upper parts of the interior. There are simple modern furnishings.

Chester-le-Street (Co. Durham)

When the bishop and community of Lindisfarne were finally forced to leave in 875 after a number of Viking raids, there followed a long period in which they travelled from place to place, taking with them their holiest treasures. These treasures included the body of St Cuthbert, relics of other saints and bishops and the famous Lindisfarne Gospels (now in the British Museum). For some time they stopped at Whithorn in Galloway (Scotland), and later they were at Crayke (Yorkshire). Eventually in 883 they settled at Chester-le-Street. The community had established good relations with the Danish king of Northumbria, Guthred, whose principal centre was York. Although it is uncertain whether Guthred was a Christian, they were given lands by him, and built a church in the centre of the former Roman fort. This was now the cathedral for a vast diocese extending from the Forth to the Tees, and to the east and west coasts. Nothing is known of the structure. In 995, when again threatened by Viking attacks, the community moved for the last time, again taking their treasures with them, and settled at Durham.

The former cathedral continued as a parish church. In 1286, Bishop Anthony Bek established a college of a dean and seven prebendaries in it. This was dissolved in 1547. The church is large-scale and fine, though it has no clerestory. Constructed of ashlared sandstone, it dates mainly from the thirteenth century. It has a spacious nave of five large bays, with aisles under low-pitched lean-to roofs. The arcades have double-chamfered arches on tall cylindrical pillars; an extension of the original construction is indicated by double responds three bays from the chancel arch. There is a west tower standing on quite slender pillars and arches, internally reading almost as a sixth bay of nave. Externally, it forms an impressive west end. The tower is broad, and turns octagonal immediately above roof level, with long bell-openings of cusped Y-tracery. Above are battlements, pinnacles, and a tall, plain stone spire reaching 158 feet, added about 1400. Most of the varied aisle windows are renewed. There are Early English north and south doorways; the elaborate south porch in gothick style is of 1742. Attached near the east end of the north aisle is the Lambton Pew, dating from 1829; this replaced a larger medieval attachment of which the mostly blocked arcade remains partly visible. Also Early English is the aisleless chancel. It has two authentic south windows, each a lancet-pair with a pierced spandrel. There are beautiful triple sedilia with deeply moulded trefoiled arches resting on quatrefoil shafts. With them goes the piscina. A large sacristy and organ chamber on the north side are partly late medieval in their structure.

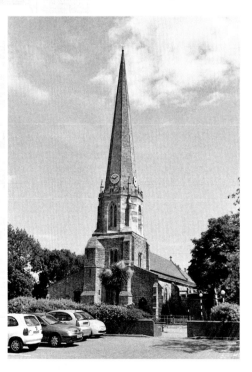

Chester-le-Street church

Unfortunately, plaster has been removed from the interior, the roofs are Victorian, and Victorian stained glass makes it dark. Most remarkable among the contents is the set of fourteen recumbent effigies in the north aisle. Known as the Lumley Warriors, they all commemorate Lumleys; five are genuinely medieval, but most are Elizabethan imitations of medieval work. They are identified by Elizabethan tablets on the wall behind them, and were assembled about 1594 by John, first Lord Lumley, in a striking expression of family pride.

In the late fourteenth century the north tower arch was blocked and the aisle here converted into a cell for an anchorite, unusually with rooms on two levels. It has a very narrow squint aligned on the high altar. After the Reformation it was enlarged and became an almshouse. It now forms an excellent small museum.

Crediton (Devon)   Plate 2

A monastery that became important was established here in 739. When the large diocese of Sherborne was divided, about 909, a diocese for Devon was created, with the monastery of Crediton becoming the bishop's seat. As a cathedral it was served by secular clergy. A new church was constructed. Some references to Bishops Tawton appear in the time of the first two bishops: it was perhaps used temporarily before the church at Crediton was ready. In about 1043, under Bishop Lyfing, the diocese absorbed that of St Germans, which covered Cornwall. Leofric, appointed

Crediton church: the chancel

in 1046, was the last bishop of Crediton: in 1050 he moved the see of the united diocese of Devon and Cornwall to Exeter.

Crediton continued as an important collegiate church. In the twelfth century it was reorganised by Bishop Warelwast to have twelve prebends. The church was rebuilt in this period. Its annual income was given in 1535 as £332; it was dissolved around 1547, but continued as a parish church. The church remains structurally complete and is splendid, with a length of about 225 feet. It is cruciform and regular, with aisles throughout, a central tower and an eastern Lady Chapel. Although what is seen now is mostly Perpendicular, Norman work remains in the crossing and transepts The crossing is relatively low, and has Norman pillars with shafts, scalloped capitals and arches of two unmoulded orders which, however, are pointed. Externally

the main part of the tower is Early English, with two lancet openings each side flanked by blank trefoiled lancets. Above are later battlements and large octagonal corner pinnacles. The transepts are lower than the nave and chancel; their details are mainly Perpendicular, but Norman flat buttresses remain on the north side. At the east end, the Lady Chapel projects two bays beyond the flanking chapels; it has Perpendicular windows but a few details show that it is basically Early English.

The nave and chancel are uniform Perpendicular structures, built in the early fifteenth century: the nave has six bays, the chancel five. They have battlemented parapets, low-pitched roofs and large traceried windows in the aisles and clerestory, all internally shafted. The arcades have two-centred arches on pillars of four shafts and four large waves, with capitals only to the shafts. The battlemented south porch, probably an early sixteenth-century addition, has a good stone vault and a room above. On the south side of the chancel is a large three-storeyed attachment, much altered but basically of the thirteenth century. The top storey, thought to have been the chapter-house, contains many interesting artefacts.

The timber roofs are now good Victorian replacements. It is a pity that plaster has been stripped from the walls. On the east wall of the nave, an assertive display of canopy work, statuary and mosaics is a memorial of 1911. There are large and elaborate triple sedilia; though badly mutilated, they retain much original colour. Also of interest are the Norman font and some mural memorials.

An enterprising initiative was undertaken in 2007, with support from the Heritage Lottery Fund, to find the Anglo-Saxon cathedral. The search used ground-penetrating radar, both inside and outside the church. It perhaps shows the limitations of the technique that no definite conclusions were reached, though it is thought likely that the cathedral was on the present site, and that it was largely of timber.

Dommoc (Suffolk)

In about 630, Sigeberht, already a Christian, became king of East Anglia. Around the same time Felix, a Burgundian, came to England and was sent by Archbishop Honorius to East Anglia. Under the king, Felix established a see of East Anglia at Dommoc (sometimes spelt Domnoc or Dumnoc) probably in 631, and was consecrated its first bishop. Felix became known as the 'Apostle of the East Angles', and revered as a saint. Several other bishops followed, but about 673–80 the diocese was divided with the creation of a second East Anglian see at Elmham. In the ninth century East Anglia suffered perhaps more than any other part of England from attacks by the Danes and Vikings. For almost a century after the death of the last king, Edmund, at the hands of the Danes about 869, there are very few records of any Christian life, and no names of bishops. The see of Dommoc never recovered: when bishops resumed in the mid-tenth century, East Anglia again became a single diocese, with its see now at Elmham.

Despite much academic discussion, there is still no firm agreement on the location of Dommoc. Bede (*c.*672–735) implies that it was a former Roman place, but gives no other indication of its position. Since at least the fifteenth century, Dunwich has usually been regarded as Dommoc. This remains the popular assumption and is perpetuated, for example, by the existence of a suffragan bishop of Dunwich. Its plausibility is strengthened by the fact that it became an important medieval town: it had a harbour, was made a borough in 1199, and from the late thirteenth century sent two members to parliament. But it suffered severely from coastal erosion, and lost its importance. The last of its many medieval churches fell into the sea early in the twentieth century, and the village that remains today occupies just the inland fringe of the site. Some authorities still favour it as the site of Dommoc, but others have argued for Felixstowe, 25 miles down the coast at the south-eastern tip of Suffolk. The place name immediately makes this identification plausible. Moreover, it was indeed a Roman place: the Roman fort of Walton Castle was lost to the sea in the eighteenth century. Discussion continues, however, and there are even suggestions of other locations in Suffolk.[2] Neither Dunwich nor Felixstowe offers much likelihood of normal archaeological investigation. All it seems safe to conclude is that Dommoc is probably under the sea.

Dorchester (Oxfordshire)   *Plates 3 and 4*

This place, today only a village, is remarkable for its early history and importance as a see; in addition, it has a church still standing that is of outstanding splendour and interest. It was a Roman town, of which some traces can still be seen. In 635 the Italian Birinus, having been sent by Pope Honorius I, baptised the hitherto pagan King Cynegils of Wessex. He was given Dorchester to be the see of Wessex, and became its first bishop. Later in the century, however, Dorchester was replaced by Winchester as the cathedral for Wessex, while a new see was also established at Leicester and Dorchester ceased to be the seat of a bishop. However, Dorchester is unique in having been a cathedral on two separate occasions, for quite different dioceses. The see of Leicester was destroyed in the Danish invasions of the ninth century, and probably in 869 Dorchester became the bishopric for a great Mercian diocese extending from the Thames to the Humber. Dorchester remained in this role until Remigius, who in 1067 became the first Norman bishop, removed the see to Lincoln in 1072–3.

Dorchester continued as a church of secular canons, but was refounded by Bishop Alexander of Lincoln as an Augustinian abbey in about 1140. In 1225, a shrine was erected for Birinus, and Dorchester became a place of pilgrimage. Probably as a consequence, there was much subsequent extension and rebuilding. Nevertheless, this was not a wealthy abbey: it was dissolved with the lesser monasteries in 1536, when its annual value was given as £190. Just the parochial nave would perhaps have been preserved, but heart-warmingly the whole was bought for £140 by a layman, Richard Beauforest, and bequeathed to the parish. Apart from the seventeenth-century rebuilding of the tower and the partial demolition of the north transept, the entire church survives intact. Nothing remains of the monastic buildings except the probable guest house west of the church, now used as a museum.

Surprisingly, the church breaks the almost universal convention for 'great churches' by having neither triforium nor clerestory. Its plan, too, is idiosyncratic, and not cruciform. It is, however, on a very large scale and of superb quality: it is 227 feet in length, and is especially remarkable for the exquisite and unusual Decorated work of the eastern limb. Its structure has long held many puzzles, but some have been excitingly resolved by studies during a major programme of conservation and improvement in 2001–7. It has developed from an aisleless, cruciform Norman church, of which the rather battered and patched north wall of the nave remains. Earlier suggestions that this wall might somehow relate to the pre-Conquest cathedral have now been confirmed: it includes at its east end an area of Anglo-Saxon masonry, surrounding the blocked site of an arch that probably opened to a north porticus. Moreover, the west wall of the partly-existing north transept may be in part the east wall of this porticus. Further Anglo-Saxon foundations perhaps underlie the west end of the nave. Though fascinating, these fragments are insufficient to give us a picture of the Anglo-Saxon cathedral as a whole.

Surprisingly, more of the existing structure may perhaps have cathedral origins. According to William of Malmesbury in the early twelfth century, Remigius began to build a new cathedral here. Only a few years were available before the move away beginning in 1072, but it is proposed that much of the lower part of the present nave walls dates from this period. It may then have stood unfinished; the rest of its Norman work was probably built after 1140 for the Augustinian abbey.

On the south side there is now an aisle as tall as and slightly wider than the nave, of fine Decorated work, with four large three-light south windows. A low, late-Perpendicular south porch is partly of timber. This aisle surprisingly ends to the east in a largely blank wall, originally the west wall of the former south transept. The aisle has an arcade of three great bays, with rich details: attached to one pillar is a remarkable large corbel, its carving apparently representing sleeping monks. East of the slim chancel arch, lofty unmoulded round arches opening towards the former transepts have been shown to be cut-back Norman work, which originally had openings at two levels. At the west end, the attractive, broad battlemented tower is of three stages, partly in a chequer of flint and stone. It is dated 1602, but incorporates a little of its fourteenth-century predecessor.

If the western half of the church is rather strange, the eastern half is glorious. It is predominantly Decorated. There is a relatively narrow north aisle, originally of about 1250 but remodelled later in that century; it has rich, shafted geometrical windows. The south side continues a broad aisle similar to that of the nave. To the east this has two large three-light windows, and curiously just its eastern section is vaulted, in two bays by two (the actual vault being a Victorian restoration). Both of the three-bay arcades of the chancel are splendid Decorated work, and are similar but not identical. The sanctuary, of one further bay, is the climax. It is exceptional in both its lavishness and its originality, and its three great windows are unique. On the south, the four-light window has unusual tracery, and below it are four extraordinary small windows of sinuous spherical triangle form, with much ballflower. They open internally through the lavish triple sedilia and the piscina recess. The great east window most unusually is filled from the base with reticulated tracery; it is supported by a central buttress for most of its height, a later medieval reinforcement. These windows both incorporate figure sculpture in their tracery. Most amazing is the north window, which is a Jesse tree, with wavy, irregular tracery forming the branches. It has even more sculpture, and retains much of its original glass. All three windows are encrusted with ballflower, and their sculpture is mostly unmutilated.

Fine architectural details are everywhere, inside and out. Conservative nineteenth-century restoration includes the timber roofs. The west parts are largely bare of furnishings. On a circular stone base, the font is Norman, of lead: a particularly good example. In the south choir aisle are four tomb-chests with fine recumbent effigies; one is probably a retrospective memorial to an Anglo-Saxon bishop. Also here is a 1964 re-creation of the destroyed shrine of St Birinus, incorporating a few original fragments.

In 2001, a cloister gallery of oak with a roof of Cotswold stone tiles was created against the north side, the site of the former south walk of the cloister. It contains a fine display of architectural fragments.

Hexham (Northumberland)

This began as a Benedictine monastery founded in about 674 by Wilfrid, then bishop of York. In 677 or 678 Wilfrid was removed from the bishopric, following which the diocese of York was divided, with the creation of a see at Hexham and the re-establishment of that of Lindisfarne. These two dioceses between them covered Bernicia (the northern half of Northumbria). Wilfrid himself was bishop of Hexham for a time before his death in 709. However, the see ceased in about 821 after the Viking raids began, and the monastery also came to an end. They were not rein-stated after the troubles. In about 1113 Hexham was re-founded as an Augustinian priory. This was dissolved in February 1537. Surprisingly, this followed a period of resistance by the canons, which, however, did not prejudice its physical survival: much of the priory church as it then stood became the parish church. It stands today, a splendid, large church of exceptional interest and beauty. Its present length is nearly 250 feet. It is often called 'abbey', but this is historically incorrect.

Perhaps the most amazing thing here is the survival of the original crypt, dating from about 675. It much resembles that of almost the same date at Ripon; this crypt, however, is built of Roman stones, many of which still show inscriptions or carving. Its principal chamber contains three niches for lamps; relics will have been displayed here. This cham-ber is flanked by passages, and there are two smaller chambers. A little further east, foundations of an apse, probably of the same period, have been found, but nothing else of the layout of Wilfrid's church is reliably known. Some Anglo-Saxon architectural fragments are set in niches in the north nave aisle.

The eastern limb was built about 1180–1250. It is a splendid example of Early English work, largely uniform, though with many variations of detail. The transepts are four bays long, and have east aisles; the aisled chancel has six bays. Arcade pillars have four major keeled shafts; capitals

Hexham Priory, from the north

are either moulded or have stiff-leaf, and (except in the south transept) the arches have multiple deep mouldings. The trifor-ium openings are subdivided into two and are richly treated, with deep mouldings, shafts and in some cases dog-tooth. The clerestory, externally set in blank arcad-ing, has single lancets, and opens internally with tripartite openings. There are excel-lent fifteenth-century low-pitched timber roofs. Single lancets also light the aisles, which have quadripartite vaults with deeply moulded ribs. However, the east wall and much of the east bay are of 1858: they are in a good Early English style, but replace a different previous east end which had five low fourteenth-century chapels.

Both transepts have further notable details. The north transept has exquisite trefoiled wall arcading and two tiers of three great north lancets. Unusually, the slype is formed within the south transept. A platform is above, reached by a splendid

broad flight of steps: the monastic night stair. The crossing tower is late thirteenth century, and is not tall or elaborate.

Whatever nave was standing then was probably destroyed by the Scots in 1296. It seems to have been rebuilt in the fifteenth century, but whether it was completed is unknown; it largely disappeared after the dissolution. There was a north aisle only. The nave was excellently re-created in 1907–8 by Temple Moore, in a quiet Decorated style. It incorporates the ancient south and west walls up to 8 or 10 feet high, with doorways west and south. The cloister stood on the south; much of the west range and a little of the east range still exist. A ruined Norman gatehouse stands to the north-east.

Many of the contents are of exceptional interest. These include many Roman pieces, probably from the nearby Roman town of Corbridge: most striking is a large first-century memorial to one Flavinus. A remarkable Anglo-Saxon relic is the Frith Stool, a finely preserved stone seat now in the centre of the chancel: it was probably the bishop's throne, and may even go back to Wilfrid's day. A carved cross is probably of the eighth century. Displayed in a glazed niche is a small Anglo-Saxon chalice. There are stalls with carved misericords. Fine timber sedilia date from the fifteenth century. Two chantry chapels are partly or entirely of timber. Most remarkable is a large ensemble in the chancel made up of three major fifteenth-century timber pieces all with well-preserved paintings. These are: a large lectern with associated screen; four panels depicting the Dance of Death; and a former reredos with seven large paintings of Anglo-Saxon bishops. One of the bishops is Wilfrid. Further fine painted panels, again including representations of former bishops, appear on the veranda-type timber pulpitum screen, which is of about 1500.

Hoxne (Suffolk)

The name is pronounced 'Hoxn'. This is another confusing case about which historical information is limited. A see certainly existed here, but it may have always been one of two held by a single bishop, and was perhaps subsidiary. In a field at Hoxne stands a Victorian memorial supposedly marking the site of the martyrdom of King (later Saint) Edmund, probably in 869, though most scholars now believe that this took place elsewhere. As we have seen, attacks by the Danes caused the extinction of organised Christian life in East Anglia from that period until the mid-tenth century. It seems that Church administration first returned to Suffolk under the oversight of the bishop of London (whose diocese included the adjacent Essex); the will of Bishop Theodred, made between 942 and 951, shows that he had a see at Hoxne as well as in London. In Norfolk, Elmham was re-established a little later, with a bishop consecrated in or soon before 955. At some time, certainly by 1040, Hoxne became a joint see with Elmham. It ceased when the see of Elmham was moved to Thetford in about 1072. Hoxne's entry in Domesday Book confirms that it had been a see for Suffolk.[3]

The cathedral was dedicated to St Aethelberht, and was served by secular priests. Confusion has arisen over its site, which this discussion attempts to resolve. Also in Hoxne at an early period was a chapel dedicated to St Edmund, in which it is said that the saint's body rested until its translation in 903 to Bury St Edmunds. In 1101 Bishop Herbert de Losinga gave to his new foundation of Norwich Cathedral the church of St Peter and the chapel of St Edmund, both at Hoxne. In about 1130, a small priory of Benedictine monks was established at Hoxne as a dependency of Norwich. This priory was dissolved in 1538, and virtually nothing remains of it; the site is now occupied by Abbey Farm, with a modest farmhouse partly of timber-framed Elizabethan work. It has often been assumed that this later religious house was successor to the earlier. However, of the two churches referred to in 1101, it was the chapel of St Edmund that was rebuilt and became the church of the priory. That this chapel was the former cathedral of St Aethelberht is implausible. We must therefore assume that the successor to the cathedral was rededicated to St Peter before 1101, and is now the parish church of St Peter and St Paul.

The church is quite large, but partly because of Victorian interference it is less attractive than some. Most impressive is its tall west tower, in four stages, with diagonal buttresses and a polygonal south-east stair turret. Its plinth has a panelled frieze, and its buttresses and stepped battlements have flushwork; the west doorway is enriched by fleurons and shields. The south side of the nave has tall two-light Perpendicular windows and a large Decorated porch. There is a north aisle with a fourteenth-century arcade in six small, low bays; in syncopation with it are five small Perpendicular clerestory windows, corresponding with the south side. The Perpendicular-style chancel has been rebuilt. Roofs over the nave and aisle are mainly old. The octagonal font is later fifteenth-century work, with seated figures round its stem and panels with the symbols of the evangelists alternating with shield-bearing angels. Its considerable damage was probably inflicted by William Dowsing, the Suffolk iconoclast of 1643–4. There is a large medieval iron-bound chest. Above the arcade are four large panels of medieval wall painting, bright but too decayed for enjoyment. Most of the aisle is given over to displays of local history and agricultural implements.

Leicester

A diocese for the Middle Angles was probably established in about 680. It is not certain that the see was immediately in Leicester, but by 737 it certainly was. It ended, however, around 869 in the Viking conquest of the region, and was moved to Dorchester. It was not until 1926–7 that Leicester became a see again. Despite extensive archaeology in the centre of the city in recent years, the location of the early cathedral is still not definitely known. It has long been thought, however, that its site was that now occupied either by the church of St Mary de Castro or by the church of St Nicholas. Present opinion fairly confidently favours the latter.[4]

Leicester was an important Roman city. Its most spectacular visible Roman site is that of the baths, with the massive Roman feature known as the Jewry Wall still upstanding on its east side. The church of St Nicholas stands immediately to the east, with its west wall parallel to and about 2 yards from the Jewry Wall. Excavation has shown foundations of early walls connecting the two, suggesting that the first church made use of the Roman structure (which may explain the surprising survival of the latter). Despite much nineteenth-century renewal, the church retains a strikingly venerable appearance; it is an especially evocative sight from the west, appearing above the Roman masonry. The church is partly of Anglo-Saxon work, though it seems unlikely that anything visible precedes the Viking period.

This is not a large church. Its roofs are low-pitched. Almost all windows are renewed and internally the walls are stripped of plaster. The nave, built of rubble and incorporating much Roman brick, is thought basically to date from about 900. Its only obvious Anglo-Saxon features are two double-splayed windows in the north wall, now internal; their arches are turned in brick. A large blocked round arch in the west wall may be either Anglo-Saxon or Norman. A central tower was inserted in the early Norman period. Externally this shows some courses of Roman brick laid in herringbone fashion, above which are two stages of Norman blank arcading, the upper intersecting and incorporating the two-light belfry openings. There is a straight parapet. Inside, it stands on excellent Norman arches of two unmoulded orders with simple

Leicester St Nicholas, with the Jewry Wall

imposts; one stage of blank arcading is above. The north arcade is of two similar Norman arches and is cut through the earlier wall below the ancient windows. On the south side, a single broad arch of brick replaced the arcade in 1829–30. Both sides have a modest Perpendicular clerestory. The south doorway is Norman, covered by an attractive partly late-medieval timber-framed porch.

The north transept and north nave aisle are Victorian replacements. The chancel, which droops south, has a blocked arch to a former north chapel. There is no south transept; the aisle continues uniformly to the east end. Its two-bay arcade to the chancel is of striking Early English work, the pillar and responds having freestanding shafts. There is an arched piscina and triple arched sedilia, much renewed. The good octagonal Perpendicular font came from elsewhere. An extraordinary Victorian pulpit with wrought-iron rail is wrapped round the south-west tower pillar.

Lindisfarne (Northumberland)

Lindisfarne, or Holy Island, off the Northumberland coast (to which it is connected by a tidal causeway), is one of the most exciting and beautiful of the places connected with the early history of Christianity in England. Following the unsuccessful first attempt by Paulinus as bishop of York to evangelise Northumbria in 625–33, the next king, Oswald, invited Aidan from Iona in 635. Aidan was Irish, and so the Christianity he brought was on the Celtic model. He established a monastery on Lindisfarne and became bishop of Northumbria. In the 660s York was re-established and for a time Lindisfarne was no longer a see; but it resumed with the division of the diocese of York in about 678, though with a smaller diocese.

Lindisfarne's most famous figure was Cuthbert, who arrived in the 670s and was reluctantly bishop from 685 until his death in 687. His body was enshrined in 698. Lindisfarne became an important artistic as well as religious centre; the *Lindisfarne Gospels* were probably created in the early eighth century. In 793 it suffered its first Viking raid. Further raids followed, but apart from a short period at Norham the community held out at Lindisfarne until 875. They then left, taking with them their treasures, including the body of St Cuthbert, and set out on the wanderings that ended at Chester-le-Street. Later, at Durham, the community still remembered its roots in Lindisfarne, and for a short period in 1069–70 came here to escape the Conqueror's 'harrying of the North', once more bringing the body of the saint with them. Soon after this, Durham became a monastic cathedral, and a Benedictine priory subject to it was established at Lindisfarne. The position close to the Scottish border later meant more troubles, and in the fourteenth century the monastic precinct and buildings, including the church, were fortified. The priory continued until the reign of Henry VIII when, with its annual income of £48, it was dissolved with the smaller monasteries in 1537.

A timber church was built under Aidan, and another constructed later is also reported as having been of timber; but little is known of the early monastery. However, today there are two churches here: the parish church of St Mary and, just east of it, the ruined priory church. That these churches have an approximately axial relationship suggests that both may be successors to churches of the early period here. Whether or not that is so, there is no reason to identify one in preference to the other as successor to the site of the ancient cathedral. In fact, though not immediately obvious, the earlier fabric is in St Mary's.

St Mary's church is an attractive, largely Early English and Decorated building. It is towerless, but its west gable carries a large eighteenth-century stone belfry. It has a long chancel and a nave of four bays with aisles under low-pitched lean-to roofs. There is no clerestory. The north arcade is mainly of about 1190, while its partner dates from about 1300. All windows in the chancel are lancets, including a fine group of three to the east. Also Early English is the chancel arch. Immediately above the arch, however, the top of a previous narrower, round arch is visible, and higher up is a rectangular opening, probably originally a doorway, with long-and-short through-stones. These features must be Anglo-Saxon. Their date is unknown, but it is perhaps unlikely that they go back to before 875. An active Christian community continued here in late Anglo-Saxon times, as shown by many of the interesting carved stones now in the excellent museum.

Lindisfarne: the chancel of the church of St Mary and the ruined priory church

The priory church was built in the early twelfth century. Though not very large, it was of remarkable richness and sophistication, and in design closely related to Durham Cathedral. It remains as a substantial ruin, but its sandstone ashlar is much eroded. There were rib vaults throughout. Part of the six-bay north arcade of the nave survives, and, like Durham, has pillars alternating between cylindrical and compound forms, with the former given giant zigzag, lozenge or fluting. Above, now all destroyed, there was a triforium and a tiny clerestory squeezed under the vault. The north aisle wall is complete and has mostly Norman windows, one surviving transverse arch, and the springers of the vault. Most of the west front survives (actually rebuilt in 1855–6 after collapse, though this is not apparent). It has a triforium of unmoulded round arches on columns with cushion capitals. Outside, the portal has four orders and is enriched with shafts and chevron. Big square flanking turrets simply contain stairs, but by their size, projection and nook-shafted corners give an impression of twin towers.

Much remains of the transepts. Both had an apsidal eastern chapel; that on the south side still has most of its half-dome vault. The north-west and south-east crossing pillars survive to full height, with intriguing fragments of high-level passages. Remarkably, the heavy, chevron-enriched diagonal rib of the crossing vault still stands; that it survived the loss of the tower seems almost miraculous! The original chancel was quite short, with an apse, but later in the twelfth century it was extended, with a straight east wall. This part now has the frames of several large (probably Perpendicular) windows.

There are also extensive remains of the monastic buildings on the south side. Surprisingly, they were not conventional in layout, and there may not even have been a chapter-house.

Lindsey (Lincolnshire)

Lindsey was an early Anglo-Saxon kingdom, covering much of what is now Lincolnshire; it was eventually incorporated into Mercia. The diocese was established in 678, but it was extinguished as a result of the Viking troubles in the ninth century. It became part of the diocese of Dorchester; on two occasions in the tenth century it was revived for a decade or two, but it did not continue.

A cathedral is recorded as having been built by Bishop Cyneberht, who died in 732; it had an apse and stood in a city. However, the site of this cathedral is a puzzle that is still a subject of debate today.[5] In 803 its location was described as *Syddensis civitas*, and another form of this name is *Sidnacester*: but we do not know where this was. Many locations have been suggested, principally Caistor, Horncastle, Lincoln, Louth and Stow (though it is questionable whether some would qualify as a city). It was for many years widely assumed that it was Stow, 9 miles north-west of Lincoln, and that the existing remarkably large and very interesting partly Anglo-Saxon church there was the cathedral. There is even a brass plate in the church stating this. However, this attribution is now discredited. Although the use of the name *Syddensis* is a puzzle, modern opinion favours the location as having been Lincoln.

The present cathedral of Lincoln was established in 1072–3, probably in a pre-existing minster. However, its dedication is to St Mary, whereas we know that the cathedral of Lindsey was dedicated to an apostle. It is therefore proposed that the early cathedral was elsewhere in Lincoln, perhaps what was later known as the church of St Peter at Pleas (which was destroyed in 1549). Another theory is that the see was peripatetic. It has also been argued that, at least in the early ninth century, the bishop was associated with two churches, one in Lincoln and the other not far distant: either also in Lincoln or at Stow or Bardney. A further possibility is that, despite the difference in dedications, Lincoln's existing cathedral of St Mary is indeed the direct successor of the ancient cathedral of Lindsey. Perhaps, as at other Anglo-Saxon sites, there was more than one axially related church building, one of which was dedicated to an apostle and another to St Mary. Such a pair of dedications occurs in other cases, such as at Wells. When succeeded by a single building, only one dedication might be taken forward. Probably only archaeology could settle this problem.

North Elmham (Norfolk)

About 673–80, the diocese of Dommoc was divided to create a second East Anglian see, almost certainly at Elmham, although the name is not reported until 803. A long sequence of bishops is recorded, but not for a period of almost a century from about 850, the worst period of attacks by heathen Vikings and Danes. Bishops also cease at this period for Dommoc, where they never resume. From the mid-tenth-century recovery, Elmham was the see for the whole of East Anglia, though at least by the mid-eleventh century it was shared with Hoxne. The cathedral was served by secular canons and continued until about 1072 when the first Norman bishop, Herfast, under the policy that sees should be in important towns, moved it to Thetford.

In North Elmham, well cared for by English Heritage, there is the ruin of a cruciform church of stone, 131 feet in external length. For many years this was regarded as the Anglo-Saxon cathedral: a unique survival. As late as the 1970s, following excavations in the 1950s and 1960s, respected authorities dated it to the late tenth century. Now, however, most scholars (though not all) believe that the Anglo-Saxon cathedral was always of timber and that the existing ruin was a large private chapel built in about 1100 by Herbert de Losinga, the first bishop of Norwich. The bishops continued to have a palace here long after the see had departed. Excavation evidence nevertheless supports the view that the present site was indeed that of the cathedral. The arguments that the ruin is of Norman date derive from its architectural features and also from a later documentary reference to the cathedral as having been a *sacellum ligneum*, a timber church.[6]

So modern tourist notices direct visitors to 'North Elmham Chapel' rather than 'North Elmham Cathedral'. It is still a fascinating site, and is that of a cathedral. A further interesting, if confusing, aspect of the ruin

North Elmham chapel, from the south-east

is that most surprisingly it was transformed by Bishop Despencer into a small castle or fortified manor house in about 1388. It is surrounded by large banks and ditches, constructed when it was fortified. Much of the structure now stands about 10 feet high. Most of the subdividing walls belong to the military conversion. Considered as a Norman chapel, it is both idiosyncratic and remarkably large. It has a long aisleless nave, transepts and a broad eastern apse, but no chancel. There is a west tower of the same width as the nave; two smaller towers stand against the west sides of the transepts. External re-entrant angles have an unusual feature called quadrant pilasters, which are one of the arguments for the Norman date. The west tower has a large semi-circular stair turret projecting at its south-east corner, which was given a partner to its east in about 1388 in order to provide a twin-towered entrance.

Dating of the church is not the only controversy here. Documentary references to the see simply call it Elmham. There is in Suffolk a place called South Elmham, which also possesses a remarkable ruin of an early church (see p.45). However, all authorities agree that, at least in the latter part of the Anglo-Saxon era, the see was at North Elmham.

Below the present bishop's throne in Norwich Cathedral, there is a battered stone throne that may well be Anglo-Saxon and may have previously been in Elmham Cathedral.

Ramsbury (Wiltshire)

On the subdivision of the diocese of Sherborne in about 909, Ramsbury became the see for Wiltshire, to which Berkshire was added some years later. Hereman, appointed bishop in 1045, also became bishop of Sherborne in 1058, and the diocese of Ramsbury returned whence it had come 150 years before. However, Hereman was referred to in 1075 as bishop of Sherborne and Ramsbury, so perhaps Ramsbury retained some cathedral role. If so, this ended shortly after with the removal of the see of Sherborne to Old Sarum. It has been a parish church ever since, set in what is now an attractive large village or small town.

A curious distinction here is that of the ten bishops who held the see, three subsequently became archbishop of Canterbury. Ramsbury is a rather shadowy cathedral. It was not monastic, but as Bishop Hereman complained of the lack of an adequate community of clerks in the 1050s it may not have had a properly organised college of canons either. Occasional references to bishops as of Sonning (Berkshire) or of Wilton (then the administrative centre of Wiltshire) have led to claims of cathedrals in those places, but probably they simply had episcopal residences. Nothing is known physically of Ramsbury cathedral, but it seems probable that the present church is on its site. It may always have been of timber.

Nevertheless, there are some impressive Anglo-Saxon relics here. They were discovered when part of the south aisle wall of the church

*Ramsbury church:
Anglo-Saxon
cross shaft*

was demolished during restoration in 1891. Now displayed on a platform in the north-west corner, they include three large fragments of a cross-shaft and two coped tomb-covers. They all have striking and well-preserved Anglo-Saxon carved interlace and other interesting motifs. They are usually dated late ninth century, in which case they predate the creation of the see. Might they, however, be a little later, and the tomb-covers perhaps have been for bishops?

The church is large by parish church standards, but unspectacular. Its earliest dateable parts are thirteenth century. Roofs throughout are low-pitched, and the battlemented aisles, probably widened in the fourteenth century to take in former transepts, are particularly broad. The massive but plain west tower is Decorated, in three stages, with over-large angle buttresses and a large south-east stair turret. There are four-bay arcades: their two east bays are Early English, with tall, acutely pointed arches, while the west bays go with the tower. The chancel arch (of horseshoe shape because of spreading) is also Early English. A modest clerestory carries a good late-medieval roof with moulded beams, bosses and some tracery. The chancel is long but relatively low. Though mostly Early English, its windows are all now Perpendicular. It has a depressed plaster barrel ceiling and is relatively unrestored. Puzzling remains on the north side may have been large Early English blank arcading. A very fine trefoiled piscina recess with Purbeck marble shafts is squeezed between a window and a great memorial of 1689. There is a good sixteenth-century canopied tomb-chest of Purbeck marble. Opening east from the north aisle is a large late-Perpendicular chapel: though now used merely for storage, this is the only spectacular architecture here. It has very large windows and rich image niches, and contains three battered medieval tomb-chests.

St Germans (Cornwall)

As with many Cornish churches, an early origin is suspected, perhaps in the time of its dedicatee St Germanus, who was bishop of Auxerre in Burgundy in the early fifth century; but nothing is known. After the integration of Cornwall into Wessex under King Athelstan, a bishop was established in about 936. There had been earlier bishops in Cornwall; we know of one in about 865. However, the Church in Cornwall had hitherto been Celtic, and it is not clear where the bishops were located or even whether they had a fixed see. It is also uncertain whether the first two bishops after 936 were at St Germans or Bodmin, but subsequent bishops were certainly at St Germans. When Bishop Burhwold died in about 1043, he was succeeded by Lyfing, who was already bishop of Crediton (and, curiously, also of Worcester). This was the end of the separate diocese of Cornwall until it was re-founded in 1876. Secular canons continued at St Germans until the late twelfth century, when Bishop Bartholomew replaced them with Augustinian canons and the church became a priory. In the sixteenth century it had an annual income of £227. Following its dissolution in 1539, the greater part of the church continued in parochial use.

The church is quite large and impressive, and of unusual character. Its great feature is the twin-towered west front, which apart from the upper parts of the towers is of unaltered late-Norman work. Standing forward under a gable is a portal of seven orders, richly ornamented with chevron. Above is a graduated trio of shafted windows. The towers have flat buttresses and small Norman windows. Higher up, the north tower turns octagonal: this is Early English, with simple lancets and battlements. The upper part of the south tower is Perpendicular. This west end is equally fine inside; however, whereas the exterior has only round arches, pointed arches are also employed here, mostly in two unmoulded orders. Capitals have volutes or scallops.

St Germans church

The body of the church is confusing, particularly inside. It is also over-restored and internally stripped of plaster, to ugly effect. Roofs are renewed. It was never cruciform, originally simply having an aisled nave and an aisleless chancel. The chancel, reportedly consecrated in 1265, was walled off from the rest after 1539 and left to decay; it seems that its partial collapse in 1592 may have also brought down other parts of the building. On the south side, instead of the former narrow aisle, there is now a great structure wider than the nave itself, in two parts. The eastern section is Decorated, with varied windows, a large and rich piscina recess under a gable with flanking pinnacles, and a mutilated ogee tomb-recess. West of this is a still wider Perpendicular section of four bays, with very large four-light windows, internally richly shafted. The entrance doorway at the south-west is a reset Norman piece, covered by a battlemented porch partly of the nineteenth century but partly Perpendicular, having a barrel vault with ornamental ribs.

Between this aisle and the nave is a six-bay arcade. The two west bays are late Norman, with massive cylindrical pillars, scalloped capitals, and pointed arches of two unmoulded orders. Above is exposed part of a former clerestory window, with bold zigzag. The remaining bays are puzzling: they have slimmer monolithic granite pillars and capitals of Norman appearance, but arches of Perpendicular type. It is suggested that they date from after the 1592 collapse. On the north side, unfortunately, the arcade and aisle were demolished in 1803, though a transept-like family pew then constructed has an arch largely of reused Norman work. This is now the organ chamber, battlemented, with vestries to its east. Most furnishings are Victorian. There are some substantial mural memorials and a great monument of 1722 by Rysbrack. The damaged font is perhaps of about 1200. Close to the church on the north side, in extensive parkland, stands the large mansion of Port Eliot, which incorporates a few fragments of the monastic buildings. Excavations east of the church in the 1920s exposed some foundations of the former chancel and perhaps also of the pre-Conquest cathedral.

Selsey (West Sussex)

The flat Selsey peninsula at the south-west corner of the long county of Sussex was perhaps effectively an island when in 680 or 681 the turbulent bishop Wilfrid arrived, having been exiled from his see of York. He established a monastery and worked to evangelise the population, but left about 686 on his restoration to York. Probably in 705 Wilfrid's foundation became the rather surprisingly situated cathedral for the new diocese of Sussex. Little is known of its history through the following three and a half centuries. There was probably disruption caused by Viking raids from about 860. In its later years it seems to have been served by canons. The last Anglo-Saxon bishop was ejected in 1070;

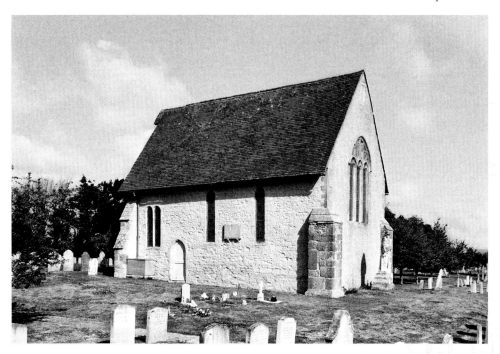

the new bishop, Stigand, in accordance with Norman policy, in 1075 removed the see to the important town of Chichester.[7]

    Selsey: the chapel of St Wilfrid

Ever since first stated by the Elizabethan historian William Camden, it has often been said that the site of the Anglo-Saxon cathedral now lies under the sea. This, however, is fiction. There is good evidence that after 1075 the former cathedral became the parish church, standing at what is now known as Church Norton. Nothing, however, is known about its structure. Also discredited is a former view that two important sculptured panels in Chichester Cathedral are Anglo-Saxon work and must have come from Selsey.

The church was rebuilt in Norman times and later, and continued as the parish church until 1865. It was then largely demolished, but its Norman arcades and other features were re-erected on a new site in the modern centre of population almost 2 miles away. The chancel, however, was left standing. It has an isolated and attractive setting, close to the waters of Pagham Harbour, a nature reserve. In 1917 it was rededicated as the chapel of St Wilfrid; it is now in the care of the Churches Conservation Trust. It is Early English, with two lancets each side and other windows now Perpendicular. Its west wall is the blocked former chancel arch. A string-course runs around the interior, and there are twin arched recesses for piscina and credence. A damaged Tudor tomb-chest serving as Easter Sepulchre retains some attractive carving.

Sherborne (Dorset) *Plates 5 and 6*

Sherborne is one of the most splendid and interesting of the former Anglo-Saxon cathedral sites. A religious house was founded here perhaps in the seventh century. In 705, the great diocese of Winchester, which had hitherto covered the whole of Wessex, was divided, with Sherborne becoming the cathedral for the western part. Aldhelm was its first bishop. It remained a cathedral for 370 years. In about 909, however, with the creation of the dioceses of Crediton, Ramsbury and Wells, its diocese was reduced to only Dorset. In 998 it was one of the cathedrals into which Benedictine monks were introduced. In 1058, the diocese of Ramsbury was re-incorporated, but in 1075 the see was moved to Old Sarum. Sherborne continued as an important Benedictine abbey, and in the sixteenth century had an annual income of £682. In the late fourteenth century, a church of All Hallows was built immediately to the west to replace the previous use by the parishioners of the abbey nave. Following the dissolution in 1539, almost the entire abbey church was purchased by the parish (for 100 marks plus £260 for the roofing lead and bells), and the church of All Hallows was demolished. The monastic buildings stood on the north side; considerable sections survive, forming part of Sherborne School.

Most of the church is now of fifteenth-century Perpendicular work. However, considerable Norman parts remain and also, though less obviously, significant Anglo-Saxon work from its cathedral period.[8] Indeed, remarkably, it is clear that the basis of the present plan is Anglo-Saxon, though the aisles were then narrower and the chancel probably much smaller than today. This explains why this important abbey church has a nave that, with only five bays, is short by Norman standards. The present total length is 245 feet. The Anglo-Saxon cathedral though shorter at the east end was longer at the west: it was of impressive size, probably only a little smaller than that at Winchester.

Though there can be no certainty, it is thought that much of the Anglo-Saxon work is of the early eleventh century. The only part readily visible is the present west wall, of rubble masonry. In its north part it has a small doorway showing long-and-short work and a lesene running round its west side. This is now externally covered by a small lobby. A larger blocked doorway in the south aisle is mainly Norman, but has one Anglo-Saxon jamb. Excavation has shown that outside the wall stood a large tower, with flanking western transepts or porticus. The long-and-short north-east quoin of the north porticus has been exposed to a height of 14 feet incorporated in the monastic west range. In front of the tower was a further short structure, perhaps an entrance vestibule. This area was later covered by the church of All Hallows; this has made the west front of the abbey appear particularly confused because still attached to it are the east responds of All Hallows. Above is a large Perpendicular window with multiple transoms; however, its lowest part is a nineteenth-century downward extension that involved the discovery but destruction of an Anglo-Saxon window that once opened from the lost tower to the nave.

The arcades of the nave are of beautifully panelled Perpendicular work. However, they are surprisingly irregular in layout; the great five-light clerestory windows above are laid out independently of them. It is thought that at least in part they encase Anglo-Saxon work. The west, north and south arches of the crossing are Norman. So apparently are the pillars, but their form is unusual and they are believed to be Anglo-Saxon work refaced and remodelled by the Normans. Lastly, much of the external north face of the north transept, covered by a surviving monastic building, is of Anglo-Saxon masonry to its full original height.

Apart from the south transept, almost the entire church is vaulted. Most of the vaults are fan vaults, and they are the abbey's greatest glory. In the three-bay chancel, the mid-fifteenth-century high vault is the earliest major fan vault anywhere. The whole structure of the chancel is fifteenth-century, with very large clerestory windows of six lights. Panelling continues below them down to the arcade arches. Outside, there are flying buttresses and the panelled parapets have pinnacles. The transepts, though given Perpendicular windows, are Norman in much of their structure. The upper part of the tower is Perpendicular, with twin two-light belfry openings.

There is a fine late-Norman south porch, vaulted, with much chevron. Regrettably, however, its former Perpendicular upper storey has been replaced by a Victorian neo-Norman one. Chapels are attached east of both transepts, west of the south transept, and north of the north chancel aisle. The east end has a Perpendicular ambulatory. Opening east from this is the Lady Chapel, of which the west bay is a noble Early English piece with a quadripartite vault, stiff-leaf capitals and rich marble shafting. Two further bays have been destroyed, but a new second bay was added in 1921–34, in a delicate and exquisite Perpendicular style, with a depressed lierne vault. The architect was W.D. Caröe. Part of a Perpendicular chapel also remains on the south side here, and has an engaging Elizabethan domestic facade from the period when this part of the church was used as a house.

The abbey contains many fine memorials, including several twelfth- or thirteenth-century effigies of abbots. There are also two large late sixteenth-century monuments. Though the stalls are mainly Victorian, they retain their medieval carved misericords.

South Elmham (Suffolk)

This is perhaps the most baffling of the many puzzling sites discussed in this chapter; moreover, whether it was actually the site of a see is very doubtful. As already seen, there was an East Anglian see described as

Elmham, but East Anglia contains two such places: North Elmham in Norfolk, and, 30 miles away, South Elmham in Suffolk. The connection between the two remains unknown. Moreover, both have a remarkable ruin of an early church. Scholars now generally agree that the see was in its later years at North Elmham. Some, however, believe that in the period before the Danish raids it was at South Elmham. It is suggested that when re-established in the mid-tenth century on a new site, this was called North Elmham to perpetuate the original name. However, positive evidence is lacking. The position of South Elmham in the same county as Dommoc would seem surprising for the second see of East Anglia, especially if Dommoc was indeed Dunwich, which is only 13 miles away.[9]

This is a most evocative and fascinating site to visit. South Elmham is a group of seven small villages. Standing among trees in the parish of South Elmham St Cross, far from any road, is the ruin known as the Old Minster. This is substantial, just over 100 feet long, but with no surviving architectural detail. Parts have their original wall surface of roughly coursed flints, but no quoins remain. It is of three cells. The square western cell is the most complete, standing uniformly about 15 feet high. A very ragged gap in the west wall probably represents a doorway with a window over. Gaps north and south were windows, apparently single-splayed and not very small. East of this, the next cell is longer but much more ruinous; a part at the north-east lies fallen. Little remains of the eastern cell, which is narrower; a limited excavation in 1963–4 showed that it was apsidal.

This excavation also discovered in the foundations a fragment of a probably tenth-century tombstone, implying that the structure must be of this period or later. The ruin has some resemblance to that at North Elmham and it has been suggested that it, too, was a private chapel built for Bishop Herbert de Losinga. South Elmham Hall was certainly a residence of the bishops of Norwich in later medieval times. However, there seem many reasons to doubt this theory. The differences between the two ruins appear as marked as their similarities. The ruin is half a mile distant and on the other side of a stream from the hall, hardly appropriate for a chapel belonging to it. Moreover, the word minster was used for the already disused building as early as the fourteenth century, and this would hardly apply to a private chapel. So what the ruin represents is a mystery; whether it was somehow connected with the former see of Elmham cannot be said. South Elmham remains a haunting place with much scope for speculation.

Notes

1. An authoritative treatment is given in Taylor, H.M., *St. Wystan's Church, Repton: A Guide and History* (1989, reprinted 2002: guidebook available in the church at the time of writing).

2. The arguments are summarised in Campbell (2000), pp.108–10. See also Wade-Martins (1980), pp.4–5.

3. Wade-Martins (1980), p.6; Campbell (2000), p.110.

4. At the time of writing, discussions are on the websites of University of Leicester Archaeological Services and the East Midlands Archaeological Research Framework Project in the School of Archaeology and Ancient History in the University of Leicester. See also Rodwell (2009), p.25.

5. Gem (1993); Leahy (2007), pp.119–21; Sawyer (1998) pp.78–81, 149–54, 247–52; Stocker (1993).

6. For the original reassessment of the date of the ruin, see Heywood (1982), pp.1–10. Opposing arguments are given in Batcock, N., 'The Parish Church in Norfolk in the eleventh and twelfth Centuries' in Blair (ed.)(1988), p.190, n.4. See also Campbell (2000), pp.110–12.

7. Hobbs (ed.) (1994) chapters one and three.

8. RCHME Dorset, vol. I (West) (1952), pp.xlvii–l and Addendum (1976), pp.li–lvii; Taylor and Taylor (1965, 1965 and 1978), pp.540–3, 991–2.

9. *Victoria County History (VCH) of England: Suffolk II* (1907), p.4, n.3; Wade-Martins (1980), pp.5–6; Campbell (2000), p.109.

2

LOST CATHEDRALS OF THE LATER MIDDLE AGES

This chapter looks at cathedrals established or proposed between the Norman Conquest and the Reformation that have not endured. In all cases, their end as cathedrals came during the later Middle Ages. No medieval cathedral has ceased since 1539, notwithstanding the severe damage inflicted on some, notably Carlisle and Lichfield, during the Civil War and Commonwealth, and despite the worst efforts of Hitler at Canterbury, Exeter, London and elsewhere. (St Paul's in London was destroyed as a result of the Great Fire of 1666, but was rebuilt.) Some of those in this chapter functioned as cathedrals for several centuries, some for only a few years. Others are proposals that were begun but ultimately came to nothing. The proposals of Henry VIII do not appear: they are the subject of chapter three.

After the Norman Conquest, Stigand, the last Anglo-Saxon arch-bishop of Canterbury, was in 1070 deposed and imprisoned. He was replaced by Lanfranc, who remained archbishop until his death in 1089. Lanfranc was an Italian by birth, but had in 1042 become a monk of Bec in Normandy, and rose to be a prominent churchman and an ally of Duke William, the future Conqueror. As head of the English Church, Lanfranc continued the process of replacing Anglo-Saxon holders of important positions with Normans. He instituted some reforms, but did not change the existing dioceses. Soon after his time, however, two new dioceses were created, with their cathedrals at Ely and Carlisle. Following the establishment of the latter in 1133, the diocesan map of England remained unaltered for the next 400 years.

We saw in chapter one that within the dioceses, however, there were changes. The removal early in the Norman period of some Anglo-Saxon sees to new locations was the result of Lanfranc's policy that bishops' sees should be in major towns. This policy was formalised in 1075 at a meeting known as the Council of London, though such moves had already been encouraged since a council in Windsor in 1072: the decisions to transfer from Dorchester to Lincoln and Elmham to Thetford were both made before 1075. Sensible the policy may have been, but viewed with hindsight it was hardly successful: in the majority of cases the changes had a destabilising effect. Six moves resulted from the policy, of which only two endured: those of Selsey to Chichester and Dorchester to Lincoln. In two others – of Sherborne to Old Sarum and Elmham to Thetford – the move turned out to be only interim: there later followed a further move to a more suitable location. In the cases of the moves from Lichfield to Chester and Wells to Bath, a complex chain of events was set in motion in which the final result, four and a half centuries later, was that both sees were back in their original locations.

At Chester, after about twenty years the see moved on to a third location, Coventry. Disputes and difficulties over the following century and a half, however, led eventually to the diocese having the title Coventry and Lichfield, with a cathedral in both places. Much later, in the dissolution of the monasteries under Henry VIII, despite the appeals of the bishop the monastic cathedral of Coventry came to an end. The diocese was rationalised to have only the one cathedral at Lichfield, the place that had previously had that role between 668 and 1075. A comparable process happened with the move of the see of Wells to Bath: this, too, eventually became a diocese with two cathedrals: the diocese of Bath and Wells. Bath was a monastic cathedral. This case has a further similarity to that of Coventry and Lichfield in that for a period a third church also became involved: this was Glastonbury. In 1539, this diocese too returned to having only the one cathedral at Wells, as it originally had from 909. So associated with each of these dioceses there are two former cathedrals. Thus as a consequence of Lanfranc's policy there were created six cathedrals that subsequently came to an end. Five of these are the most important buildings discussed in this chapter.

The reasons behind the creation of the dioceses with two cathedrals, and some other cases that appear in this chapter, have to do with the nature of the monastic cathedral.[1] (As we saw in chapter one, a diocese with two cathedrals was also possible in Anglo-Saxon times, but its character and reason for existence seem to have been quite different.) As already mentioned, in later medieval times about half of the cathedrals of England were served by monks. Monastic cathedrals were almost unique to this country (the only other parallel instances are Downpatrick in Ireland and Monreale in Sicily). St Dunstan, archbishop of Canterbury 960–88, was a great monastic reformer: the establishment in many of England's monasteries of a strict observance of the Benedictine rule was due to him. His support for monasticism also led to the four cathedrals of Canterbury, Sherborne, Winchester and Worcester being reorganised in this period to have a Benedictine monastic community. No further cathedrals then became monastic before the Norman Conquest. The first Norman bishop of Winchester wished, with the king's support, to replace his monks by secular canons. However, he was overruled by Lanfranc, who became a supporter of the monastic cathedral and encouraged his bishops to make further cathedrals monastic. This change was carried out at Durham and Rochester in the next few years. The new cathedral established in 1095 at Norwich was given a monastic community. The dioceses newly created at Carlisle and Ely took as their cathedrals churches that were already monastic, and so became monastic cathedrals. This also applied to the new cathedrals at Coventry and Bath. As a result, there were now ten monastic cathedrals. All were Benedictine except for Carlisle, which was Augustinian. Nine cathedrals remained secular.

However, cathedrals having a monastic chapter turned out to be a source of difficulty. In a cathedral served by a college of secular canons, the bishop was head of the community. He had control over it; he could use the positions in it to exercise his patronage; he was assisted by a supportive chapter of canons. In a cathedral served by a monastic community, although the bishop was titular abbot, the real head of the monastery was the prior. The prior had the power in the community, and he and his monks were largely independent of the bishop. This could lead to problems and divisions; the monks could thwart the bishop's wishes. Many subjects, such as aspects of finance or the patronage of dependent churches, offered potential for disputes. By the last quarter of the twelfth century hostility among the bishops towards monastic communities in their cathedrals had become widespread. This reached a climax during the time of Baldwin, archbishop of Canterbury 1185–90. At a meeting of bishops in Westminster in 1189, it was proposed that those who had a chapter of monks should together support the prosecution of a case in Rome to bring the monastic cathedrals to an end. In the event, however, Baldwin held back, and other than for a few years at Coventry no monastic cathedral was converted to a secular constitution. The pope was the ultimate resort in cases of contention, and popes were generally supportive of monastic communities.

An extraordinary dispute took place between Archbishop Baldwin and his monastic community at Canterbury. Baldwin made two successive attempts to create a secular establishment as an alternative to the cathedral, at Hackington and then at Lambeth; the latter was continued by his successor Hubert Walter. Both were strongly opposed by the monks, and passions ran high. The dispute became a widely discussed cause célèbre, but ultimately the monks held sway.

Following these episodes, the situation had to be accepted. Some difficulties continued; at Durham, strife between the bishop and the monks seems to have been fairly continual through the thirteenth century. It was in this period that in each of the two dioceses already discussed the compromise was finally agreed that there should be two cathedrals, one monastic, the other served by secular priests. Having a secular cathedral enabled the bishops of these dioceses to avoid most of the difficulties associated with the monastic cathedral.

As the Middle Ages wore on, bishops of monastic cathedrals generally came to work well enough with their monastic chapters. Not until 1538, at Norwich, was any monastic cathedral converted to a secular constitution; and this was in the context of the rapidly advancing dissolution of the monasteries. The rest followed soon after, under government direction. It is interesting that although monasteries have returned in the last two centuries or so, the monastic cathedral remains extinct. This is despite some interest having been shown in it by the revived Roman Catholic Church. For almost sixty years, a monastic pro-cathedral functioned at Belmont (see chapter six). Moreover, when setting up Westminster Cathedral at the end of the nineteenth century, Cardinal Vaughan for a time hoped to have a monastic community; but in the event the idea was abandoned.

Bath (Somerset) *Plates 7 and 8*

First founded perhaps in 675, this became an important Benedictine monastery. In 1088, John de Villula became bishop of Wells, and two years later moved the see to the monastery of Bath. Construction of a new cathedral was begun soon after; it was perhaps completed about 1170. Meanwhile, the canons of Wells continued to argue that theirs was the rightful location of the see. Bishop Robert, 1136-66, ruled that bishops should be elected by the chapters of Bath and Wells conjointly. In about 1176, even though the see was still at Bath, interest in Wells was such that construction began there of what became the present cathedral. Further difficulties arose in 1192 when Savaric became bishop without the involvement of the Wells chapter. He then made the see joint between Bath and Glastonbury, but this arrangement lasted only a few years before reverting to Bath. After another disputed election, and the involvement of Rome, in 1245 an enduring agreement was at last reached whereby the diocese had two sees and was entitled Bath and Wells. It continued as such until 1539. After the thirteenth century, however, Bath was clearly the lesser partner. By the fifteenth century it seems to have been in decline, and the church in bad condition.

Finally, Oliver King, who became bishop in 1496, determined on a complete rebuilding of the church. This began in about 1500 and by 1539 the new church was completely roofed and in use, although some work, such as vaulting the nave, remained to be carried out. In this year the monastery was dissolved and the church lost its cathedral status, with Wells becoming the sole cathedral of the diocese – although the diocesan title remains Bath and Wells to this day. The church was offered to the town for 500 marks, but the offer was declined. Accordingly, like so many, it was on the path to destruction: this wonderful church was very nearly lost. It was stripped of roofing lead, glass, iron and any other valuable materials, and the shell sold. The south transept and south aisle were partly demolished. However, in 1572, the then owner Edmund Colthurst gave it to the town to become its parish church. That this happened is remarkable: perhaps a part was played by local pride in what was a splendid and modern building, together with memories of its past cathedral greatness. The repair campaign was a major effort. Queen Elizabeth visited in 1574, and gave her support. The chancel was brought into use in 1576, a date that also appears prominently on a buttress of the south transept. Not until the early seventeenth century, however, did the nave and south transept again have roofs.

Bishop King's church is a unique and magnificent building.[2] A remarkable aspect, however, is that it represents a substantial reduction in size from its predecessor. A factor was presumably the decline in its importance as a cathedral; did it also show a recognition that the great days of medieval monasticism were over? It has a simple plan with an aisled chancel of three bays, a crossing with transepts, and an aisled nave of five bays, and occupies the site of just the nave of the Norman church. Its external length is about 230 feet, making it at that time easily the country's shortest cathedral. However, there are indications at the east end that an ambulatory and presumably an eastern chapel were intended, so had those been constructed it would have been longer and less simple. Moreover, it is of cathedral scale and quality: the vault is 78 feet from the pavement, the crossing tower is 162 feet high and the aisled width is that of its Norman predecessor. It was built under the direction of the great royal master masons Robert and William Vertue, and is one of the finest buildings of the last years of the Perpendicular style. Indeed, among them it is the only major cruciform church, most others being of different types: college chapels such as King's College Chapel, Cambridge, or parts of larger buildings, as Henry VII's chapel at Westminster Abbey. Although the only major gothic building in this predominantly Georgian city, it somehow harmonises with its surroundings. It bears the name Bath Abbey, although strictly that title has not been correct since 1090.

It is uniform and regular, of limestone ashlar inside and out. The crossing is narrower east-west than north-south; the transepts are correspondingly narrow, particularly noticeable in their very tall five-light end windows. The large tower is in two stages, with polygonal buttresses. Engagingly, on the turrets flanking the main window the west front has angels climbing up and down ladders, supposedly commemorating a dream of Bishop King. Inside, the arcades, which are not especially high, have four-centred arches and minimal capitals only on the shafts in the cardinal directions. There is no triforium but the five-light clerestory windows are particularly large and lofty, making the interior very light.

Crowning the composition are splendid fan vaults. The vaults of the aisles have pendants. In the chancel the vaults are medieval; those of the crossing and south transept are of the seventeenth century, while in the nave they are Victorian. The enormous east window has a square head, which clashes rather curiously with the vault.

The only later additions are a seventeenth-century vestry and a cloister-like addition of 1925–6 on the south side. In the chancel is the beautiful chantry chapel of Prior Bird, with another fan vault. Memorial tablets, mostly to the fashionable of Bath society in the eighteenth and early nineteenth centuries, almost completely cover the aisle walls. Before Victorian restorations, the interior was divided by a choir screen on which stood the organ.

Bury St Edmunds (Suffolk)

A scheme of the 1070s and 1080s to move the see of East Anglia to the abbey of Bury came to nothing (see Thetford, p.63). Bury St Edmunds Abbey is examined in chapter three.

Chester (St John)

The see for the ancient diocese of Mercia was long at Lichfield, then (as now) a relatively small place; so in accordance with Archbishop Lanfranc's policy, Bishop Peter in about 1075 moved it to the much more important town of Chester. It took as cathedral the church of St John the Baptist, just outside the walled area, which was perhaps of early origin and had in 1057 been re-founded as a college by Leofric, Earl of Mercia. However, the next bishop decided to move the see to Coventry instead; the move received papal approval in 1102, and Chester returned to its previous status as a collegiate church. Nevertheless, in what rather over a century later became the diocese of Coventry and Lichfield, Chester retained a special status almost as a third cathedral, and the title Bishop of Chester was still sometimes used. Nevertheless, when Henry VIII's new diocese of Chester was formed in 1541, it was the Benedictine Abbey of St Werburgh that became its cathedral. The college of St John was dissolved probably in 1547.

What is to be seen today is basically a cruciform Norman church, fully of 'great church' character, with arcade, triforium and clerestory. However, it has been sadly mutilated, and is truncated in all four directions. Also lost is its central tower. Following the dissolution, parts were abandoned. In 1574 the north-west tower collapsed, possibly causing the loss of the western part of the nave, and there was further damage in the Civil War. The existing structure was probably begun during its cathedral period.[3] However, it was not then completed, and there was perhaps a lengthy break before work resumed towards the end of the twelfth century.

The external appearance is now uninspiring: a massive, effectively tower-less hulk, predominantly of the restoration by R.C. Hussey, seeming early Victorian in character though mostly carried out in 1859–66. Ruins are prominent at both the west and east ends. The former is of the former north-west tower. Following its first collapse in 1574 it was rebuilt and as shown in old photographs was very tall; but it collapsed again in 1881. Its massive base remains. Just to its east stands the impressive north porch, which is Early English. It was destroyed in the 1881 collapse but rebuilt in replica, and its outer arch has the spectacular total of eight orders; the doorway inside has seven and though restored is genuine Early English work. As the western part of the nave has gone, the doorway now opens only to a Victorian passage leading to the church. Some way beyond the present east end, the ruined original east wall of the chancel still stands, with a Norman arch. This probably originally opened to an apse, which was later replaced by a chapel, perhaps longer. Much survives of the two flanking east chapels. That on the north side is of fine Perpendicular work, while that to the south is Decorated, a largely complete shell, retaining its vaulting springers and some good details.

Unlike the exterior, the interior is very authentic. Just one bay of the chancel survives from an original five, its arcade arches enriched with rolls; the bays were smaller than those of the nave. On the north side the Norman triforium remains, without subdivision; in place of the aisle here there now stands a minimal tower of 1886–7, with a frilly pyramidal top. The wall of the south chancel aisle has Norman blank arcading, and continues beyond the present east wall. The crossing remains complete,

Chester St John

with impressive Norman arches of three unmoulded orders, resting on
scalloped capitals. Both transepts now project no further than the aisles,
their side walls externally cut off to form crude buttresses. Of the nave,
four bays remain from an original seven, with thick cylindrical piers,
circular scalloped capitals, and arches again of three unmoulded orders.
The triforium and clerestory are entirely Early English, both having a
wall passage and four richly shafted openings to each bay. An oddity is
that in the clerestory only alternate arches open in a lancet window: this
can never give a symmetrical bay. Of the walls of the nave aisles, only
that on the north side is ancient; it has broad shafted lancets. Attached
south of the chancel is a large square late thirteenth-century building,
vaulted from a central column and with a ruined upper storey. This is
said to have been the chapter-house.

*Chester St John:
the ruined east
end, looking east*

What remains of the south transept and south chancel aisle now forms
the Lady Chapel, with a fine screen of 1660 and a reredos of 1692 having
scrolled pediments. A probably fourteenth-century painting of St John
the Baptist survives on a nave pillar. In the north-west corner of the
church are collected many interesting relics: pre-Conquest cross heads,
coffin lids with varied decoration, and some medieval memorial effigies.

This remarkable survival surely deserves to be better known! Though
much damaged and externally unimpressive, a good deal still stands of a
major early Norman church, almost certainly conceived as a cathedral.
When completed it was around 280 feet long, making it comparable
with several of the early Norman cathedrals (the first cathedral at Old
Sarum, for example, was considerably smaller). It gives us a rare view of
what a lesser Norman cathedral was like.

Coventry (St Mary) (Warwickshire, now West Midlands)

Long before the time of the cathedrals known here today – the great parish-church cathedral wrecked in 1940, and its modern successor – Coventry had a major medieval cathedral. The cathedral of St Mary was much larger than either of those others, but it was the only cathedral to be physically destroyed as a result of the dissolution of the monasteries.

A Benedictine abbey was founded perhaps in the 1020s by Earl Leofric and his wife, Lady Godiva, and dedicated in 1043. Some years after the see of Lichfield had in about 1075 been moved to Chester, Bishop Robert de Limesey decided to move it again, to Coventry Abbey. Papal approval was granted in 1102, and building of a Norman cathedral began soon after. However, a major new church was also being built at Lichfield, and bishops from Roger de Clinton (1129–48) onwards took much interest in it. They usually continued, however, to use the title Bishop of Coventry. Construction of Coventry Cathedral was badly disrupted in 1143 when it was seized and fortified by Robert Marmion during the civil war between King Stephen and the Empress Matilda. It may have again been interrupted by an episode beginning in 1189, at the height of the feeling against monastic cathedrals under Archbishop Baldwin. Led by Bishop Hugh Nonant, the monastic pre-cinct was broken into and the monks driven out; some of the bishop's own blood is said to have been spilt in the church. He then set up a secular chapter. Nevertheless, in 1197 the monks finally obtained a papal mandate and were restored. Disputes continued between the canons of Lichfield and the monks of Coventry over elections of bishops; these were finally resolved in 1248. By this time the bishops were usually styled as of Coventry and Lichfield, with a cathedral in both places. This arrangement continued unchanged for the next three centuries.

The monastery was dissolved in 1539. Bishop Lee pleaded for the cathedral's continuance; several attempts to save it were also made by the mayor and aldermen. Although nothing was conceded, it seems that doubt was felt: surprisingly, the cathedral remained with the Crown and apparently stood barred but essentially undamaged until 1545. Then, however, it was sold, and destruction began. Unlike the case of Bath, there was no late reprieve, and though in the seventeenth century much still stood, almost all had vanished by the later nineteenth century. Meanwhile, the title of the bishopric remained Coventry and Lichfield, but in the 1660s was adjusted to be Lichfield and Coventry. Coventry was dropped from the title in 1837 when the archdeaconry of Coventry was transferred to the diocese of Worcester.

The cathedral was probably completed with the twin-towered west front in the second quarter of the thirteenth century. Part of the north-west tower survived into the nineteenth century, and drawings show its enrichment with blank arcading. In 1856–7 it was partly demolished, but its base still stands, though it is largely refaced. Virtually nothing else was

Coventry St Mary: the interior of the west end

known until 1955, when during site preparation for the new cathedral, the bases were exposed of two polygonal chapels of what was probably a chevet of three at the east end. Parts of these remain visible adjacent to the west side of the present cathedral (though, alas, some further work then exposed was destroyed). In stages since then, much more of the cathedral has been revealed, especially in major archaeological investigations between 1999 and 2003 as part of the Phoenix Initiative, a Millennium project. Most of the nave and parts of the monastic buildings are exposed, and the area has been laid out as the Priory Gardens. Some wall bases stand a few feet high, and glass installations rest on the pillar bases of the nave. A bridge spans the west end, and a large visitor centre has been constructed.

With its length of over 430 feet, this cathedral was longer than that of Lichfield. It is often suggested that it had three spires, but there is no real evidence for this (though there was clearly a liking for tall spires in medieval Coventry – three still stand). Internally the Early English west end stands 6 feet and more high, with the fine west arcade responds showing multiple keeled shafts. The towers stood outside the aisles, making a facade about 140 feet across. A partly sixteenth-century building covers most of the west side here. Including the tower bay, the nave had nine bays; its east bays were Norman while the west part was Early English, the change taking place further west on the south side. From the absence of finds of vaulting material, it is thought that the high roof was of timber. Fragments of Perpendicular window tracery suggest modernisation of the fenestration. In the crossing and north transept, evidence was found that the Norman work was later remodelled or rebuilt. Pieces of ballflower ornament imply Decorated work, while a boss of about 1400 indicates vaulting. Most of the chancel remains unexcavated. The remains of the chevet are probably of the fifteenth century. This was a long chancel, and it seems that the original Norman structure was at least extended and probably remodelled or rebuilt.

The monastic buildings were terraced down the slope to the north; the chapter-house was rebuilt in the Decorated period, with a polygonal apse. Extensive standing remains have been exposed of the buildings immediately to its north, now called the Priory Undercrofts. Displayed in the visitor centre are many architectural fragments, mostly Decorated or Perpendicular. Computer animation reconstructions are shown of the cathedral nave and the chapter-house.

Glastonbury (Somerset) *Plate 9*

This outstandingly historic and once exceptionally magnificent Benedictine abbey is one of the most important places discussed in this book. Its period as a cathedral, however, forms only a minor and incidental part of its history. Its earliest associations are legends: that the first church was constructed in the first century by Joseph of Arimathea, and later that King Arthur and Queen Guinevere were buried here. Baseless these stories may be, but they were believed in the later medieval era, and Glastonbury remains one of England's most venerable religious sites. The earliest firm fact seems to be the founding or re-founding by King Ine of Wessex about 700. Foundations of Anglo-Saxon churches have been excavated. After the Norman Conquest, a completely new church was built. Through all these years, however, west of the monastic church there stood what was known as the *vetusta ecclesia* or old church, which was of wattle or timber and of unknown age but regarded as especially holy. This was another example of Anglo-Saxon buildings in axial relationship. In 1184, however, everything was destroyed in a great fire, including the *vetusta ecclesia*. All was subsequently rebuilt. With a sixteenth-century annual income given as £3,311, Glastonbury vied with Westminster as the country's wealthiest abbey. Its dissolution in 1539 involved a shocking episode: the elderly Abbot Whiting refused its surrender and he and two of his monks were convicted of treason and executed on Glastonbury Tor.

Glastonbury stood within the diocese of Somerset, which from 909 had its cathedral at Wells, just over 5 miles away. In the late eleventh century, as we have seen, the see moved to Bath, but instability then continued for almost a century and a half. Bishop Savaric, 1192-1205, whose seat was at Bath, with the assistance of Richard I had himself appointed abbot of Glastonbury. This was vigorously opposed by the monastic community, who saw it as a usurpation of their rights; the bishop's taking possession of the abbey is said to have involved physical violence. He then made his title Bishop of Bath and Glastonbury. The next bishop, Jocelyn (1206–42), was still using this title in 1215 when he was a witness to Magna Carta. Meanwhile, however, the monks of

Glastonbury had taken their case to the pope, and eventually in 1218 the dispute was resolved in their favour. Glastonbury's short period as a cathedral ended.

Demolition of the main cloister buildings since the dissolution has been almost complete. Fortunately this is not so for the church where, though destruction has been severe, enough remains to be enjoyed and to give a good appreciation of its size and character. All the surviving parts retain their ashlar facing in good condition, with exquisite architectural detail. It was on an enormous scale, and at about 580 feet in length was exceeded only by Old St Paul's in London. This exceptional length is in part due to its having long chapels appended at both ends. Unusually, the Lady Chapel is at the west: it was built in 1184–6 immediately after the fire, on the site of and as successor to the *vetusta ecclesia*. It is now the most complete part of the ruins. Originally freestanding, it is a four-bay rectangle in a rich, very late Norman style. Its details, including intersecting blank arcading inside and out, are exquisite but entirely round-arched, with sophisticated chevron. There are prominent square corner turrets and very richly carved north and south doorways.

The main church, also begun soon after the 1184 fire, by contrast exclusively employs pointed arches, yet also prominently uses chevron ornament, in a slim and elegant form. Capitals have stiff leaf. In what can still be seen, the style appears to have remained largely consistent throughout. It was cruciform, with a nave of nine bays, transepts with

Glastonbury Abbey, looking east from the Lady Chapel

east aisles and also east chapels, a chancel of five bays, an ambulatory of two bays, and a long eastern chapel. There were west towers. Of the eastern limb, most of the south aisle wall stands, and parts of the east and north walls. Windows are single, very large lancets. The ambulatory and the east bay of the chancel were a fourteenth-century extension. The eastern chapel, now seen only in excavated foundations, was added in the early sixteenth century to contain the remains of Anglo-Saxon kings including Edgar (943–75). Both east piers of the crossing stand high, with flanking arches to north and south, and give good knowledge of the full elevation of the church. The triforium had three trefoiled arches per bay and was framed by a giant order rising from the arcade. The clerestory had single lancets, with a wall passage and triple internal openings. Also surviving are the beginnings of the chancel elevation: they show busy Perpendicular panelling, from which a remodelling comparable to that at Gloucester is supposed. Much of the east side of the north transept stands, and one of its chapels is still almost perfect. Of the nave, a section of the south aisle wall is left. The cloister was on this side. Also surviving is the west portal, of rich mid-thirteenth-century work in four shafted orders. This opens into a three-bay galilee, constructed to link the Lady Chapel to the nave. Beneath the Lady Chapel and part of the galilee a large crypt was inserted much later, of which the vault of the east bay still stands.

The site was purchased by the Church of England in 1907. It is beautifully laid out, with foundations exposed or marked. A little masonry has been added to the ruins in a few places to ensure stability. A few outer buildings survive, notably a gatehouse and the great abbot's kitchen. There is a large and interesting museum, with many fine architectural fragments and some memorial effigies.

Hackington (Kent)

Baldwin of Exeter became archbishop of Canterbury at the beginning of 1185; he had been the choice of the king, Henry II, who had rejected several nominations by the monastic chapter of Canterbury. Relations between the monks and the archbishop were therefore immediately strained. In 1186–7, having obtained a papal bull, Baldwin began the foundation of a major college dedicated to SS Stephen and Thomas of Canterbury at Hackington, just outside Canterbury. This was to have at least forty canons, and the political aspect of Baldwin's move is illustrated by the inclusion among these of the king and the bishops. For them, vicars would be endowed to take part in the daily life of the college. It seems likely that Baldwin intended the chapter of this college to replace the Canterbury monastic chapter. He may also have planned to set up an archiepiscopal throne in the collegiate church, which would thereby be a cathedral, either in addition to or in replacement of the existing cathedral of Canterbury. However, the prior and monks of Canterbury were bitterly opposed to the scheme, seeing it as causing them to lose both power and income. Building began, and the first clergy moved in in 1188. The prior appealed to the pope, but at this time without response. The archbishop had the support of the king. At the height of the dispute, from January 1188 to August 1189 the archbishop had the monks blockaded within their own monastic buildings; the liturgy in the cathedral ceased. Henry II then died, and was replaced by Richard I. Both Baldwin and Richard were now anxious to depart on the Third Crusade. In November 1189 Richard visited Canterbury and a compromise was agreed whereby the college would be abandoned; however, Baldwin could instead establish a college at Lambeth (see below).

Whatever had been constructed at Hackington had been demolished by 1191. Nothing is known of it, and even its site is uncertain; it was not directly connected with the still-existing partly Norman parish church. It would be interesting to know whether it was on a cathedral scale.

Lambeth (London)

After the defeat of Archbishop Baldwin of Canterbury in his plan to establish a college at Hackington (see above), he determined instead on establishing one at Lambeth. It was to have the same dedication as its predecessor. Its objectives, presumably, were similar but with the added convenience of being situated on the Thames just opposite Westminster. Baldwin may have envisaged it as a future cathedral in the capital for the archbishops. Construction was probably begun in 1190, on a site acquired by an exchange of lands with the bishop of Rochester. Meanwhile Baldwin went to the Holy Land, where he died in November 1190. Building seems to have continued for a while, but in 1192 was stopped by edict of Pope Celestine III. A new archbishop, Hubert Walter, was appointed in 1193; in 1196 he decided to resume the project at Lambeth. However, it proved as contentious as before. The prior and monks were opposed, while King Richard supported the archbishop. After the king's death in 1199, Pope Innocent III ordered the dissolution and demolition of the college. Walter was given permission instead to establish a new foundation in a different location at Lambeth, to be of Premonstratensian canons.

The archbishop never acted on the new proposal. However, this may be the origin of Lambeth Palace, which was begun in the early thirteenth century and is to this day the London home of the archbishops of Canterbury. The abandoned college probably stood just north of the present palace grounds. Nothing is known, and the site has never been investigated. As at Hackington – perhaps even more so – one could wish to know the scale and nature of what was being built.

Old Sarum (Wiltshire)

The see of Sherborne, which as we saw had absorbed that of Ramsbury in 1058 under Bishop Hereman, was, under the same bishop, moved to the important town of Sarum from 1075 in accordance with the decree of the Council of London. This was a hill town: it had been an Iron Age hill fort, and is readily approached only from the east. Many of the houses must have stood outside the fortifications, presumably on the east side. A Norman castle had already been constructed on what had been made a high central mound. Around this is a large ring of land at a lower level, surrounded by a further earthwork. In this area, construction of a cathedral was quickly begun, with consecration in 1092. It was later enlarged. However, there were disadvantages to the situation on this hilltop site: it was cramped and exposed, water was difficult to obtain, and life in such close proximity to the military became increasingly uncomfortable, especially after 1139 when the Crown ceased to allow the bishops to be responsible for the castle. Eventually the decision was made to move both town and cathedral to a new site 2 miles away in the valley to the south. Once papal approval had been granted, construction began in 1220 of what was to become Salisbury Cathedral. In the early fourteenth century, stone from the old cathedral site was incorporated in the walls built round the Close in Salisbury. By the time of the antiquary John Leland's visit in 1535, the old town was almost deserted. He reported that just a chapel of Our Lady still stood: this may or may not have been a part of the former cathedral.

This is a beautiful and evocative place, still outside the built-up area of Salisbury. It is in the care of English Heritage. The earthworks are very impressive, and there are considerable masonry remains of the castle. Of the cathedral below, following excavations of 1909–15 the plan is laid out in the grass; some parts still show a little flint masonry or the lowest courses of ashlar facing. Interestingly, even in its short life it had quite a

Old Sarum Cathedral, looking west

complicated building history. As first built in the eleventh century, it was very modest, with a length of just under 200 feet: it had a short apsidal chancel with flanking chapels, a crossing with transepts each having one apsidal east chapel, and an aisled nave of seven bays. There was probably a central tower; a former view that the thickness of the transept walls implied that they were towers as at Exeter is now discredited. In the first half of the twelfth century, the cathedral was dramatically extended to the east. New three-bay transepts with both east and west aisles were constructed; these incorporated the west walls of their predecessors, so that the nave was extended by one bay to reach the new crossing. There followed an aisled chancel much longer than the original. It ended straight, with an ambulatory from which opened three chapels, all facing east, the central one longer; these were internally apsidal but externally square. Probably in the second half of the century the west end of the cathedral was extended, almost certainly with twin towers. A porch was also added to the south transept. The external length was now about 330 feet.

In the twelfth century a cloister was constructed, unusually on the north side of the chancel: it was at a lower level, and the north chancel aisle wall still stands about 8 feet up from it, though with no features. More remains, however, of a rectangular building attached to the north side of the north transept. This was formerly rib-vaulted in four bays by two; an arched recess remains intact in its south wall. The structure above this undercroft was either a large sacristy or the chapter-house. Some of the display panels around the site have attractive illustrations of what the cathedral may have looked like. Interesting architectural fragments from here are displayed in Salisbury Museum. Three twelfth-century memorials of bishops, originally at Old Sarum, are now in Salisbury Cathedral; two are tomb-slabs with effigies.

Thetford (Norfolk)

In about 1072, Herfast, the first Norman bishop of Elmham, began the transfer of his see to the much more important town of Thetford. There it took over an existing religious house of pre-Conquest origin known as St Mary the Greater, which was probably served by secular canons. However, Thetford was at this time in decline, and it seems that the move was seen as only temporary, with the intention of moving on to the great abbey of Bury St Edmunds. There was an obstacle to this: when, in 1020 under King Cnut, Bury had been made into a monastic house, it had been granted exemption from episcopal control. Herfast probably expected that he could overturn this, but Abbot Baldwin fought to retain the abbey's independence, and Herfast's plan was defeated in 1081 when the exemption was confirmed by both king and pope. Plans now changed to a move to Norwich, which took place in about 1095 under the third Norman bishop, Herbert de Losinga.

After this, St Mary the Greater may have continued to be served by secular canons. However, in 1103–4 Roger Bigod founded a Cluniac priory at Thetford. This initially occupied the former cathedral, but immediately began building in a different location, to which it moved in 1114. The cathedral site seems then to have been unused until 1335, when it was taken over to become a new Dominican friary founded by Henry, Duke of Lancaster. Dissolved in 1538, in 1566 its site became that of the grammar school, which it still is today. Significant fragments of the friary church remain, partly incorporated in the school buildings.

Nothing is known of the former cathedral or its buildings. The site was extensively investigated in 1998 by the television series *Time Team*. Much was learned about the friary, but though it was particularly hoped that remains of the cathedral would be found, nothing was identified. This is perhaps not surprising. Whereas by the early twelfth century Norman building or rebuilding of most cathedrals that were continuing had begun, it is unlikely that this happened at Thetford, as the bishops had no intention of remaining there. Thus the idea that Thetford once possessed a Norman cathedral is almost certainly unrealistic. This would explain why, on the foundation of the Cluniac priory, the former cathedral and its buildings were thought inadequate for anything more than temporary occupation. Taking into account that the cathedral of North Elmham is now considered likely to have always been of timber, it may be that this was true also of St Mary the Greater. By 1335 probably nothing remained on the site.

Westbury-on-Trym (Bristol)

Westbury is now part of the northern suburbs of Bristol. In medieval times the area lay near the southern extremity of the diocese of Worcester, which had a monastic cathedral. A religious house was established at Westbury in Anglo-Saxon times, and by the end of the twelfth century was collegiate, with a dean and five canons. From 1286, Bishop Giffard had plans to increase the number of canons at Westbury by nine and to establish it as a second cathedral in his diocese. His motives were perhaps twofold: to counterbalance his monastic chapter, and to strengthen his presence in the important town of Bristol. However, the scheme was opposed by the prior and monks of Worcester. Despite the quarrel being taken to the pope and the king it remained unresolved, but after Giffard's death in 1301 nothing more is heard of his plan. The idea was revived, however, by Bishop Carpenter in 1455; he reorganised and enlarged the college and began to use the title 'Bishop of Worcester and Westbury'. He also added to the church and built a large quadrangle of collegiate buildings, part of which still stands. But after his death in 1476, no more is heard of Westbury as a cathedral. When the new diocese of Bristol was formed in 1542, it took as its cathedral the abbey

of St Augustine near the centre of the city. The college of Westbury was dissolved in 1544.

As a collegiate church, this is an attractive and interesting example. However, its length is only about 135 feet, and no part of it even approaches cathedral stature. This seems surprising considering the ambitions of Giffard and Carpenter and the fact that the latter, at least, was responsible for some building work. Would a major rebuilding have followed had Westbury been properly established as a cathedral? The church has a west tower, a nave with broad aisles, and a chancel flanked by chapels. Windows are mostly Perpendicular, and large. Roofs are low pitched, with battlements throughout; the nave has a modest clerestory. The nave arcades, in three large bays, are thirteenth century. All else is Perpendicular, though not uniform. The tower is quite impressive, in four stages. The eastern limb, set noticeably crookedly with respect to the nave, has three bays and the unusual and attractive feature of a polygonal apse. Between the sanctuary and the south chapel there survives the cadaver effigy of Bishop Carpenter, now set in a Perpendicular-style tomb-chest with openwork sides, dating from 1853.

Notes

1. Knowles (1963), chapters VII, XVIII, XXXIII and XXXVI.
2. Davenport, P., 'The Cathedral Priory Church at Bath' in Tatton-Brown and Munby (eds.) (1996).
3. This view on the date of the Norman work differs from that stated in this author's book on collegiate churches. Architectural and archaeological authorities vary: for example, Carrington (1994), p.72; Gem, R., 'Romanesque Architecture in Chester c.1075 to 1117' in Thacker (ed.) (2000). However, a historical view argues for a date during its cathedral period (Professor Christopher Brooke, pers. comm.).

3

NEW CATHEDRALS PROPOSED UNDER HENRY VIII

As we have seen, no changes took place in the number of dioceses through the last four centuries of the Middle Ages.[1] However, this diocesan organisation was far from perfect. The dioceses were very unequal in size: although a few were quite small, the largest, particularly those of Coventry and Lichfield, Lincoln and York, were enormous. As we saw earlier, the diocesan structure was still in part derived from the political map of Anglo-Saxon England. Moreover, several counties that had been separate dioceses through part of the Anglo-Saxon period but had then been merged into larger dioceses remained so, as in Devon and Cornwall, Wiltshire and Dorset, and Norfolk and Suffolk. The dioceses were generally much larger than those of most other Western European countries. Some cathedrals were also located far from centrally in their dioceses; Lincoln, for example was near the northern end of its territory. Especially considering the difficulties of transport in medieval times, it must often have been difficult to operate an efficient diocesan system.

We first hear of a plan to address these inadequacies being put forward by Thomas Wolsey, Henry VIII's lord chancellor. In 1524 Wolsey had already, with papal approval, dissolved over twenty smaller monasteries in order to use their endowments for the support of his two great new academic colleges at Ipswich and Oxford. In November 1528 and May 1529, he obtained two successive bulls from Pope Clement VII that would have allowed him to dissolve some large monastic houses in order to create thirteen new cathedrals. In the event, however, nothing had been implemented when Wolsey fell from power in 1529.

At the time of Wolsey's proposal, the pope was firmly supreme over the English Church, and any idea of the complete abolition of the monasteries would have seemed inconceivable. Circumstances were very different when the idea surfaced again in 1539. The king had broken with Rome and was supreme head of the Church, and the proposal was now under his leadership. The lesser monasteries had been dissolved, and the suppression of the greater monasteries was in progress. It is clear that the motivation for reviving the plan was at least in part political. Henry and his vicar-general, Thomas Cromwell, needed parliamentary support for the final Act of Dissolution of the monasteries, which (though partly retrospective since the process had been going on since the end of 1537) was the subject of considerable discussion. It would help to achieve that support if it could be shown that the dissolution would lead to gains for society and for religion. The use of some of the dissolved monasteries to reform the diocesan system would meet that need. Another indication that measures were needed to increase support for the government's religious policy was perhaps the failed Pilgrimage of Grace rebellion of 1536–7. Accordingly, in May 1539 in the House of Lords Cromwell presented a bill to authorise the king to create and endow any number of new bishoprics with their cathedrals, and to produce statutes for them. A preamble was provided to this bill, which is in the hand of the king himself. With the spelling and punctuation modernised, it reads as follows:[2]

> For as much as it is not unknown the slothful and ungodly life which has been used among all those sort which have borne the name of religious folk, and to the intent that henceforth many of them might be turned to better use as hereafter shall follow whereby: God's word might the better be set forth; children brought up in learning; clerks nourished in the universities; old servants decayed to have living; almshouses [provided] for poor folk to be sustained in; readers of Greek, Hebrew and Latin to have good stipends; daily alms to be administered; mending of highways; exhibition for ministers of the Church. It is thought therefore to the king's highness most expedient and necessary that more bishoprics, collegiate and cathedral churches shall be established instead of these aforesaid religious houses, within the foundation whereof these other titles before rehearsed shall be established.

These objectives could hardly be disagreed with. Ultimately, however, they were realised only to a limited extent. The king's initial proposal envisaged thirteen new dioceses. In the event, by the end of 1542 six new dioceses were created. Their cathedrals were at Bristol, Chester, Gloucester, Osney (for Oxford), Peterborough and Westminster. Only five of these dioceses lasted, and neither Osney nor Westminster survived more than a decade as a cathedral. The end result was that to the canon of the English cathedrals were added four of those listed here together with one later substitute not anticipated in 1539–42.

    This chapter focuses on the cathedral proposals that were not implemented, or were abandoned after a brief existence.

There survive many documents from the government discussions on this plan. At least eight identify a set of proposed new cathedrals, which though all having many cathedrals in common also have interesting differences. None of the documents are dated, so other than by inference we do not know their order, but all probably date from the second half of 1539 or sometime in 1540. Their authors include bishops Gardiner of Winchester and Sampson of Chichester; some have annotations by others, including the king.

One of the documents, however, is entirely in the writing of the king.[3] This is the best known, and material from it has often been published. It is a single sheet, and unlike most of the others it simply lists the proposals and does not discuss their details. This is probably the earliest of the papers, in which the king lays out the idea that the bishops and other authorities were to work out in detail. It is a fascinating and evocative document. The king writes the heading 'Byshopprychys to be new made' above a broad column listing on the left thirteen new diocesan areas, bracketed together where more than a single entity, and against them monasteries, also bracketed together where necessary.

Almost all the new dioceses are formed of either one or two counties.[4] Against them, in most cases just one monastery is identified. The church of this monastery, then, was to become the new cathedral. In other cases, however, either two or three monasteries are listed. To understand this requires some consideration of financial matters.

The annual incomes of all religious houses, including cathedrals, as they were on the eve of the Reformation are as already mentioned known from the *Valor Ecclesiasticus*. This great national valuation of religious institutions was carried out in 1535 by commissioners for the king, following the act that made him supreme head of the Church in England. Almost all such foundations obtained most of their income from an endowment largely of land, though augmented from other sources, such as the gifts of the pious.

Two incomes are associated with a cathedral: one for the bishopric (that is, the bishop and the diocese), the other to support the cathedral and its establishment. We have seen that cathedrals in the Middle Ages were either monastic or secular, so the income of the cathedral establishment would support either the cathedral priory or the cathedral's college of canons; the costs of the two were similar. The wealthiest cathedral was Canterbury, which was monastic: its bishopric had an annual income given in 1535 as £3,233 and its cathedral priory £2,349, for a total of £5,582. Lichfield, which was secular, might stand as typical, with figures respectively of £795 and £1,075, totalling £1,870. Smallest in income was Rochester, another monastic cathedral: its respective numbers were £444 and £486, totalling £930. No doubt the king would not wish to commit more financial support than necessary, but each new diocese might require an income of the order of £1,000. (This is supported by another document from this period[5] that calculates the total annual income of the religious houses of England and Wales, and then subtracts an annual allowance of £18,000 for the establishment of eighteen new bishops and their cathedrals. This seems to be, however, the only suggestion that so large a number of new cathedrals was ever considered.) What was necessary for a particular cathedral would depend partly on the establishment planned for it, which would be related to the size of its diocese. Rochester again furnishes an example, for as well as having the smallest income, it also had the smallest diocese.

Of the single monasteries identified in the list, most had incomes close to or over £1,000; in the cases of Bury St Edmunds, Gloucester, Peterborough, St Albans and Westminster, well over. In these, the income of the dissolved monastery was sufficient (perhaps more than sufficient) for the support of the proposed cathedral and its bishopric. In the case of the diocese proposed for Oxfordshire and Berkshire, two monasteries are identified: Osney and Thame. Osney had an income of £654, while Thame had £256, giving a total of £910. Osney was to be the cathedral, and was indeed so elevated, this being one of the proposals actually implemented. The role of Thame was only to contribute its revenues: like almost all other dissolved monasteries, its church and buildings were to be destroyed or sold for what they would fetch. Similarly, in the proposals where three monasteries are listed, the incomes of all three were to be appropriated to the new see, but only one church was to be preserved as the new cathedral. There are three such proposals. While the king does not explicitly identify which was to be the cathedral in these cases, it is clear when considered in conjunction with the other documents that he intended it to be the first named. The incomes of the monasteries in these schemes are all much smaller than those where a single monastery was listed. For example, of Dunstable, Newnham and Elstow the incomes were respectively £344, £284 and £284. Dunstable was to be the cathedral; the total income of £912 from the three monasteries would be sufficient to fund the cathedral and diocese. Newnham and Elstow were in the intended diocese, so their endowment estates should be located conveniently to be managed as one with those of Dunstable for the new cathedral. Similar considerations apply in the other two groups of three; however, as we will see, in the case of the diocese of Cornwall there were second thoughts about which church should be the cathedral.

This listing of multiple monasteries has confused some writers, who have supposed that any mention of a church in this or the other documents means that it was to become a cathedral. Consequently, mistaken statements may be encountered indicating that it was planned to elevate to cathedral status such churches as Elstow or Thame, which were actually only to contribute revenues.

Broadly, the scheme as drafted by the king seems a sound reform. The creation of new dioceses in the form of counties or pairs of counties would have made for a much more uniform diocesan structure across the country. The largest dioceses would have been broken up into smaller units. Not all was ideal: for example the cathedrals of Peterborough and Waltham were placed peripherally in their planned dioceses. However, the other documents, probably written later, represent a working out of the proposals, in which there were changes and potentially improvements. They include several other proposed cathedrals that were not in the king's draft, and also some further religious houses that were to contribute only their revenues. Intended dioceses are only occasionally shown in these other documents (but when they do appear they agree with the king's list).

Most of the other documents are long, of multiple folios. They mainly address the 'proportions' of the proposed new cathedrals: the financial and administrative aspects of their establishments. They show, sometimes in meticulous and beautifully written detail, the positions that were to be associated with the respective cathedrals, with the associated stipends. These positions include not just the dean and prebendaries, the singing men and choristers, but also many other posts such as porter, butler, chief cook and undercook. Other expenses such as alms are also listed. Some also identify candidates for particular principal positions, including bishops. In the following table, the monasteries (and in two cases colleges) appearing in each document are listed. A is the king's plan, presumed to stand first in time; the order of documents B to G is arbitrary; H corresponds with what was implemented and so is last. The order of the entries in the table is that of the king's document, followed (in arbitrary order) by those appearing only in other documents.

Diocese	Monastery or College	A[3]	B[6]	C[7]	D[8]	E[9]	F[10]	G[11]	H[12]
Essex	Waltham	X	X	X			X		
Hertfordshire	St Albans	X	X	X	X		X		
Bedfordshire and Buckinghamshire	Dunstable Newnham Elstow	X X X		X	X	X		X	
Oxfordshire and Berkshire	Osney Thame	X X	X X	X	X X	X X	X X	X X	X X
Northamptonshire and Huntingdonshire	Peterborough	X	X	X	X	X	X	X	X
Middlesex	Westminster	X	X	X	X	X	X	X	X
Leicestershire and Rutland	Leicester	X					X		

Gloucestershire	Gloucester	X	X	X	X	X	X	X	X
Lancashire and the Archdeaconry of Richmond	Fountains	X		X	X				
Suffolk	Bury St Edmunds	X							
Staffordshire and Shropshire	Shrewsbury Wenlock	X	X Xᵃ	X	X	X		X	
Nottinghamshire and Derbyshire	Welbeck Worksop Thurgarton	X X X							
Cornwall	Launceston Bodmin St Germans Plympton	X X ᵇ		X X X	X Xᶜ X	X X	X X	X X X	X X X X
	Bristol			X	X	X		X	X
	Chester Wenlock		X X	X	X	X	X X	X	X
	Colchester			X	X	X		X	
	Guisborough Beverley			X	X		X X		
	Southwell				X	X		X	

a The three folio sides occupied by this proposal have later been struck through[13]

b Shows Launceston and Bodmin 'with another'

c One of the lists in this composite document shows Bodmin alone; the other shows 'Bodmin, Launceston and St Germans'

It can be seen that five proposed cathedrals appear that had not been in the king's draft: Bristol, Chester, Colchester, Guisborough and Southwell. Of these, Southwell is unique in that it was a college rather than a monastery. One of the further religious houses appearing as contributors of endowments is also a college: this is Beverley. Two of the documents show fourteen cathedrals, one more than the king's total, but most have fewer: while new proposals appear, others disappear. In any case (as discussed later), unlike the king's draft most of these documents were probably not intended to represent a complete scheme.

Three of the new proposed cathedrals were almost certainly replacements for three that had appeared in Henry's draft: Southwell for Welbeck, Chester for Fountains and Colchester for Waltham. Each new proposed cathedral would have a diocese the same as, or similar to, that of the cathedral previously identified. We can see or at least guess at the reasons for dropping some of the original proposals. The most obvious reason was timing. It was found that several of the monasteries appearing in the king's list had already been dissolved and also sold or leased to a secular owner, so were beyond recall. In the case of Welbeck, having been dissolved on 20 June 1538, it was leased on 26 February 1539, almost certainly before the king wrote his list. Presumably problems of communication meant that this was unknown to the king and his advisers at that time, but it was no doubt soon discovered, and this proposal appears in none of the other documents. Instead, Southwell was introduced as its replacement for the same diocese of Nottinghamshire and Derbyshire, its college being dissolved for the purpose in August 1540. Even where a monastery had been dissolved but not sold, its organisation and personnel would have gone, so it would be harder to reinstate. In those new cathedrals that were actually established, former monks were often re-employed. The Benedictine abbey of Chester was dissolved at the beginning of 1540; on its creation as a cathedral in August 1541, the dean was the former abbot and four of its six prebendaries had been monks.

The new diocese of Chester included the area proposed in the king's scheme for Fountains, but it had further territories as well. Although we do not know why the proposal for Fountains was abandoned, it may be that it was recognised that, in its remote situation and without even a village outside the gates, it could never have functioned successfully. The decision seems to have been made fairly early, as Fountains Abbey was sold on 1 May 1540. As for Colchester, it is in Essex, the diocese identified for Waltham; though we do not know why it was introduced it seems that it must have been an alternative to Waltham. Since both Waltham and Colchester appear in document C, it might be thought that they could not have been alternatives. Similarly, both Fountains and Chester appear in documents C and D. However, this probably illustrates that these documents did not represent complete schemes but were working drafts: presumably all the proposals in them were afloat at the time these particular documents were written, even though a decision would soon be made between those that were incompatible. Another example of this is the appearance of Wenlock twice in document B, once as a supplier of endowments to Shrewsbury and again in a similar role to Chester.

However, two of the new proposals, Bristol and Guisborough, seem simply to have been new ideas. In the case of Bristol, it is clear that the reason for its introduction was pressure from the civic authorities, who wished to obtain for their very important town the dignity of a cathedral city. As a result Bristol seems (as we will see later) an awkward addition squeezed into the scheme with little real justification. Why Guisborough was introduced is not apparent; perhaps it was in recognition that the proposals for Fountains (or Chester) and Welbeck (or Southwell) still left the diocese of York as unduly large.

Implementation of the scheme took some time. Many of the monasteries involved were dissolved in 1539; on 23 March 1540 Waltham was the final surrender of an English monastery. The first new cathedral, Westminster, was created in December 1540, with the other five following in 1541 or 1542. As long as a proposal for a former monastery was open, it was kept as Crown property, and no action was taken towards its destruction. Once its proposal was dropped, however, it was disposed of like any other.

While many factors played a part in the development of the proposals, ultimately politics and the king's need for money probably determined the reduction in the scale of the scheme from the thirteen cathedrals first proposed to the six actually created. By 1541–2, the drama of the Tudor religious changes had moved on; the dissolution of the monasteries had been completed. The project for new cathedrals had largely served its political purpose. Renewed war with France and Scotland threatened (and indeed happened in 1543). So the king wanted the smallest expenditure on new cathedrals that seemed acceptable.

Despite the careful consideration that went into the proposals, some of what was implemented has an appearance of compromise and expediency. The diocesan changes produced some serious peculiarities. Worst was the new diocese of Bristol, which was largely formed by the county of Dorset even though that was completely separated by many miles from the cathedral and the small further area of the diocese around Bristol. The creation of the dioceses of Peterborough and Oxford out of that of Lincoln left a substantial remaining part of the original diocese now detached from the rest. Taking Middlesex as the diocese of Westminster from the diocese of London put the two dioceses and cathedrals in an uncomfortable relationship. The new diocese of Chester, taken partly from the diocese of Coventry and Lichfield and partly from that of York, was very large. The dioceses as implemented were not necessarily as they had appeared in the king's plan. That of Osney, originally to have been Oxfordshire and Berkshire, was in the event only Oxfordshire. That of Peterborough, originally proposed as Northamptonshire and Huntingdonshire, was actually Northamptonshire and Rutland.

Many of the churches of both implemented and abandoned proposals were fully of cathedral stature. However, size and architectural quality were probably only incidental factors in the considerations of the king and his advisers. Of the proposals not implemented, at least Shrewsbury Abbey and the priories of Launceston or Bodmin would probably have been, by medieval cathedral standards, surprisingly modest. Of the six cathedrals actually created, Gloucester, Peterborough and Westminster are of high rank. Chester is comparable with the lesser medieval cathedrals, as probably was Osney. Bristol, considering that when made a cathedral in 1542 it had no nave, was surely inadequate. Indeed, though its quality is wonderful, it is small as a cathedral even with the Victorian nave it now has. The events of 1545–6 at Oxford (discussed under Osney, p.84) illustrate this further.

Some of the churches proposed as cathedrals in abandoned plans have been lost completely. Westminster of course remains complete, though not functionally a cathedral. Dunstable, Shrewsbury and Waltham have survived in part. Fountains is a famous, exceptionally complete ruin; much more scanty but nevertheless impressive ruins remain of Bury St Edmunds and Guisborough. It is interesting to note the extent to which the unrealised plans of 1539–42 were finally implemented in the nineteenth or twentieth century (see chapter five). Cornwall became a diocese, but with a newly built cathedral at Truro. There is a diocese of Suffolk with its cathedral at Bury St Edmunds, though this is a lesser building than was the abbey. Most remarkably, the churches of St Albans and Southwell have survived and have finally become cathedrals, both with a diocese at least similar to that proposed in 1539–40. St Albans was purchased by the townspeople for £400 to become their parish church, and was raised to cathedral status in 1877. Southwell has an especially surprising story. Although its college had been dissolved for the cathedral scheme, it was not yet clear at this period that there would be a general dissolution of the colleges; so after the abandonment of its proposal, it was reinstated as it had been by Act of Parliament in January 1543. It was then again dissolved in 1548 in the final dissolution of the colleges under Edward VI. However, it was once more re-founded under Queen Mary, and continued during Queen Elizabeth's reign, when new statutes were given. It was finally dissolved in 1841, becoming simply parochial until made a cathedral in 1884.

The documents here considered include some other interesting related matters. Also addressed in King Henry's paper and most of the other documents are the seven monastic cathedrals of Canterbury, Carlisle, Durham, Ely, Rochester, Winchester and Worcester. These were to continue, but be transformed into secular cathedrals. Accordingly, they required similar considerations for their new establishments as did the cathedrals to be founded from former monasteries. They were of course all implemented, and were given an organisation similar to that of the newly created cathedrals. Together the two groups are known as the cathedrals 'of the new foundation'. As we saw in chapter two, the monastic cathedrals of Bath and Coventry were not to continue, and they are not mentioned. Surprisingly, one other monastic cathedral does not appear. Norwich had already surrendered itself to the Crown in 1538 and been granted licence to organise its own conversion into a secular cathedral. In 1539–42 it was left untouched in its new form. However, it was eventually surrendered again in 1547, and reconstituted to be like the others of the new foundation.

The king's preamble to the 1539 Act also indicated that new colleges would be created out of former monasteries, and these too appear in the documents. Three were proposed: Burton upon Trent (Staffordshire), Thetford (Norfolk) and Thornton (Lincolnshire). Burton and Thornton indeed came to exist. They were not academic colleges. The foundation of these new colleges may have had a further political purpose, suggesting that no general dissolution of the secular colleges was intended. In fact, a gradual process of dissolution had already begun. Burton was again dissolved in 1545 and Thornton in 1548. Their brief collegiate reincarnation did not save their churches from ultimate destruction.

A further surprising proposal appearing in document F was for re-founding the three great existing colleges of Beverley, Ripon and Southwell. Presumably some of their revenues would have been taken from them in the process. Through the remaining years of Henry's reign, the Crown continued to extract money from the Church where opportunity presented. This resulted in considerable reductions in the endowments of the cathedrals, both those of the new foundation and the hitherto untouched cathedrals 'of the old foundation'. It was this climate that also led to the loss of Osney in 1546.

We should not be excessively regretful over this story of the cathedrals that might have been. Had circumstances been different, some more major monastic churches might indeed have been saved as cathedrals, and of course one must wish that this had happened. But considering the scale of the artistic loss caused by the dissolution of the monasteries, the sober fact is that the creation of half a dozen more cathedrals could only have preserved a small fraction. Rather than lament what did not happen, it is better to be grateful for what did. Henry's scheme has given us several worthy additions to the canon of the English cathedrals. Even more importantly, the medieval cathedrals, both secular and monastic, survived the period of the Reformation essentially undamaged and with only one physical loss. Had the English Reformation resembled that in Scotland, not only would no monasteries at all have been saved by becoming cathedrals, but perhaps half or three-quarters of the medieval cathedrals would have become ruins or disappeared altogether.

Bury St Edmunds (Suffolk)   *Plate 10*

This was one of the greatest and most powerful of Benedictine abbeys, and had a correspondingly exceptional church. The earliest religious house here was founded in about 633 in the first days of Christianity in East Anglia. Its fame came from the acquisition in 903 of the remains of the sainted King Edmund, martyred by the Danes in about 969. In 1020, Benedictine monks replaced secular canons. As we have seen, it evaded plans in the 1070s to make it the cathedral for East Anglia. The church was rebuilt on a very lavish scale from about 1090, with completion of the west front around a century later. Incidents in a rather stormy subsequent history included damage in 1327 by rioting townspeople, after which the precinct was fortified. The net income recorded in the *Valor* was £1,656; dissolution took place in November 1539. Though identified as a new cathedral in the king's plan, it appears in none of the subsequent documents; the reason is not obvious. It was sold, and most of the buildings became a convenient quarry for the townspeople. What remains of the church is terribly ruinous: just rough cores of flint-work, all dressed stone having been removed. However, the plan is clear and enough survives to give a strong impression of the scale. Unusually detailed building records still exist to tell us more than is now visible.

This was the largest church in East Anglia, larger than Norwich or Ely. Its length was 505 feet. The framework remained to the end largely Norman. A Lady Chapel was added in about 1265 beside the chancel on the north side. Later changes included construction of a new crossing tower in 1361–87 and rebuilding of the west tower in about 1435–65 following a partial collapse. A fire in 1465 then required major repairs, and high vaults were inserted throughout. The chancel was of five bays with an apse, an ambulatory and three radiating apsidal chapels; all these stood over a crypt. The transepts had the exceptional length of five bays; each had east aisles and also two apsidal east chapels. The nave had twelve bays and then an immense west front wider than any other in the country. A great tower stood over the centre of the front, which had three giant round arches open to the west. To each side were large, two-storeyed apsidal chapels, and outside these were octagonal towers. All four towers eventually had timber spires. The cloister stood on the north side.

The remains of the church comprise two distinct sections; the greater part is beautifully displayed by English Heritage. Most of the ruins are low, but some crags stand high. A good deal survives of the transepts and crossing, including the south-west and north-east crossing piers and the north wall of the north transept, with its large window opening. The remains of the chancel are largely of its crypt. Little stands of most of the nave. Largely separate from all this is the west front, forming the most impressively massive part of the ruins. Amazingly, it has seven houses built into it, which are still occupied. One house is Georgian and another gothick, but most have Victorian pseudo-Norman detail. Around them, the craggy, rough masonry appears almost like a natural cliff. The outlines of the three great arches are visible. Much more detail remains behind or concealed by the houses, but is normally inaccessible. Enough evidence remains in the ruins to tell us of arcades 26 feet high, a triforium of 19 feet, and crossing arches reaching 59 feet.

The great abbey precinct still dominates the centre of the town; large sections of its wall still stand, and it contains much beautiful open space. Two wonderful, very large gatehouses are still in good condition, one Norman and the other Decorated. Their rich architectural detail gives some idea of what has vanished from the church itself. Also in the precinct are two great parish churches, one of which became the cathedral in 1914 (see chapter five). Since 2005, the abbey ruins have been overlooked by the splendid new tower of the cathedral.

Colchester (Essex)

This beautiful large town, of Roman origin, would surely have made an ideal cathedral city. Although not in the king's list, four documents show the proposal for Colchester; as already suggested, it was probably intended as an alternative to Waltham for the diocese of Essex. It would have used the abbey of St John the Baptist, an important Benedictine house founded in 1096 by Eudo, an official of the king's household. This had an annual income given in 1535 as £524 (which seems small for the cathedral purpose). The last abbot, John Beech, in 1539 was one of those few who attempted to resist the suppression: he was in consequence executed. Following the abandonment of the cathedral scheme, parts of the buildings were converted into a house, which was destroyed in a siege in 1648. The site later became that of the Colchester Garrison. There remain the main gatehouse and some sections of precinct wall, but nothing else. The main site has not been excavated, and altogether remarkably little is known about this abbey. It contrasts with the nearby smaller Augustinian priory of St Botolph, dissolved in 1536, where a substantial ruin may still be seen.

However, the gatehouse is a fine building. It is in the care of English Heritage and is in excellent condition; there were extensive repairs in Victorian times, but they are not obvious. It is Perpendicular. Both faces are battlemented and have flanking octagonal turrets carrying crocketed spirelets. Towards the town, the gatehouse presents a splendid display of panelling in flint flushwork, covering the entire surface; it also has three large canopied image niches. The side towards the abbey is plainer, with flushwork only on the battlements. The main archways are four-centred, and the lofty interior has a lierne vault. A porter's lodge, now ruinous, is attached to one side.

Dunstable (Bedfordshire)

This town, on the Roman Watling Street, was established by Henry I early in the twelfth century; he founded the Augustinian priory in about 1131. The church was not completed until the early thirteenth century. We are told that it had two west towers, but that these were brought down by a storm in 1222. The west front was then rebuilt, without towers. In about 1324, an eastern Lady Chapel was rebuilt at the beginning of a campaign that probably extended to the whole chancel, transepts and central tower. The parishioners originally had the use only of the north nave aisle, but in 1392 their takeover of most of the nave was agreed.

Dunstable Priory

Dunstable Priory

In 1533, the priory made a dramatic appearance in English history. Archbishop Cranmer, with three other bishops, sat as a court in the Lady Chapel to consider the king's divorce from Catherine of Aragon. Catherine was at this time living at Ampthill, 12 miles away; but she refused to attend. Cranmer here pronounced the marriage null and void.

The priory was dissolved in January 1540. As we have seen, because of its moderate income, the cathedral was also to have the incomes of the other Bedfordshire monasteries of Elstow and Newnham. The documents show extensive details of the intended cathedral establishment, including the name of the first bishop. After the abandonment of the proposal, the nave of the church was spared because of its use by the parish. Of Elstow, an abbey of Benedictine nuns, much of the nave and a freestanding campanile have survived; but the Augustinian priory of Newnham has all but vanished.

The church of Dunstable as it remains today is beautifully set in parkland. Despite the priory's limited income, the church was on a very large scale. A geophysical survey in 2005 revealed something of the destroyed eastern limb; it probably brought the total length to about 360 feet. As we can see from the remaining largely Norman nave, it was of splendid quality. This stands as a lovely but mutilated hulk, seven bays in length (one further bay has gone). Also destroyed is the clerestory, an alteration that, surprisingly, seems to have happened in the late medieval period; three-light Perpendicular windows were inserted in the triforium, and a battlemented parapet was provided above. So even had the church become a cathedral, it would apparently have been mutilated to this extent.

The west front is the famous feature here. It still has its tremendous late-Norman portal, with four orders of shafts and rich but decayed ornamentation. Most of the rest is Early English, magnificent but both confused and strangely one-sided. It includes two big lancets in the centre, another rich portal on the north side, several tiers of image niches or arcading, and a great north-west buttress with multiple image niches. To the south, however, it was perhaps never completed: it now stops immediately in a big Perpendicular buttress rising to a short octagonal battlemented turret. Above the north end of the front a Perpendicular tower has been added, with twin two-light belfry openings and battlements. Was this tower constructed at the time of the demolition of the clerestory, perhaps in the late fifteenth century?

Part of the east wall is the former priory rood screen. Otherwise, however, it has much brickwork of 1962, when also two windows were inserted. Externally the Norman north arcade respond appears here, but the south side has a mass of masonry perhaps relating to the fourteenth-century remodelling of the eastern limb. The south aisle has windows in plausible Norman style, but is externally of 1852, when a major restoration took place; it shows no sign of the cloister formerly attached here. There is a large north doorway of four orders, Norman but drastically renewed; until the dissolution it was covered by the parish porch.

Internally, the width is striking and the Norman work is authentic and magnificent. The pillars are compound, with two orders of shafts towards the arches, which have big rolls. Chevron appears only on the hood-mould. The triforium openings have rich mouldings in three orders; just the east bay has chevron. They have never been subdivided. The Perpendicular window tracery is set in the outer plane of the wall, and does not interfere. One shaft from the arcade arches across above the triforium, forming a giant order. Heavy Perpendicular reinforcement has been put into the tower bay. The west wall is superb: it is Norman lower down, but above has a wall passage with seven exquisite freestanding Early English arches; there are stiff-leaf capitals and very rich mouldings. Roofs are renewed. Just the south aisle has rib vaulting, of which the two east bays are genuine Norman work, the rest a good copy of 1852.

Two bays from the east end is a timber rood screen, of large single-light divisions and with no base: this is a rare survivor of its type, and belongs to the period after the parish takeover of the nave. There are some good mural memorials and a few brasses. The large Norman tub font, with much sophisticated decoration, is a convincing re-creation from fragments found in 1852. Of the monastic buildings very little is left, though a fragment of a fifteenth-century gatehouse survives.

Fountains (Yorkshire, WR, now North Yorkshire) Plates 11 and 12

This must be the most famous ruined abbey in England, owing its celebrity to its scale, splendour and exceptional completeness combined with the beauty of its setting. Founded in 1132, it became the largest and wealthiest of the Cistercian abbeys. It owned huge moorland estates, and was the greatest producer of wool in the North of England. Its annual income in 1535 was given as £1,115. Dissolution came in November 1539. It was to have a large diocese comprising Lancashire and the extensive Archdeaconry of Richmond. It appears ill placed for much of the Lancashire part of this diocese; but as already remarked, it is its rural situation that seems most improbable when considering Fountains as a cathedral. The scheme was abandoned, and when the new diocese of Chester was created it included what had been proposed for Fountains. Fountains was sold on 1 May 1540 and it was already being stripped of reusable materials later in that year. We have its remote position to thank for the fact that little stone was robbed from it over the next two centuries and more. From 1768, as a consequence of its acquisition by William Aislaby of the adjacent Studley Royal estate, it was preserved as a feature of his landscape gardens. It is now owned by the National Trust and cared for by English Heritage.

Fountains would have been a worthy cathedral. Its external length is 402 feet, and it is all on a majestic scale. The basis is mid-twelfth-century Norman work: transepts each with two east chapels, and an aisled nave of eleven bays. These parts stand as a largely complete shell. Their work-manship is of fine quality, but the masonry of sandstone quarried from the adjacent hillside is now sadly weatherworn. In keeping with early Cistercian ideals they are stately but austere. They employ pointed main arches and have no triforium, in both ways being typical of twelfth-century Cistercian building. The nave has very tall cylindrical pillars, and the clerestory has one simple large window in each bay. Transverse arches across the aisles still stand, but not the vaults between them, which were of transverse pointed barrel form. The high roofs were of timber. Some aisle windows are later replacements, and the west front has the frame of a great window inserted in 1484. There is a low west narthex, which includes three bays of delicate open arcading on twin shafts, re-erected in the nineteenth century – a rare survival.

Vaults still stand in the east chapels of the south transept, one of which has a Perpendicular east extension. Only two of the crossing piers remain, one with enormous additional late buttressing: a tower was added or begun in the later fifteenth century, and gave trouble. Instead, a magnificent tower was added in the early sixteenth century on the north side of the north transept, built of fine limestone that remains almost perfect. It is massive, about 170 feet high, and is in five stages with large angle buttresses. Its battlements are still largely complete, and it has fine enrichment including inscription friezes and image niches, some still retaining their statues.

A very large new eastern limb was built in about 1210–40. This is of sophisticated and lovely Early English work; Cistercian austerity had by now been abandoned, though the two-storeyed elevations were continued. It was originally vaulted throughout, and had much enrichment by shafting in Nidderdale marble, now all gone. The chancel is in five bays; its aisles have lancet windows and elegant blank arcading, but the arcades have fallen. As the climax there follows a great eastern transept, known as the Chapel of the Nine Altars; only Durham Cathedral has a similar structure. Remarkably still standing are the two-bay continuations of the arcades across this, with slender pillars almost 50 feet high. Some fifteenth-century repairs and alterations are visible, which were in part a response to structural problems. The high vaults had to be removed.

Surprisingly, some internal plaster still remains, in one area even showing painted lines simulating ashlar. A few areas of floor tiles survive, as do some tomb slabs. The monastic buildings are splendid. They include all those around the cloister; much is also to be seen of outer subsidiary buildings. One of the most memorable sights in a medieval building anywhere is the great lower level of the western range, a space internally 300 feet long and 42 feet wide, retaining complete its vault of twenty-two bays by two.

Guisborough (Yorkshire, NR, now North Yorkshire)   Plate 13

The Augustinian Guisborough (or Gisborough) Priory was founded in about 1119 by Robert de Brus. Its annual value in 1535 was £628. It surrendered on 24 December 1539, but was not formally dissolved until 8 April 1540, a delay occasioned presumably by consideration of the cathedral proposal. Guisborough was not on the king's list but appears in three later documents, one of which shows its endowments being

augmented by those of Beverley Minster, which had £724. After abandonment of the scheme the site was leased and later sold; the west range
of the cloister initially became a residence, subsequently replaced by
a mansion standing further to the south-west. Almost everything was
demolished, with one major exception: the east wall of the church was
retained as a landscape feature and so remains almost complete. Of the
rest of the church only a few footings, mainly of the nave, are at present
exposed. The monastic buildings were on the south side; the wall bases
of the west range are visible, and at its south end a fragment stands up,
with an intact rib-vaulted passage. There is also a part of the main gatehouse. Though so little remains, the spectacular survival of the east wall
makes this a most beautiful and evocative site.

The church was large and magnificent, and would surely have been
a splendid cathedral. It was about 380 feet long, with a chancel of nine
bays and a nave of eight, including the west bay which had twin towers.
Most of it was rebuilt following a fire in 1289, and the east wall must
be of soon after that date. Its scale is tremendous (it shows that the roof
ridge was 97 feet from the ground), and it is of the highest sophistication. Its external ashlar is still almost perfect. Crocketed spirelets mark
the angles of the chancel and of the aisles. There are some image niches.
Only fragments remain of the tracery of the three main windows, but
their geometrical character is evident. Internally, their enrichments
include an order of continuous foliage. The wall below the great central
window was removed before 1709 for picturesque reasons. Details on
the west side tell us much about the body of the chancel. The arcade
responds have three orders of filleted shafts. There were passages at both
triforium and clerestory level, but the two stages were combined into
one composition. Springers remain of the vaults.

Launceston and Bodmin (Cornwall)

As we have seen, the proposed diocese of Cornwall is the only one
in which there is ambiguity as to which church was intended as the
cathedral. Launceston, first in the king's list, was presumably the original
proposal. However, Bodmin was clearly subsequently preferred, since
in two documents Launceston is omitted, and others refer to 'Bodmin
with Launceston and...' In the Middle Ages, despite standing on the
county's eastern boundary, Launceston was the county town, but the
more centrally placed Bodmin was larger and a more important religious centre. In the nineteenth century Bodmin became the county
town. Most documents list three monasteries in this scheme, of which
two would simply supply their endowments; in most the third is St
Germans. Launceston, Bodmin and St Germans were all Augustinian
priories with the moderate respective incomes of £354, £270 and
£227, giving a suitable total of £851. One document however shows '...

St Germans or Plympton'. Plympton, yet another Augustinian priory but just outside the county, would alone have provided £912.

The priories of Launceston and Bodmin are similar in many ways. Both were completely destroyed above ground after their dissolution. At both the excavated wall bases of a part of the church are now displayed, along with a collection of archaeological fragments. In each case further material is in the town's museum. Launceston was founded about 1126, replacing an earlier monastery in a different location. Most of the site, close to St Thomas's church, was excavated in 1886–93. The church was about 260 feet long and was not cruciform. It had a west tower; the cloister was on the south side, and the nave had a north aisle only. The chancel had flanking aisles and an eastern chapel. What is now exposed is most of the chancel, largely standing 2–3 feet high; a scheme further to investigate, consolidate and improve its display took place in 2008. From this, it is suggested that it dates from between 1290 and 1345. Features such as the bases of arch responds show good architectural detail. Many of the collection of separate carved stones appear Perpendicular. A simple Norman doorway now forming the entrance to the White Hart Hotel in the market square may have come from the priory.

Bodmin too was founded in the early twelfth century; a previous religious house probably stood on the site now occupied by the parish church of St Petrock, 150 yards to the north-west. The late eighteenth-century Priory House, now local government offices, replaced the west range of the cloister buildings. North of this are exposed the foundations of the north-west corner of the church, excavated in 1985–6. This had a tower, and had been largely rebuilt in the Perpendicular period. The rest has not been excavated and its plan and extent remain unknown. Many archaeological fragments are displayed in the public gardens on the other side of the house. The tomb of Prior Vivian, who died in 1533, was moved to the parish church at the dissolution.

St Germans appeared in chapter one (interestingly, it resembles Launceston in not being cruciform). Plympton is in a condition similar to that of Launceston and Bodmin.

Leicester

It has sometimes been said that the cathedral proposal for Leicester applied to the church of the great Newarke College, which had a sixteenth-century annual income of £595. However, it is now clear that Leicester Abbey was intended.[14] Founded in 1143, this was one of the largest of Augustinian houses, with an annual income given in 1535 as £951. Its principal appearance in history was as the location of the death and burial of Cardinal Wolsey in 1530. It was dissolved in August 1538 and leased on 24 March 1539: so this had probably already happened before use as a cathedral was proposed, causing the failure of the scheme.

The site, a mile north of the city centre, is in the large and beautiful Abbey Park. Much of the north and east sides of the precinct wall
still exist. The only substantial standing structure is a largely ruined
mainly Elizabethan and Jacobean mansion, Cavendish House; this is on
the site of the main gatehouse, but nothing medieval is now visible. Of
the church and cloister buildings, the foundations were excavated in
1929–32. They were then treated in an unusual way: the entire plan was
marked out in rubble masonry a foot or so high. The reliability of their
layout has been questioned, but reappraisal in the early twenty-first century has shown that they are generally trustworthy.[15]

The church was a little over 340 feet long. It was largely complete
by the end of the twelfth century, and little is known about any later
remodelling. It had an aisled nave of nine bays and a westwork with a
single large tower, referred to in the 1538 or 1539 survey of the Crown
Commissioners as 'a hyghe squayr Tower stepyll standying at the West
end'. The chancel had aisles with three-bay arcades and an aisleless sanctuary beyond. Opening from the aisleless transepts were large chapels
flanking the full length of the chancel aisles. These were probably later
additions. A memorial to Wolsey has been set up in the north chapel,
thought to have been the Lady Chapel.

Osney (Oxfordshire)

The story of Osney (or Oseney) Abbey is particularly sad. It stood just
west of the centre of Oxford, having been founded in 1129 by Robert
d'Oilly the Younger as an Augustinian priory. Raised to abbey rank
about 1154, it became one of the most important Augustinian houses. It
was in the king's list of proposed cathedrals, where as we saw its income
was to be supplemented by that of Thame, a Cistercian abbey. Following
its dissolution in November 1539 it indeed became the cathedral of the
new diocese of Oxford in September 1542. The last abbot, Richard
King, was made bishop. Its future should have been secure. But this was
not so, and Osney has the sorry distinction of having functioned as a
cathedral for several years yet still ultimately being destroyed.

In 1525, Thomas Wolsey, Henry VIII's chief minister, had founded the
great academic Cardinal College in Oxford. Its site was largely provided
by the Augustinian priory of St Frideswide, which had been dissolved
for the purpose in 1524. When in 1529 Wolsey fell from power, much
of his college had been built, though it was far from complete. All construction ceased, but in July 1532 the king re-founded it as King Henry
VIII College. Wolsey's college was to have had a great new chapel, but
in 1529 this had only just been begun. Although three bays of the nave
of the former priory church had been demolished to make way for the
great court of the college, the rest still stood and served as the college
chapel. In 1545 a new scheme was devised whereby Osney Cathedral

Prospectus Ruinarum Abbatiæ de OSNEY, juxta Oxon:

Osney Abbey: the ruins as they stood in about 1640 (c. 1661, engraving by Wenceslaus Hollar; the details are presumably largely imaginary). (By kind permission of the University of Southampton)

and King Henry VIII College were to be amalgamated, with the former priory church of St Frideswide becoming the cathedral. By this the Crown could both sell Osney and regain some of its revenue. The two establishments were surrendered in May 1545, and the scheme was completed by the foundation of Christ Church in November 1546, one of the last acts of the king's reign. Christ Church is an institution of unique dual function, with its church serving as both college chapel and cathedral. Removal of fittings from Osney began in 1545. Among these were the bells, including the famous Great Tom, which (though recast) now hangs in Tom Tower above the entrance to Christ Church. Osney rapidly became a ruin. Stone was taken for Christ Church, and more for Civil War defences; the last of the church, the great west tower, was demolished in about 1650.

Most of the site of the church now lies in a cemetery, though its extreme east end is under the railway. It was probably considerably over 300 feet long. Much of the structure was of the thirteenth century. It had a central and a very tall west tower. The nave apparently had double aisles: a characteristic which, among the English cathedrals, it would have shared with Chichester. There seem to have been five east chapels beyond the high altar, including a central Lady Chapel, and another Lady Chapel on the north side of the chancel.[16] Almost the only thing now visible is a square, stone-built subsidiary building of unknown function, standing away to the south-west. It has a blocked two-light square-headed Perpendicular window and, in a spur of wall projecting from one corner, a broad, depressed Perpendicular archway. At the time of writing it is unused and stands in semi-derelict surroundings partly used as a boatyard. Of the supporting abbey of Thame, rather more survives than of Osney, though nothing of the church.

It is ironic that it was the lesser of Oxford's two Augustinian monastic churches that finally was saved and became the cathedral, even though as early as the 1520s it had been dissolved and partly demolished. The greater Osney, still flourishing at that time, went on to become the cathedral in 1542. Yet ultimately it was destroyed. Had it continued, Oxford would have had a cathedral certainly larger and probably more splendid than the beautiful but undeniably small building that it has.

Shrewsbury (Shropshire)

As a location for a see, this beautiful and important ancient town would seem ideal. Its Benedictine abbey was founded in 1083 by the Norman earl, Roger de Montgomery. It was dissolved in January 1540. Its annual income, given as £532, would have been small for a cathedral, so it is not surprising that one of the documents shows it augmented by the £401 of the nearby Cluniac priory of Wenlock. After the abandonment of the cathedral proposal, the nave of the church survived in parochial use. It remains today, though it was damaged in the Civil War. In the 1920s it was again the subject of a cathedral scheme, but this once more came to nothing. The nave is in part early Norman, perhaps as early as the late eleventh century. The destroyed eastern parts were investigated by resistivity and radar surveys in 1995–6, which indicated a chancel with an eastern apse (so perhaps remaining Norman to the end), and a presumably later square-ended eastern chapel. The full length was apparently just over 300 feet. Though the surviving nave is large and interesting, it must be admitted that by cathedral standards it is disappointing.

The nave as built was six bays in length; of its arcades, the three Norman east bays remain. They have short, thick circular columns, shallow capitals and arches of two unmoulded orders. There is no ornamentation. Above is a triforium of similar form, unattractively filled in by S. Pountney Smith in 1861–3 as windows with polychromatic stone-work. The clerestory, which had been removed in 1704–6, is now a good re-creation of 1894 by J.L. Pearson. The aisles have mostly later windows and curious plastered ceilings (on the north side with cross gables) of 1729; the springers remain of former (or intended) groin vaults. To the west the Norman arcades end in an especially massive pillar with a thick pilaster, thought originally to have marked the division between the parochial and monastic sections. West of these is now a late fourteenth-century Perpendicular structure, though still within the Norman aisle walls. There are two narrower bays of well-moulded arcade, with large three-light clerestory windows and no triforium. Then comes the tower, with a very tall arch. It occupies the space of one and a half Norman bays and, unusually, includes clerestory windows. This Perpendicular work is quiet, but it is well preserved and unlike the Norman part has suffered no mutilation.

Externally the west front is the finest feature. It has a little Norman work low down. The splendid west window has seven lights. This is flanked by two richly canopied image niches, and has a great crocketed ogee hood-mould rising to the belfry stage. There are twin two-light belfry openings, between which the west side has another canopied image niche with a statue said to be of Edward III. The plain battle-ments are a repair following Civil War damage. There is a north porch externally of quite ambitious Perpendicular type, in three storeys; inside, however, it has a Norman tunnel vault, and covers a fine Norman door-way of three orders. The cloister was on the south side, but a road now runs here, built in 1836 by Thomas Telford.

Shrewsbury Abbey

In 1886–8, a new east end was added to the designs of J.L. Pearson. His first plans envisaged a splendid, full-sized structure with a crossing tower, but financial constraints caused what was built to be much less than that. The crossing was re-created, in excellent Norman style. The transepts, however, do not project beyond the aisles, though keying on their wall-ends shows that continuation was intended. At low level, battered pieces of the Norman transept west walls still project further on both sides. Pearson's chancel has three short bays with single-bay flanking chapels. It is in Early English style and elegantly vaulted. This is a fine addition, although internally it seems rather bare and its length insufficient for the scale. It brings the total length to 211 feet.

The church contains a notable series of medieval memorials, mostly with recumbent effigies; many came in the eighteenth or nineteenth century from other churches in Shrewsbury and elsewhere. There are also some fine later memorials. The very large circular font bowl is thought to be an inverted Roman pillar base. There is what is believed to be a fragment of the shrine of St Winifred, of late fourteenth-century work.

Waltham (Essex)

An early church here was re-founded by Earl Harold, later king, as an important college of secular canons; a new church was built, which was consecrated in 1060. Harold prayed here before the Battle of Hastings; it is said that his body was subsequently returned here for burial. The church was again rebuilt from about 1090. In 1177, it was re-founded by Henry II as an Augustinian priory, which was elevated to abbey rank in 1184. This became one of the wealthiest Augustinian houses, with an annual income in 1535 of £900.

After its re-founding by Henry II, a great Early English building campaign created monastic buildings and a church on a very large scale. Most remarkably, although a complete new cruciform church was built which had a nave of seven bays, four-bay transepts with east aisles and a chancel of four bays probably also with a retrochoir and eastern Lady Chapel, this did not entirely replace its predecessor. Attached to its west, the old nave, crossing and transepts were kept. The cloisters stood north of the new nave. The function of the retained Norman parts in this vast church is not certain, but they may have served the parish. After the dissolution, and the abandonment of the cathedral scheme, destruction did not begin until 1544; the old nave became the parish church and the rest was completely demolished. Most of the area is now parkland, with a few post-Reformation brick walls. A late twelfth-century vaulted passage survives at what was the north-east corner of the cloister, giving us our only glimpse of the huge, lost Early English structures of the abbey. Much was superficially excavated in 1938–9, though not the very east end of the church. The total length including the old nave may have approached 500 feet.

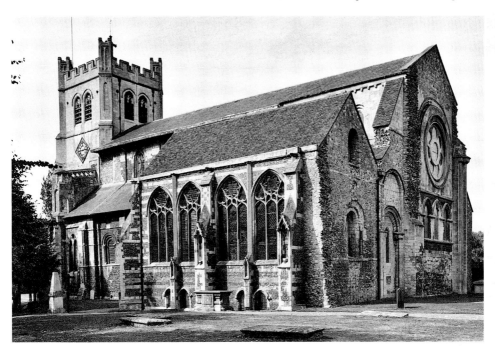

Waltham Abbey

The nave is a splendid structure of the early twelfth century, in seven bays. It has cylindrical pillars, alternate ones being made compound by large shafts north and south. The two east pillars have great spiral grooves of the type familiar from Durham Cathedral; west of these is a pair of pillars having a giant zigzag pattern. Cushion capitals carry round arches in two orders, with zigzag and chevron ornament. The triforium openings are undivided, but have shafts and capitals implying that subdivision was intended. Each clerestory bay has a single window, with a wall passage and sophisticated tripartite internal openings, again with much decoration including chevron. There is a flat wooden ceiling strikingly painted in 1859–60 with a design copied from that at Peterborough. This is appropriate; but few would say of the east wall, also of this time, with its heavy and elaborate features including a wheel window. It was designed by William Burges.

The aisles retain some of their externally shafted Norman windows, with small circular openings above. There is no sign that the aisles were ever vaulted; they are now open to the lean-to roofs above the triforium. The west arcade pillars are especially large, indicating that west towers were constructed or intended. In the early Decorated period the west front was rebuilt, with polygonal corner turrets, openwork parapets and a very fine doorway. However, much of this is now hidden by the tower, which is built against the front. The tower is large and attractive, in four stages, its lower part faced with flint and stone in a chequer pattern. It is a rarity in that it dates from the reign of Queen Mary, built in 1556–8 after the collapse in 1552 of the former central tower

Waltham Abbey

(probably as a consequence of the loss of abutment from parts that had been demolished). The two west bays inside are curiously mutilated by the removal of their arcade arches, and apparently the alteration of the triforium and clerestory arches to pointed form; this was presumably the beginning of an unfinished remodelling scheme.

Attached on the south side towards the east is a beautiful Decorated chapel, raised over a vaulted crypt. It has four south windows and a remarkable broad and straight-headed west window of six lights with an internal plane of simpler tracery. Its east wall is the west side of the former south transept, and preserves a large doom wall painting. Externally, the lower part of this wall has flint masonry laid in a herringbone pattern: recent investigations have shown this to be a surviving fragment of Harold's church. There are some fine memorials and a charming later seventeenth-century hexagonal pulpit.[17]

Welbeck (Nottinghamshire)

This Premonstratensian abbey was founded in 1153–4. It was one of the largest houses of the order. When in 1512 Pope Julius II granted a bull exempting the English Premonstratensian houses from foreign jurisdiction, he and the king (Henry VIII) formally recognised Welbeck as the principal house of the order. Perhaps the king remembered it from that time when making the cathedral proposal in 1539. However, it had an annual income given in 1535 as only £249 and was therefore also to be given the revenues of the other Nottinghamshire houses of Thurgarton and Worksop, both

Augustinian priories and valued respectively at £259 and £239. However, like Fountains, Welbeck had no village, so its suitability as a cathedral location would seem questionable. Moreover, as we have seen, it had almost certainly already been leased before the time of the proposal.

Welbeck Abbey is now a great mansion, largely of the seventeenth century and later, and long the seat of the dukes of Portland. It is particularly known for the extraordinary underground rooms and tunnels built for the fifth duke in Victorian times. After being used as an army college for sixty years, in 2005 it returned to being entirely a private home. In what is now the basement level of the house there survives the vaulted west range of the medieval cloister buildings. This is of the thirteenth century and is seven bays long by two wide, divided into two sections by a passage. There are also several relatively recent subdivisions. Its east side has a doorway that formerly opened onto the cloister: this is of about 1190, and is round-arched with deep mouldings. In a room a little to the north-east is a further medieval feature: a thin wall running north-south with an opening that has Decorated sunk quadrant mouldings. Intriguingly, its position suggests that it may have been part of the church: if so, could it have been part of a screen? There have been no archaeological investigations, and nothing is reliably known.[18]

Unlike Welbeck, something still stands of the church of Thurgarton, and a great deal at Worksop.

Westminster (London) *Plates 14 and 15*

This unique and wonderful church had unclear origins, though probably early. It became a Benedictine abbey in the tenth century under Dunstan. Edward the Confessor in the last Anglo-Saxon years re-endowed it and began a great rebuilding: this was in the Norman style, but it has all since been replaced. It was also Edward the Confessor who gave it its unique royal and national position; it has been the scene of every coronation of an English monarch since that of William I on Christmas Day 1066. As we have seen, it was perhaps the country's wealthiest monastery. It was dissolved in January 1540. Because of its unique importance and position in national life, it could not be destroyed, and this was almost certainly the reason for its inclusion in the king's cathedral scheme. The proposal was implemented, and in December 1540 it became the cathedral for the county of Middlesex. As already mentioned, this did not appear to be a satisfactory arrangement, so it is not surprising that the new diocese only ever had one bishop: it ceased in 1550, returning to the diocese of London. Westminster continued for a period nominally as a second cathedral in that diocese, served by canons. Under Queen Mary, however, in 1556 it was re-established as a Benedictine abbey. It was still an abbey at the coronation of Queen Elizabeth, but in July 1559 in the Elizabethan religious settlement it was again dissolved. In 1560 it became what it remains today: the Collegiate Church of St Peter, Westminster. It keeps the name 'abbey' by tradition.

This is thus an exceptional survivor among the English monastic churches, standing complete and with much of its complement of buildings. Physically it has the stature of a cathedral of the highest quality and on the greatest scale. The length is 531 feet. The present building was begun at the east end in 1245 under Henry III, and in the initial very dynamic building campaign the chancel, transepts and five bays of the nave were completed. Following the king's death in 1272, construction ceased. Work resumed on the nave in 1376, though when it stopped in about 1520 the west front was still incomplete. The towers were finally completed in 1734–45 to the design of Nicholas Hawksmoor. No central tower was ever built. The nave has twelve bays including the bay of the towers. There are transepts of four bays with east and west aisles, and the chancel has four bays followed by an apse with an ambulatory and four radiating polygonal chapels. The original eastern Lady Chapel was replaced in spectacular style in 1503–12 as the chapel of Henry VII.

Remarkably, the design of the abbey is strongly French in many ways, no doubt expressing the preferences of Henry III. Above all this applies to the height: with its vault approximately 102 feet from the floor, it is the loftiest medieval church in England. Internally this makes it seem tall and narrow, though it is in fact of typical cathedral width. Also French is the apsidal plan of the east end (though there are Cistercian parallels, some of which appear in chapter eight). Lancet windows are not employed: all windows have bar tracery, which was then one of the latest French developments. Not at all French, however, is the possession of long transepts; nor does the nave have double aisles, as would be typical in France. The arcades have very tall cylindrical pillars of Purbeck marble with four detached shafts, carrying moulded capitals and acutely pointed, richly moulded arches. Their spandrels have diaper enrichment. The triforium stage has twin two-light openings, in two planes; they open to a gallery (another English feature). Above is a clerestory of tall two-light windows. The vaults are quadripartite with a ridge rib. Interestingly, the continuation after 1375 retains the same proportions and general style, with alterations only to details. Changes include the abandonment of diapering, the adoption of pillars with eight attached shafts and the use of octagonal rather than circular capitals on the shafts. Only in the west front, inside as well as out, does the full Perpendicular style appear.

Hawksmoor's towers employ a modified Perpendicular style, and though classical and gothick motifs also appear they are a fine and appropriate completion of the front. At the east end, however, the chapel of Henry VII contrasts with the rest. It is glorious: perhaps the most lavish, sumptuous and daring exposition of the late Perpendicular style in existence. It has aisles, and its east end is apsidal. Both outside and in, no area is left unornamented. Externally, it has an amazingly undulating shape, and its surfaces, whether of masonry or glass, are a continuous grid of close panelling. There are openwork flying buttresses and ornate great pinnacles encrusted with niches. Internally, two aspects are especially memorable. First are the extraordinary vaults: they are all fan vaults with pendants, and the main vault has tremendously orna-mented transverse arches. Secondly, the chapel retains an almost unique array of undamaged original sculpture, including many statues in niches.

Two general considerations affect appreciation of the abbey. One is restoration, which has been going on since long before the Victorian years. Externally, most has been renewed, not always faithfully to detail. Inside, however, though restorers have been active, much remains untouched, and indeed there are many wonderful, authentic features. The second consideration is the contents, especially memorials. No other church is so filled with monuments, dating from medieval times up to the present; many are large and obtrusive, and half-conceal the architecture. Some are uniquely fine, although the dominant aspect must be their historical interest. There are also other remarkable fittings, notably the Coronation Chair of 1300–1. Still in the feretory behind the partly medieval reredos in the chancel is the thirteenth-century shrine of Edward the Confessor, as reinstated under Queen Mary after it was dismantled in 1540.

The ritual choir extends three bays into the nave, ending in the pul-pitum screen, now mostly of 1828. A curiosity of the planning is that a cloister walk passes through the west aisle of the south transept, in a kind of box. The cloisters are of the thirteenth and fourteenth centuries; the outstanding octagonal chapter-house dates from about 1245–50. A few eleventh-century Norman parts still remain among the monastic buildings.

Notes

In the following, LP refers to Brewer, J.S., Gairdner, J. and Brodie, R.H., (eds.) *Letters and Papers, Foreign and Domestic, of the Reign of Henry VIII* (22 vols, London 1862–1932).

1. This chapter owes much to Knighton, C.S., 'Collegiate Foundations, 1540 to 1570, with special reference to St. Peter in Westminster' (unpublished Cambridge Ph.D. dissertation, 1975), and to generous further assistance from Dr Knighton. See also Knowles (1959), pp.164, 358–9, 389–92; Scarisbrick (1988), pp.63–4. It seems likely that further research could reveal yet more about this fascinating episode in Tudor history.
2. BL Cottonian MS Cleopatra E.IV, fo. 366 (LP XIV, i, 868(2)). Printed in Cole, H., *King Henry the Eighth's Scheme of Bishopricks* (London: 1838) pp.75 6.
3. BL Cottonian MS Cleopatra E.IV, fo. 365 (LP XIV, i, 868(3)) Printed in Strype, J., *Ecclesiastical Memorials* (1721), I, ii, p.406.
4. The proposed diocese of Staffordshire and Shropshire was presumably a mis-take, since the already existing secular cathedral of Lichfield is in Staffordshire. (Might Cheshire rather than Staffordshire have been intended?)

5. BL Cottonian MS Cleopatra E.IV, fo. 312 (LP XIV, ii, 428).

6. PRO E 315/24, fos. 5–30 (old foliation) (LP XIV, ii, 429). Printed in Cole, *op. cit.* Fewer cathedrals are detailed than in other documents, possibly because some folios are missing.

7. PRO E 315/24, fos. 36–78 (old foliation) (LP XIV, ii, 429). Printed in Cole, *op. cit.* The writer is Stephen Gardiner, bishop of Winchester.

8. PRO E 315/24, fo. 79v (old foliation) (LP XIV, ii, 429). Two lists are written on this folio, in different hands, with similar but not identical contents. The list given here combines the two.

9. BL Cottonian MS Cleopatra E.IV, fo. 363 (LP XIV, i, 868(4)). Printed in Strype, *op. cit.*

10. PRO SP 1/154, fos. 86–93 (LP XIV, ii, 430).

11. PRO SP 1/243, fos. 49–55 (LP Add, 1457).

12. PRO SP 1/154, fo. 94v (LP XIV, ii, 430(2)).

13. The Wenlock reference in this is wrongly transcribed in LP.

14. The entry in folio 90v of document F says '*Leycester colleg' ibm [ibidem]*'. This has been read as 'College at Leicester' and assumed to mean Newarke College. Dr Knighton (pers. comm.) has shown that this entry is a later, misplaced, insertion; it is on two lines, probably meaning 'Leicester [Abbey]' and 'College in the same place'. Leicester contained, as well as Newarke College, a smaller college of St Mary de Castro, which was a property of Leicester Abbey. The inference is that the revenues of both Leicester Abbey and the college of St Mary de Castro were to be allocated to the new cathedral.

15. Story, Bourne, and Buckley (2006), pp.1–69.

16. *Victoria County History (VCH) of England: Oxfordshire IV* (1979), p.365. This largely depends on early documentary sources; little is known archaeologically. See also Blair, J., 'The Archaeology of Oxford Cathedral' in Tatton-Brown and Munby (eds.) (1996), p.100; Sharpe (1985), pp.95–130

17. The considerable recent archaeological investigations are summarised in Huggins, P.J., 'The Church at Waltham. An Archaeological and Historical Review' (2000, unpublished typescript available in the abbey at the time of writing).

18. Hamilton Thompson (1938), presents a proposed interpretation of the supposed church fragment. Green and Bewley (1998) offer a suggested plan of the whole, based on dowsing. Both seem highly questionable.

4

LOST PREDECESSOR CATHEDRALS

Most of the cathedrals of the canon, as we see them now, are not the first to have stood in these places. Many have completely replaced an earlier cathedral, or indeed have had more than one such predecessor. Moreover, some of the cathedrals that stand today once had significant parts of their structure that have since been lost or replaced by later work. This chapter looks at these lost predecessor cathedrals and parts of cathedrals.

Only addressed are predecessors that were themselves cathedrals. Some cathedrals succeeded an earlier religious house that was not the seat of a bishop: the church of such an earlier house is only discussed where, as at Exeter, it then became the cathedral. The cathedrals to be considered for predecessors are the seventeen medieval cathedrals of the canon, together with the two that ceased in 1539: Bath and Coventry. The cathedrals created under Henry VIII and those of the 'extended canon' have, with one exception, no cathedral predecessors, and since becoming cathedrals have remained essentially unaltered: they are therefore not considered here. The exception, because of its unique early history, is Ripon.

It may with truth be said of a particular cathedral that it is, for example, the third to have stood on its site. However, this could be misleading in that what has often happened has been a process of continuous development. Typically, an earlier building was extended, or just a part of it was rebuilt larger or in the style of the day. This may have happened in successive building campaigns until, after a century or two, the previous building had been entirely replaced. It was usually only in the aftermath of the Norman Conquest that a later building completely superseded an earlier one with little or no structural relationship between the two. In these cases, even the exact site and the orientation of the new may differ from those of the old. A similar fresh start was made at St Paul's Cathedral in London following the Great Fire.

The lost predecessor cathedrals are divided by their dates into two very different groups. Over half of the twenty cathedrals discussed in this chapter began in Anglo-Saxon times: these are the cathedrals of Canterbury, Durham, Exeter, Hereford, Lichfield, London, Ripon, Rochester, Wells, Winchester, Worcester and York. All of these, then, had at least one Anglo-Saxon predecessor cathedral. As indicated earlier, all these predecessors have been completely destroyed above ground level: in none of the existing buildings does there remain (as far as we know) any standing Anglo-Saxon fabric. So, as with most of the lost Anglo-Saxon cathedrals discussed in chapter one, our knowledge is largely limited to information from early documents and what has been discovered by archaeology.

Some of these cathedrals of the years before the Norman Conquest (a period of up to four and a half centuries) probably had a sequence of Anglo-Saxon buildings, successively enlarged or replaced. Documentary evidence sometimes indicates the enlargement or rebuilding of a previous church. Some were probably of timber, especially in the early years. Until the 1960s, little was known about any of these Anglo-Saxon predecessors of existing cathedrals (Rochester was to some extent an exception). This remains the case with the majority. However, excavations principally at Canterbury, Exeter, Lichfield, Wells and Winchester have revealed much, and indeed have shown the spectacular results that can be achieved by modern archaeology. Nevertheless, some even of these studies have been limited in their scope. Moreover, as already remarked, knowledge of possible timber-built cathedrals is almost non-existent. The potential for future investigations is large.

Some of these places illustrate that theme of major early Anglo-Saxon sites, discussed in chapter one, of there having been multiple separate churches or other religious structures aligned on an east-west axis.

Of course, no Anglo-Saxon cathedral was on the scale of the medieval cathedrals as we know them. Some were nevertheless large, no doubt among the greatest buildings of their time. We know enough about the size and character of Canterbury, Winchester and (discussed in chapter one) Sherborne to be able to judge that even by the standards of later centuries they must have been impressive. Canterbury and Sherborne were basilican structures and must have formed fine internal spaces. Winchester, which had grown by the joining of separate buildings, was perhaps internally more divided into multiple interlinked parts so that its full size would have been felt less. These three are likely to be representative of the character of others of the Anglo-Saxon cathedrals.

Despite seeing the plans recovered by archaeologists, perhaps also with conjectural drawings of their appearance, it may still be difficult for us to form a good impression of the character of an Anglo-Saxon cathedral. Some further sense of what they were like may perhaps be gained from the surviving larger Anglo-Saxon churches, such as

Barton-upon-Humber (Lincolnshire), Brixworth (Northamptonshire), Deerhurst (Gloucestershire), Great Paxton (Huntingdonshire, now Cambridgeshire), or Worth (West Sussex).

The predecessor cathedrals that date from since the Norman Conquest are a very different subject. It is a remarkable fact that in every continuing see other than Wells the Anglo-Saxon cathedral was completely replaced by a Norman building. In some, the rebuilding began within twenty years of 1066, and was pushed through with such energy that it was complete before the beginning of the twelfth century. The rest were complete, or nearly so, by the end of that century. The Normans, especially in their early years, could put up cathedral fabric more rapidly than was done at any subsequent period (at least, before the nineteenth century). The will and the organisation that made this possible illustrate the Norman determination to make the conquered country their own. We may note that the consecration of a Norman cathedral normally marked not the completion of the whole but of sufficient to be usable, usually at least the eastern limb.

So, except for Wells and Salisbury, every medieval cathedral was at one time a wholly or largely Norman building. Most have since been partly or completely rebuilt, though Chichester, Durham and Norwich still retain almost the whole of their Norman framework. Much of the Early English, Decorated or Perpendicular work in our cathedrals stands in place of destroyed Norman parts. At Canterbury, Rochester and York, early Norman work was replaced by structure of a later Norman period. Norman cathedrals have largely or completely disappeared at Bath, Coventry, Exeter, Lichfield, Lincoln, London, Worcester and York.

As is probably true of every period, the builders of the medieval era believed that, in replacing earlier work by that of their own time, they were creating something of greater beauty. This was one motivation for the later reconstruction of Norman cathedrals or parts of cathedrals. It might apply particularly to the chancel, since this was considered the most important part; moreover, since medieval churches were usually built from east to west, it was generally oldest and so might appear the most stylistically outmoded. Chancels were also often rebuilt for functional reasons. Most Norman cathedrals had a relatively short chancel. By the later twelfth or early thirteenth century, developments in the liturgy were demanding more space. So these Norman chancels were frequently either extended or rebuilt on a larger scale. Another reason for reconstruction of the chancel was a change in ideals of planning: Norman east ends were usually apsidal, whereas the subsequent preference was for a square east end. Among the cathedrals in this chapter, the only Norman apsidal termination to remain is that of Norwich.

Another reason for the extension of the eastern limb might be to create a worthy setting for the shrine of a saint. Possession of the body or other relics of an important saint was important for a cathedral or monastery, as it would attract pilgrims and their contributions. The remains were sometimes at first enshrined in a crypt, but they were often later moved to a place of greater honour in the eastern limb. In the great late twelfth-century rebuilding and enlargement of the chancel of Canterbury, a major requirement was to create a setting for the shrine of St Thomas à Becket. Space was needed not just for the shrine itself but to allow for the access and circulation of pilgrims.

Also growing in this period was the cult of the Virgin Mary, often expressed (as in several churches already discussed) by the addition of a substantial Lady Chapel, most frequently at the east end.

Rebuilding might also be driven by disaster. Sometimes this was a structural failure: towers fell only too often, sometimes bringing down adjacent parts of the building. The other frequent cause of devastation was fire, perhaps caused accidentally but on occasions by war or riot. In the subsequent repairs or rebuilding, vaulting might be inserted to reduce the vulnerability to fire.

In seeking to understand lost structure of cathedrals built since 1066, archaeological investigations are not only based on excavation. Although it might seem that complete replacement has taken place of, say, a Norman chancel, some of the earlier building may still be present, incorporated in fabric that has actually been remodelled rather than completely rebuilt. It may be visible only in hidden places, such as above vaulting. Even when rebuilding was indeed complete, there was often a period in which a section of the old structure remained in use while the new fabric was being built, and this coexistence may have influenced the new building. Archaeologists, starting in many cathedrals with the ground-breaking investigations of Professor Robert Willis (1800–75), have often shown great ingenuity in discovering in the standing structures indications of their architectural history.

In this context, a welcome development in recent years has been the appointment of cathedral archaeologists. Also, since the 1980s, excellent scholarly studies of many of the cathedrals have been published (some appear in the bibliography), generally containing a series of contributions by experts on topics including archaeology and architectural development.

Because these predecessors of all periods have been succeeded by a later cathedral, we may not regret their loss in the way that we do, for example, churches destroyed in the dissolution of the monasteries. However, they are all of great interest, and some must have been wonderful buildings. In our present state of knowledge, four may be singled out as particularly noteworthy. These are the Anglo-Saxon cathedrals of Canterbury and Winchester, the Norman cathedral of York, and the pre-Great Fire cathedral of London.

Bath (Somerset)

As we have seen, Bath had cathedral status from 1090 to 1539; a Norman church was begun soon after 1090. We are told that, at the death in 1122 of Bishop John de Villula, the lower vaults were complete. The whole was finished in about 1170. It was realised in the later nineteenth century that the present early sixteenth-century church that replaced it occupies just the site of its nave. Various limited investigations have together resulted in considerable knowledge of the Norman cathedral.[1] The floor of its nave was about 6 feet lower than the present level, so small excavations in the church have shown extensive survival of the bases of piers and walls. The nave had nine bays, the west bay probably having twin towers. Incorporated in the present east end are some standing Norman fragments, most obviously the arch that led from the south aisle to the south transept. From these, a good deal can be said about the lower elevation of the transepts and nave. Two-bay arcades probably separated the transepts from the crossing. Confusion over the position of an 1895 excavation discovery of a fragment of an apse seems to be the origin of a widely-published plan showing a conjectured eastern limb of four bays plus apse. More recent investigations have indicated that this was wrong: rather, the chancel was short, having only one bay and an apse with an ambulatory and three radiating apsidal chapels. Documentary evidence indicates construction of an eastern Lady Chapel in the 1260s. Without that chapel (which is unexcavated), the length was just under 350 feet.

Incorporated in the seventeenth-century vestry east of the existing south transept, some Norman masonry from the former cloister has been identified, standing in part 14 feet high. Outside the present south chancel aisle are the 'Heritage Vaults', opened in 1994, where among much else of interest are many fine carved fragments from the Norman cathedral.

Canterbury (Kent)

Canterbury has a unique place in English history. It is indeed 'the Cradle of English Christianity', and its cathedral was England's first (excepting any unknown late-Roman structures). Though not so intended by Pope Gregory when he sent Augustine on his mission, by the accidents of history it has remained the mother church of English Christianity, and more recently of worldwide Anglicanism. On Whit Sunday 597 in Canterbury, soon after his arrival in England, Augustine baptised King Aethelberht of Kent. The king gave Augustine an ancient church of Roman work for his cathedral, which was repaired and consecrated to Christ, probably in 602. Several later enlargements of this cathedral are recorded; and the monk Eadmer described it in its final state before destruction by fire in 1067. Canterbury has been relatively well served by early writers, and the information they have provided remains important in interpreting and supplementing what has been learned from archaeology.

In 1993, replacement of the paving of the nave and its aisles allowed archaeological investigation of what lay beneath. The revealed foundations were largely examined only in situ, rather than being removed: this strategy limited what could be learned, but also preserved the archaeology for potential future investigations.[2] What was exposed was much of the Anglo-Saxon cathedral, the remains being less than a foot below the floor surface in places. The present building follows its alignment, but with its centre-line about 16 feet further to the south. Three main phases of construction were identified. The first began as a nave and apsidal chancel, with perhaps later porticus to north and south and a narthex to the west. It is thought that this may indeed be Augustine's original church, though no direct evidence of Roman origin was identified. In a perhaps subsequent development, the lateral porticus were extended west as aisles. In the next phase, probably in the first half of the ninth century, the previous church was partly or completely demolished and a much larger replacement constructed, extending west to more than twice the previous length. The new church had aisles and a large square central tower. Its foundations were widened in a later remodelling, probably to enable the walls to be raised in height. The final phase was probably constructed in the early eleventh century, perhaps following a sacking by the Danes in 1011. A large westwork was added,

Canterbury: the Anglo-Saxon cathedral as it might have appeared in about 1025 (1997, copyright Canterbury Archaeological Trust)

extending north and south to hexagonal stair towers with an externally polygonal apse projecting west. Also at this period, towers were added flanking the church towards its east end; the south tower was probably that called St Gregory's Tower, and contained the main entrance. The eastern parts were not exposed in this investigation, but we know from documentation that there was an apse, which may relate to fragments exposed below the present crypt in 1895. The cathedral was thus 'bi-polar', having apses at both ends. It was of sophisticated design and workmanship. Its overall length may have been over 250 feet, making it one of the largest English churches of its time. From documentary evidence, it is thought that a church or chapel of St John the Baptist stood immediately to its east and in axis with it. This was constructed under Archbishop Cuthbert (740–60): it was a baptistery church and perhaps also used as burial place for the archbishops.

Under the Norman Archbishop Lanfranc, a new cathedral was built in the remarkably short period of about 1071–8. Its dimensions and character were closely similar to those of the abbey of St Étienne at Caen, begun about 1064, of which Lanfranc had been abbot. It is suggested that he used the same master mason for the new job. Its foundations carry the present Perpendicular nave, transepts and crossing, but above ground only fragments remain, including some incorporated in the upper levels of the west end and the transepts. Its character was probably fairly severe. Two-bay arcades crossed the entrance to the transepts. The eastern limb was short, with a main apse and apsidal endings to the aisles; the transepts also had apsidal east chapels. Its north–west tower stood until 1832, and was recorded in beautiful measured drawings by J.C. Buckler, which show it as sophisticated and enriched by blank arcading.

In the time of the next archbishop, Anselm, under priors Ernulf and Conrad, the eastern limb was replaced on a spectacularly larger scale, with east transepts and an eastern apse and ambulatory. Known sometimes as Conrad's glorious choir, it was consecrated in 1130, and was of a lavish richness that must have contrasted with Lanfranc's work. It was gutted by fire in 1174, following which the central vessel was demolished and replaced by the present great structure, and the whole extended even further to the east. However, the outer walls and chapels and the eastern transepts with their towers and pairs of apsidal east chapels largely survive, as does the exceptionally spacious and splendid crypt beneath.

Carlisle (Cumberland, now Cumbria)

Established in 1133, this was the last English medieval see to be created. The area had been Scottish until it was occupied by William II (Rufus) in 1092. A house of Augustinian canons was founded by Henry I perhaps in 1122; when its church was begun is uncertain, but much was probably built before it became a cathedral. It was of relatively moderate dimensions. Nothing remains of its chancel, it having been replaced by the dramatically larger structure begun in about 1225. Discovery of the position of a former eastern apse has been claimed, but this is doubtful. The north transept and tower have been replaced by Perpendicular structures, but Norman work remains in the south transept and crossing.

The Norman nave has suffered a major misfortune, all but two bays having been demolished during the Commonwealth for the sake of their stone. It is uncertain whether it originally had seven or eight bays, but seven is now thought more probable.[3] Both before and since this demolition, the nave served as the parish church of St Mary; in 1870, it was replaced as such by a new church of St Mary built just south-east of the cathedral. One could perhaps wish that here Victorian zeal might instead have been devoted to rebuilding the lost nave bays. The new St Mary's ended in demolition in 1954.

Chichester (West Sussex)

The see for the diocese of Sussex was established in this former Roman town in 1075, on its transfer from Selsey by Bishop Stigand. It took over what was previously an Anglo-Saxon minster church of St Peter; no remains of this have been identified. Construction of the new cathedral is now thought to have begun within a year or two of the move. There was a fire in 1114, but the cathedral was probably largely completed in the 1120s. Essentially this Norman building still stands today, though with extensive and interesting alterations and additions. The only substantial part to have been destroyed is the original apsidal east end with its ambulatory and three radiating chapels, which was replaced by a square-ended retrochoir in the major repairs that followed a fire of 1187. Also replaced have been the former apsidal east chapels of the transepts.[4]

Coventry (St Mary) (Warwickshire, now West Midlands)

As discussed in chapter two, a good deal is now known about the cathedral that was begun soon after 1102 and destroyed after 1545. We also know that some development took place during its lifetime, but at present almost nothing can be said about what was replaced.

Durham

We saw in chapter one that Viking raids compelled the Community of St Cuthbert to leave Lindisfarne, to settle in Chester-le-Street, and later to leave there, always taking with them the relics of the saint. Finally, in 995, led by Bishop Aldhun, after a short period at Ripon, they settled in a strongly defensible position at Durham. A timber church was erected, in which the relics of the saint were placed; this was known as the *Alba Ecclesia* or 'white church', no doubt because it was white-washed. Meanwhile, construction of a stone church was begun; it was consecrated in 998 and the saint's relics were moved to it. This, too, is often referred to as the white church. Its west tower was completed in the early eleventh century. This Anglo-Saxon building remained until it was demolished for the beginning of the Norman cathedral in 1093. No structural remains of it have been identified; from documentary evidence it has been thought that it was cruciform and possessed two towers. It has also been proposed that it stood immediately south of the present cathedral, in the existing cloister garth.

There are, however, remarkable Anglo-Saxon things still to be seen in Durham. These include considerable sculpture, some of it found in 1874 in the foundations of the Norman chapter-house apse. After the destruction of St Cuthbert's shrine in about 1538, his remains were reburied, and are still in the cathedral today. Very remarkably, his coffin, believed to have been made in 698, though decayed, has survived; it is no longer in his grave and, with its fragments reassembled, is on display. It is a unique piece, with very interesting carvings and inscriptions. Also shown are items that were placed in the coffin with the saint, including his pectoral cross. Further pieces displayed are a stole and maniple thought to have been given by King Athelstan in the 930s; they are exceptional examples of Anglo-Saxon embroidery.

The great cathedral begun under the first Norman bishop, William of St Carileph, stands almost complete to this day. Only the original eastern termination has been destroyed; excavation has shown that it had a main apse and lesser apses for the chancel aisles.

Ely (Cambridgeshire)

A religious house founded in 673 by Etheldreda, subsequently enshrined as the great saint of the place, later became a Benedictine abbey. Rebuilding began in 1083 under Simeon, the first Norman abbot, and the eastern limb was sufficiently complete in 1106 for the saint's relics to be translated into it. Only in 1109 was the see established: Ely (like Carlisle) differs from all the other medieval cathedrals in that the existing building was begun before it became a cathedral. It is nevertheless on the largest cathedral scale. Of the church completed by about the end of the twelfth century, only the central tower and chancel have been replaced. Excavation has shown that the chancel had four bays and a stilted apse; the aisles ended straight. Just the shafts originally rising from floor to roof at the entrance to the apse still exist.

Exeter (Devon)

An early minster of St Peter in Exeter was re-founded by King Athelstan (924–39). In 1050, when Bishop Leofric moved the see of the newly united diocese of Devon and Cornwall from Crediton to Exeter, this minster became the cathedral. It continued as such apparently without major alteration for a surprisingly long period after the Norman Conquest. Only in about 1114 under Bishop Warelwast was building begun of a Norman cathedral. This was consecrated in 1133, but not completed until about the end of the century.

Until 1971, a large church of St Mary Major stood only 25 yards from the cathedral's west front. It had been rebuilt in 1865–7 by the local architect Edward Ashworth, and was amusingly described by Pevsner in 1951 as 'major only as a disaster to the effect of the Close as a whole'. Following its demolition, an excavation took place in 1971–6, which has transformed understanding of the early history here. The Victorian foundations had destroyed any traces of previous main church buildings, but projecting beyond them on the north side were remains of two probable Anglo-Saxon porticus and, at the east end, a broad apse. These indicate an Anglo-Saxon church at least 110 feet in length. This was almost certainly the Anglo-Saxon minster, later cathedral: so after 1133 it had been reduced to parochial status. The Normans had chosen for their cathedral a site further east, more spacious and further from the city's streets, and gave it a different and more correct east-west axis than that of the minster. The excavations showed that the apse of the former minster was demolished in the twelfth century, perhaps a reduction in size commensurate with its reduced status. Interestingly, just west of St Mary Major there may until about 1300 have stood a church of St Mary Minor: was this another case of multiple axially aligned Anglo-Saxon churches?

Apart from possessing twin Norman transeptal towers, Exeter Cathedral is now almost completely a Decorated building. Study of the structure has, however, revealed much information about the lost Norman cathedral. Some lower parts of its aisle walls remain, and a few pieces of masonry are in situ elsewhere. Bomb damage in 1942 revealed significant Norman architectural fragments, including part of a large capital that showed the arcade pillars to have been cylindrical. The eastern limb ended in an apse with an ambulatory having radiating polygonal chapels; these chapels stood close to the position of the present secondary transepts. The nave was of the same length as at present, though its bay spacing was different. The Norman aisles continued beside the towers; large arches were inserted in the towers only in 1285 and 1287 when they were converted into transepts.

Hereford

This diocese was one of those established under Archbishop Theodore, in about 680. The cathedral of that period may have been replaced in the early ninth century. More certainly, in the early eleventh century it was greatly enlarged or rebuilt to become what was referred to as 'the glorious minster'. This building, however, was burnt when Hereford was sacked in 1055 by Earl Aelfgar with a force of Welsh and Irish, and apparently remained in ruins for half a century. No archaeology has revealed anything of these buildings; it is sometimes assumed that their site was just south of the present cathedral, but there is no firm evidence.

A Norman cathedral was probably begun under Bishop Reynelm (1107–15), and consecrated in the 1140s. This remains the framework of the cathedral today. Its original eastern termination has gone: excavation has shown that it had three apses. The Norman north transept has been replaced, but presumably resembled its surviving partner. Destroyed in the fall of the west tower in 1786 were the west front and west bay, and in the subsequent reconstruction the triforium and clerestory of the whole nave. They are known from old illustrations. Also removed at this time was a timber spire carried by the central tower.

Lichfield (Staffordshire)

The great figure here is St Chad, who on his appointment as fifth bishop of the Mercians in 669 established his see at Lichfield. On his death in 672, he was buried close to a church of St Mary. The first cathedral here, originally dedicated to St Peter, was built or rebuilt under Chad's successor Hedda and consecrated in 700. Chad's body was moved to it. Until recently, nothing was known of Anglo-Saxon structures here. However, excavations in 1992–4 in the present choir aisles revealed limited Anglo-Saxon remains, apparently of lateral porticus. Then, in 2003, an excavation in the second bay from the east end of the nave exposed further important Anglo-Saxon structures. These are the foundations of the west and side walls of a substantial building, and extending west from them the side walls of a further narrow chamber added later. They are interpreted as part of Hedda's cathedral of St Peter. It is also suggested that the remains under the chancel may be of the church of St Mary, the two having an axial relationship as seen at other Anglo-Saxon sites.[5] The present cathedral follows the Anglo-Saxon alignment, though is offset slightly to the north.

Remarkably, within the probable early cathedral a sunken chamber was found, with signs that it was once covered by a canopy. This is thought to have been the site of the grave and shrine of St Chad, perhaps that established by Hedda in the early eighth century. It remained here when the later medieval cathedrals were built around it, apparently until about 1320 when the saint was moved to a new shrine in the retrochoir. Most spectacularly, near this chamber were found three pieces of a sculptured panel, which fit together. This panel was made in about 800, probably during the time of King Offa when Lichfield was an archbishopric, and may have formed part of a shrine chest. Known as the Lichfield Angel, it probably represents the angel Gabriel. It is exceptionally fine and excellently preserved, retaining original paint, and is now displayed in the cathedral.

Despite the move of the see in about 1075 to Chester and then to Coventry, with a final resolution only in the thirteenth century, a large Norman church was built here from the late eleventh century. It was subsequently completely replaced by the present cathedral, which dates from about 1200–1340. The recent investigations have increased understanding of the Norman building. Its chancel had three bays with narrow aisles and an apse with an ambulatory and three apsidal chapels. A complicated evolution of this east end into the present structure has been elucidated. First, about 1150–60, a larger square-ended Lady Chapel replaced the previous eastern chapel. This and the Norman ambulatory and chapels were then replaced in a style transitional to Early English by a spacious feretory having a square east end containing four chapels. Later again, the Norman arcades and apse were replaced by the existing Early English chancel bays. The eastern limb remained in this form for about a century before the construction of the present Lady Chapel and the longer east part of the chancel.[6]

We may be grateful that Lichfield is not a lost cathedral. In 1646 and the years following, it suffered extensive structural damage; the central spire was brought down and the lead was stripped from all the roofs. Its restoration between 1661 and 1669 was a remarkable achievement.

Lincoln

Lincoln had no Anglo-Saxon cathedral, unless, as discussed in chapter one, that of Lindsey was indeed here. The see of Dorchester was transferred to Lincoln in 1072–3 under the Norman bishop Remigius. A cathedral was begun at once, and was consecrated in 1092. Following a fire in 1141, it was repaired and vaulted throughout under Bishop Alexander. In 1185, it was badly damaged by what was described as an earthquake (now suggested, however, as hyperbole for a structural failure, perhaps the collapse of the central tower!). In 1192, under Bishop Hugh of Avalon (St Hugh), a great rebuilding began that has given us the present cathedral.

The Norman cathedral has vanished but for the very west end, where spectacular Norman work, due partly to Remigius and partly to Alexander, remains as the centre of the west front. The Norman chancel terminated in an apse, with its aisles internally apsidal but externally square. There were rectangular east chapels to the transepts. The aisled

nave had a length equivalent to twelve bays. A remarkable reinterpreta-
tion of the west end was put forward in 1982.[7] In 1140, during the civil
war, Lincoln Castle was garrisoned for the Empress Matilda. Startlingly,
the cathedral, of which the west front faces the castle 200 yards away, was
garrisoned by King Stephen. The suggestion is that Remigius's cathedral,
as built, was fortified, with the whole west end to a length equivalent to
three bays forming a massive castle-like block. The episode of 1140 was
followed in February 1141 by the Battle of Lincoln, which led to the
burning of the city and cathedral. It is proposed that, in the subsequent
reconstruction under Bishop Alexander, the fortifications were removed
and the west end converted to a normal ecclesiastical form.

In the later rebuilding, which was begun in 1192, the first phase comprised a choir and eastern transepts. The eastern termination of this was
demolished in about 1256 to make way for the present Angel Choir. As
revealed by excavation in 1886, this termination was a polygonal apse
with further flanking apses of complicated and unusual form; it is still a
subject of discussion.[8]

In the later medieval period Lincoln Cathedral possessed a spectacular trio of timber spires. That of the central tower was extremely tall,
reputedly 525 feet high and the tallest in England, or even the world.
It was brought down by a storm in 1548 or 1549; the west spires were
removed in 1807.

London

Old St Paul's was the largest cathedral in England, straightforward in
plan but on a grand scale. Its later medieval length was about 585 feet,
and for a few decades in the seventeenth century it was even longer by
35 feet. It also had a famously lofty spire. It is easily the best known of
all the country's destroyed great churches. Moreover, it is almost unique
in that most of our extensive knowledge of it does not depend on
archaeology. Instead, having survived into the later seventeenth century
and being so prominently situated in the capital city, it was extensively
recorded, especially in illustrations. Finest are the many etchings by
Wenceslaus Hollar, published in Sir William Dugdale's *History of St
Paul's Cathedral* (1658). Showing the cathedral in its final state, they are
both beautiful and mainly (though not entirely) reliable. However, they
were not photographic: when it was seen by Hollar, the cathedral's condition was very bad, and Dugdale's instructions were to draw it not as it
was then but as it had been.

A cathedral was first established in 604 for Mellitus, one of the com-
panions of Augustine. As we saw in chapter one, Mellitus's mission was
not a success and in 616 he was driven out. Only with the arrival of
Erkenwald in 675 did a continuous sequence of bishops begin. This
uncertain beginning probably contributed to the thwarting of Pope

Gregory's intention when he sent Augustine that London should become a metropolitan see. The site chosen for the cathedral (in 604 or perhaps 675) was in the western part of the former Roman city. After the Romans left, the city had become derelict, and apparently remained so in this period, the Anglo-Saxon re-occupation of 'Lundenwic' being centred further west in what is now the Strand area. The exact Anglo-Saxon cathedral location remains unknown, though it was almost certainly on or close to the present site. There is no evidence that it related to any Roman Christian predecessor. The cathedral was rebuilt after being burnt in 962. Considering the importance of London, it seems probable that by the eleventh century it was large. After its destruction by fire in 1087, Bishop Maurice began a Norman cathedral. The eastern limb was completed by about 1110, and the nave was finished around the end of the century.

Internally, the Norman nave remained largely unchanged to the end. It had twelve bays, with compound pillars and large undivided triforium openings. There was a high vault, perhaps dating from the early thirteenth century. Two quite small towers probably of the late twelfth century stood outside the aisles at the west end. The transepts were of the unusual length of five bays. They had west aisles, which retained their Norman form throughout. On their east side, bays three and five from the crossing originally had an apsidal chapel. Later this side was given further chapels, effectively creating aisles that absorbed the Norman chapels, though one in the south transept retained its identity. The cross-

London: Old St Paul's Cathedral, the east end (c. 1656, engraving by Wenceslaus Hollar). (By kind permission of the University of Southampton)

ing tower was Early English, completed about 1221. A very lofty timber spire was added, which in the fifteenth century was burnt after being struck by lightning, but was rebuilt. It was a dominating feature apparently reaching nearly 500 feet. This is higher than any other in England today, though it may have been exceeded by that of Lincoln. The corners of the tower had massive external buttressing, but its stability remained a matter of concern.

The Norman chancel had perhaps four straight bays, with an apse and probably an ambulatory and radiating chapels. From about 1228, it was remodelled in Early English style, re-using parts of the Norman work including the pillars and aisle walls. Then from 1259 to about 1327 there was added a spectacular extension known as the 'New Work', bringing the eastern limb to a total of twelve bays. This was in Decorated

style and richer than the remodelled bays, with a tierceron vault and large traceried windows showing French influence. The tracery of the great east window included a spectacular rose. The New Work contained a large shrine of the former bishop St Erkenwald. The fifth bay from the crossing was wider than the rest, for unclear reasons: it perhaps implied intended eastern transepts, or it may have been in some way a consequence of the Norman apse having been here. A spacious and quite lofty crypt was beneath the whole eastern limb. The cathedral had many monuments and chantry chapels. A cloister was added in about the 1330s in the angle between nave and south transept, with the octagonal chapter-house uniquely set in its centre. Both were two-storeyed, and notably they were among the very first structures in the Perpendicular style.

In 1561, the spire was again struck by lightning, and this time not just the spire but all the roofs were burnt, though the vaults stood. The roofs were reinstated, but not the spire. However, there had been more fundamental damage, and in the early seventeenth century the state of the structure was bad. Eventually, in 1631 a major restoration began under the direction of Inigo Jones. In this, St Paul's received a treatment unique in this country (though frequent in continental Europe): the nave and transepts were externally refaced (in Portland stone) and converted to classical form. They had classical windows, pilaster buttresses, obelisk pinnacles and large volutes on the nave and transept fronts. No changes were made to the interior. Across the west front was added a spectacular Corinthian portico with columns 40 feet high and carrying a balustrade. The chancel, too, was extensively refaced, though without alteration. In 1642 however, the Civil War caused the work to be abandoned incomplete. The cathedral was very badly treated over the following years. In 1652 the removal of scaffolding left from work in progress a decade earlier led to a partial collapse of the south transept. After the Restoration, repairs started and major new alterations were

London: Old St Paul's Cathedral, from the north (1656, engraving by Wenceslaus Hollar). (By kind permission of the University of Southampton)

in prospect. Christopher Wren's involvement began, and he proposed to replace the tower with a great dome, of which his drawings remain. Then came the Great Fire of September 1666. The damage was severe; the main walls and the tower still stood, but in shaky condition. In 1668 the decision was taken to demolish completely. Wren's new cathedral was begun in 1675 and structurally completed in 1708.

Little physically survives of Old St Paul's. A few memorials are preserved in the existing cathedral. There is a collection of architectural fragments. Much of its stone is built into the present structure, visibly so in a few places in the crypt. In 2008, alongside Wren's nave, the new South Churchyard was opened: a garden that evocatively re-creates the footprint of most of the former cloister and chapter-house.

Norwich

In 1096, on a hitherto largely unoccupied site, construction of a cathedral for the newly transferred East Anglian see was begun. It was completed by the 1140s. Remarkably, this Norman cathedral remains complete in its essentials today, modified only by changes to details such as most of the windows, and additions including the high vaults and the spire. An Early English Lady Chapel added at the east end was demolished in the sixteenth century.

Ripon (Yorkshire, WR, now North Yorkshire)

This church originated in a Celtic monastery founded from Melrose in Scotland around the late 650s. Wilfrid then became abbot and reformed it to the Roman ways. When in about 668 he became bishop of York, he retained control of Ripon and in about 671–8 a great new church was built. We are told that Wilfrid brought continental masons for its construction, and that it was 'a basilica of smoothed stone … with various columns and porticus'. In about 678, Wilfrid left under a cloud for various reasons and Archbishop Theodore subdivided the large diocese of York, a proposal to which Wilfrid had objected. In a further subdivision in about 680, a diocese of Ripon was created with Wilfrid's church as cathedral. However, this did not last long. Wilfrid and Theodore were reconciled, and in 686 Wilfrid again became Bishop of York. The diocese of Ripon ceased and was incorporated back into that of York.

Ripon was later one of the three great collegiate churches of the diocese of York. In 1836 it became the first cathedral created since the 1540s. Among such cathedrals it is unique in that a see had been here before: it has a cathedral predecessor in Wilfrid's church. Amazingly, fabric of this church still exists, and is part of today's cathedral: this is its crypt, very similar to that at Hexham (see chapter one), which was also built under Wilfrid. It is by far the earliest part of any existing English cathedral, indeed the only one of pre-Conquest date, and one of the most moving places to visit. No above-ground structure remains of Wilfrid's church, and there has been little archaeological investigation. A limited excavation in 1932 exposed the foundations of two walls running east-west on either side of the crypt, under the present crossing, and also found two stone drums, thought to be column bases. One drum was removed and is now used as an altar. A re-examination in 1997 confirmed that the walls belonged to Wilfrid's church.[9]

Rochester (Kent)

The first bishop was consecrated by Augustine in 604: of English sees only Canterbury is older. In 1888, when the west front of the present cathedral was being underpinned, there were found under its northern part the foundations of the apse of a small stone-built church. Further excavation and probing in 1894 identified the plan of an aisleless nave and apsidal chancel, on a markedly different axis from that of the existing cathedral. The total external length was about 71 feet. Whether there may have been appendages such as porticus cannot be said. Does this church go back to the seventh century? Only a modern archaeological investigation might tell us, but it is comparable to other known seventh-century churches of Kent and, whatever its date, it seems likely that it was indeed a predecessor cathedral. The outline of the apse is marked in the cathedral floor. There have also been two other suggested discoveries of pre-Norman foundations: attached to the wall of the south nave aisle, and between the crossing and the north transept; but both are doubtful.

A Norman cathedral was built and almost certainly completed under Gundulf, bishop 1077–1108. Very little of this remains visible: probably just the Norman part of the crypt under the chancel and the massive, mutilated, plain tower standing slightly askew on the north side. The existing nave, though Norman, is in all visible features later, probably dating from after a fire of 1137. However, it certainly follows Gundulf's plan, and much of his fabric may be incorporated. Everything else was replaced in the great rebuilding that was begun perhaps in the 1180s. Excavations have shown that, surprisingly, the Norman east end had no apse.[10]

Salisbury (Wiltshire)

Begun on a virgin site in 1220 and completed about 1265, Salisbury Cathedral as then built still stands complete and little altered. The only major change has been the early fourteenth-century addition of the tower and spire. Nevertheless, something has been lost: a separate bell-tower that stood to the north-west was demolished in 1790. It was a massive, heavily buttressed Early English structure carrying a three-stage timber superstructure, the top part a spire reaching about 200 feet.

If the spire was original, it was then the cathedral's principal vertical accent. Salisbury's Norman predecessor was at Old Sarum (see chapter two).

Wells (Somerset)

The see of Wells was established in about 909, an existing minster of St Andrew becoming the cathedral. As we have seen in chapter two, the see was removed from Wells to Bath in about 1090, beginning a period of turbulence not finally resolved until the mid-thirteenth century. A Norman reconstruction under Bishop Robert of Lewes (1136–66) was consecrated in 1148. The present gothic cathedral is now considered to have been begun as early as 1176.

Archaeology, principally a major excavation beginning in 1978, has yielded some spectacular and exciting insights here.[11] The focus of these investigations has been east of the east walk of the present cloister. A sequence of structures was found beginning with a rectangular mausoleum remarkably thought to date from about the end of the Roman era: the fourth or fifth century. Eventually, in the late tenth century, a substantial chapel of nave and chancel was built on this site. Its axis was markedly more north–north-east to south–south-west than that of the present cathedral. This chapel was subsequently extended west to link with a structure which appears to end in an apse, now largely covered by the east cloister walk. The latter is interpreted as the east end of the Anglo-Saxon cathedral, which extended across what is now the cloister garth. Wells is thus another example of the later connection of originally separate buildings on the same axis. To the east, this axis is aligned on the spring called St Andrew's Well. To the west of the cloister, some post-Conquest buildings, presumably built while the Anglo-Saxon cathedral still stood and largely demolished in 1870, continued this axis. Further west, the market place is close to the same axis.

No excavations have been undertaken in the cloister garth, so the form of the Anglo-Saxon cathedral remains unknown. The building work of the 1140s is now thought almost certainly to have been a modification of this cathedral, not a new build. The Normans had by this time begun the complete replacement of all other Anglo-Saxon cathedrals; this lesser action may reflect the then diminished status of Wells. Wells and Sherborne were perhaps the only cases where an Anglo-Saxon cathedral received major Norman alterations.

Wells was still not unambiguously of cathedral status when the new start was made in about 1176, yet this is fully on a cathedral scale. It was laid out further to the north on a different orientation. A straight-ended chancel of three bays was built, which still exists, though it has been modified. This had an eastern ambulatory and a straight-ended eastern chapel, which were both demolished for the great eastward extension in the Decorated period. The cathedral's arcaded circular font is now thought to be of the ninth or early tenth century, though altered.

When the Anglo-Saxon cathedral was demolished and the cloister was built across its site, the ancient eastern chapel was retained as the Lady Chapel-by-the-Cloister. It was enlarged several times, and then demolished in about 1477 for a completely new structure, still on its site but now on the new orientation. This was destroyed in about 1552.

Winchester (Hampshire)

We have seen that in about 635 Birinus established the see of Wessex at Dorchester (Oxfordshire). Probably under Birinus's influence, a minster was built in Winchester in about 648 by King Cenwalh. In the 660s, the see was transferred from Dorchester to Winchester and this minster became the cathedral for the diocese of Wessex.

The 1962–9 excavations that explored the Anglo-Saxon cathedral are a landmark in modern archaeology.[12] Even its location just north of the existing nave was unknown until the mid-twentieth century. The investigations revealed a very complicated architectural history in startling and fascinating detail, yet this was done on a site from which even the foundations had been robbed in the demolition of 1093–4. What was learned from the archaeology could also be linked with the important surviving documentary evidence. Cenwalh's church was of stone, and remained the core of the cathedral for over 400 years. During this period it went through a remarkable series of transformations

Winchester: the Old Minster as it might have appeared in about 1000 (1997, copyright Winchester Excavations Committee/ Simon Hayfield)

and enlargements, achieving its final form in about 993–4. As built originally, it was cruciform: a nave with three rectangular porticus projecting from its E end, which were effectively transepts and chancel. It was substantial, with a length of about 96 feet. At some time in the eighth century the square east end was replaced by an apse. Also, some distance to its west and in axis with it, there was built the freestanding St Martin's tower. After about another century, in 862, the bishop Swithun was buried in the open area between the tower and the nave.

Under King Alfred the Great, reigned 871–99, Winchester grew to new importance, and another large church, New Minster, was built immediately to the north in about 901–3. The cathedral now became known as Old Minster. So close were the two that (according to William of Malmesbury) 'the voices of the two choirs confounded one another.' Shortly after this, broad transept-like wings were added to the west end of Old Minster, perhaps to make it appear more impressive beside the larger New Minster. Also constructed nearby in this period was a church for nuns, creating a unique group of three major churches together with a royal palace.

Later in the tenth century, Swithun became a saint and the focus of a cult. In 971 his remains were translated into the ancient nave and enshrined, but his former gravesite also continued to be revered. This heralded the final and most spectacular phase of the growth of Old Minster. A large new structure joined St Martin's tower to the nave, carrying a lofty tower and flanked by apses. A little later, St Martin's tower was incorporated in a new westwork with flanking towers. The final alterations, in the last decade of the century, included a much longer eastern apse, thought to be surmounted by a further tower, with a pair of flanking apses. In its final century of existence, this was an extraordinarily complicated structure, with four towers and three apses. The easternmost tower was crowned by a gilt weathercock. The total length was about 240 feet – similar to that of the great twelve-bay nave of the present cathedral. Internally, it was by now made up of a large number of separate but interlinked spaces. Its embellishments included wall paintings, friezes of carved stone and windows of coloured glass. It had bells, and a large organ stated to have required a team of seventy operators. Many kings were buried in it, both of Wessex and of England, including Cnut in 1035.

After the Norman Conquest, a great new cathedral was begun in 1079, set to the south-east of Old Minster so that its eastern arm could be constructed while the old building continued in use. Following the initial dedication of the Norman cathedral in 1093, Old Minster was demolished, and the new nave when built partly encroached on its site. Since the excavations, the outline of most of Old Minster has been marked with brickwork in the grass, and a granite slab identifies the site of St Swithun's original grave.

Of the Norman cathedral, the transepts, crossing and tower remain essentially unaltered. The eastern limb has gone except for its crypt; but from this together with a few indications at higher levels, much is known about its lost structure. It had an apse with a square-ended ambulatory and an apsidal eastern chapel. Also well known is the nave, which was transformed without demolition into a Perpendicular structure. Obviously visible are a few Norman shafts and capitals in its east part, formerly concealed by screens. A large tripartite structure, now believed to have been twin towers, extended beyond the present west end. Evidence remains that the transepts, too, were intended to have flanking towers, and also the east end. An intriguing conjectural view shows the Norman cathedral had it ever been completed with its full complement of seven towers.

Worcester

This see was established in about 680, in the time of Archbishop Theodore, with a church of St Peter as cathedral. However, when Oswald became bishop in 961, he moved to a church of St Mary in the same precinct (were the two churches axially related?). Here, under the influence of St Dunstan, he established strict Benedictine monastic life. Rebuilding of this church, now cathedral, was completed in 983. In 1062 Wulfstan became bishop: he was the only Anglo-Saxon bishop fully to retain the favour of the Norman kings, remaining in office till his death in 1095. Under his perhaps reluctant orders, in 1084 a great new cathedral in Norman style was begun, which in 1089 was sufficiently advanced for services to be transferred to it. Nothing is known of its Anglo-Saxon predecessors except the probability that their sites were close to that of the present cathedral. However, Oswald's cathedral is memorialised in Wulfstan's reported expression of his feelings when in 1089 he was obliged to order its demolition: 'We poor wretches destroy the works of our forefathers only to get praise to ourselves. That happy age of holy men knew not how to build stately churches. Under any roof they offered up themselves as living temples to God ... We on the contrary, neglecting the care of souls, labour to heap up stones.'

Of Wulfstan's Norman cathedral, only the crypt under the chancel and parts of the main transepts remain, the rest being replaced mostly in the thirteenth and fourteenth centuries. The crypt shows that the Norman chancel above had an apse and ambulatory, and there were three polygonal radiating chapels. Some hints of the Norman elevation also remain. A tower fell in 1175: it seems likely that this was a west tower and that the present two western bays of the nave, in a transitional style, were built to replace the previous west end.

York

In 1966, the condition of York Minster was causing serious alarm. Tell tales (glass monitor pieces) fitted across cracks repeatedly broke and it became evident that, unless action was taken, York would become a late example of the many collapses among the medieval cathedrals. Concern was greatest over the central tower, but the east front and west towers were also at risk. An appeal was launched and there followed an inspiring campaign in 1967–72 in which the resources of modern engineering were harnessed to secure the minster. Much of the work involved the foundations, and so also presented a great opportunity for archaeology. Though it had always to be subservient to the urgent engineering work, a major archaeological campaign was mounted that produced spectacular discoveries concerning both the Roman structures that had previously occupied the site and the minster's Norman predecessors. At the end of the structural work, the opportunity was taken to create a large new undercroft in the excavated area under and around the crossing, in which many of the Roman and Norman footings, and much else, can be seen.

In 627, a wooden church dedicated to St Peter was constructed, in which Paulinus, who had been consecrated as the first bishop probably in 625, baptised King Edwin. This is regarded as the first minster. Under Edwin, a stone church was begun soon after. This had a chequered early career after Bishop Paulinus was obliged to flee in 633, but it was restored in about 669 under Wilfrid. In 735 it became the seat of an archbishop. By the late eighth century it could be described by Alcuin as 'supported by strong columns ... lofty, splendid and graceful'. It was

York: the Norman minster as it might have appeared in about 1130 (1985, Crown copyright. NMR)

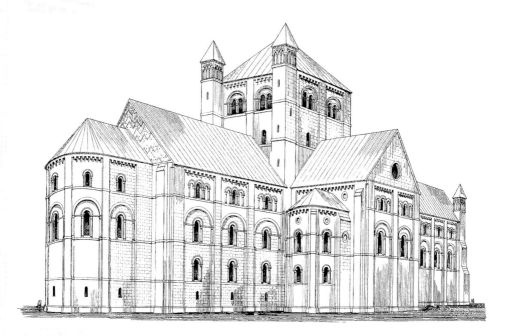

burnt in 1069 in the 'harrying of the North', but repaired under the first Norman archbishop, Thomas of Bayeux (1070–1100). Perhaps as early as 1075, the archbishop began a Norman cathedral, probably completed early in the twelfth century. The present minster, however, is entirely of the thirteenth to the fifteenth century.

No Anglo-Saxon foundations were discovered in the excavations in the minster. The location of the Anglo-Saxon minster remains unknown, though there is reason to believe that it was close by. However, many remains of Archbishop Thomas's Norman minster were revealed: because of its lower floor level, parts of its walls survive to a height of about 5 feet. It was both longer (366 feet) and wider across the transepts than the contemporary cathedral of Archbishop Lanfranc at Canterbury. However, the greatest surprise was its character: it was cruciform but both nave and chancel were aisleless. It had the remarkable internal width of over 45 feet, and has determined the width and layout of the present minster; its foundations still support much of the later structure, including the central tower. The chancel ended in an apse, and both transepts had one apsidal east chapel. A crypt lay under the chancel. The chancel walls were double, with a passage between them: what this represents remains uncertain. Externally, it was covered in an almost white render, which was lined out in red to give the effect of ashlar. Surviving capitals and other architectural fragments indicate some richness and sophistication. In several places high in the present structure, fragments of in-situ Norman masonry have been identified, including indications of its height and fenestration, which have provided evidence for a conjectural reconstruction of the upper parts. It must have been magnificent, and unlike anything else.

In 1154 Roger of Pont l'Evêque became archbishop. Under him, a new chancel was built, probably completed in the 1170s or 1180s. This was much longer and more spacious than its predecessor: it had eight bays, with aisles, eastern transepts and a square east end. A crypt was beneath, and some of the columns of this still remain to their full height of 7 feet and are complete with their capitals. They are cylindrical with four attached shafts, and their surface is incised with spiral zigzag or lozenge patterns reminiscent of the famous, much earlier pillars at Durham. Other architectural fragments and part of a doorway illustrate the sumptuous richness that it must have had throughout. All these appear Norman in character, but it is thought that the upper parts also showed some early gothic features. Other new construction under Archbishop Roger included the addition of a westwork with twin towers. This had a spectacular external display of statuary, some of which survives by having been re-used later. The next building campaign after this, beginning about 1220, was the south transept, which is the start of the minster as it stands today. Archbishop Roger's chancel survived until the late fourteenth century.[13]

Notes

1. Davenport, P., 'The Cathedral Priory Church at Bath' in Tatton-Brown and Munby (eds.) (1996), pp. 19–25, 29–30.
2. A full treatment is Blockley, Sparks, and Tatton-Brown (1997). Shorter accounts are given in Collinson, Ramsay and Sparks (eds.) (1995) pp. 33–37; Blockley and Bennett (1993).
3 McCarthy, M.R. 'The Origins and Development of the Twelfth-Century Cathedral Church at Carlisle' in Tatton-Brown and Munby (eds.) (1996).
4. Tatton-Brown, T., 'Archaeology and Chichester Cathedral' in Tatton-Brown and Munby (eds.) (1996); Hobbs (1994).
5. If so, this invalidates the old belief that Chad's original burial was outside the church now dedicated to him at Stowe, half a mile east of the cathedral.
6. Rodwell, W., 'Archaeology and the Standing Fabric: Recent Investigations at Lichfield Cathedral' in Tatton-Brown and Munby (eds.) (1996); Rodwell (2004); Rodwell, Hawkes, Howe and Cramp (2008).
7. Gem, R., 'Lincoln Minster: *Ecclesia Pulchra, Ecclesia Fortis*' in Heslop and Sekules (eds.) (1986).
8. Kidson, P., 'St Hugh's Choir' in *ibid.*
9. Bailey, R.N., 'Seventh-Century Work at Ripon and Hexham' in Tatton-Brown and Munby (eds.) (1996); also unpublished material from the cathedral.
10. Tatton-Brown, T., 'Archaeology and Rochester Cathedral' in Tatton-Brown and Munby (eds.) (1996); Ayers and Tatton-Brown (eds.) (2006).
11. A full treatment is Rodwell (2001); a shorter account is Rodwell, W., 'Above and Below Ground: Archaeology at Wells Cathedral' in Tatton-Brown and Munby (eds.) (1996).
12 The most accessible account is Kjølbye-Biddle, B., 'Old Minster, St Swithun's Day 1093' in Crook (ed.) (1993).
13 Brown (2003), pp. 1–9; Harrison and Norton (2008), pp. 53–9; Phillips (1985), *passim.*

5

POST-REFORMATION ANGLICAN CATHEDRALS

We have seen that the medieval organisation of England into dioceses left much to be desired, and that Cardinal Wolsey and then Henry VIII himself had plans for its rationalisation by the creation of new dioceses. Despite the improvements that were effected under the latter, the position remained far from ideal. Only a decade after the king's changes, interest was surprisingly again shown in the creation of a new diocese: an Act of Parliament of 1553 included the establishment of a see at Newcastle upon Tyne. This would have used as its cathedral the large parish church of St Nicholas; but on the accession of Queen Mary later in that year the scheme was cancelled. From 1550 (when the recently created diocese of Westminster ceased) no changes were made to the diocesan map for nearly 300 years. By the first half of the nineteenth century the need for change had become more pressing, with the great movements of population in the Midlands and the north associated with the Industrial Revolution. This period saw the growth of a new spirit of reform in the Church of England; it was realised that if the Church did not change it would increasingly lose touch with large parts of the population. Among the actions taken was the progressive reform of the diocesan system, partly through the introduction of new dioceses.

This started in 1836 with the creation of the diocese of Ripon, beginning a period of just over ninety years in which altogether twenty new dioceses were established, almost doubling the total. The process then ceased (though at the time of writing a dioceses commission is sitting which could lead to further changes). The new dioceses came slowly at first, and many were not founded until the twentieth century, ending with five in 1926–7. Some were the fulfilment of proposals that had previously been made in the sixteenth century. Several reinstated dioceses that had existed in Anglo-Saxon times, and had subsequently been abandoned. The dioceses created for Cornwall and Suffolk, for example, fall into both categories. Other dioceses such as those of Birmingham, Blackburn, Bradford, Manchester, Newcastle, Sheffield and Wakefield were created in areas that had once been rural or sparsely populated, but had become densely settled as a result of eighteenth- and nineteenth-century industrial growth. Most of the new cathedrals were in places that had never before had or been considered for a cathedral. However, Coventry, Leicester and Ripon had previously had a cathedral, and in the last of these it was (as discussed earlier) the direct successor to the early cathedral that now again became the seat of a bishop. Those of Bury St Edmunds, Leicester, St Albans and Southwell were in places that had appeared in the Henry VIII proposals; remarkably, as we have seen, two were able to use the actual churches of his abandoned plans.

As well as the establishment of new dioceses, other diocesan changes took place through this period, some of them surprising. For example Essex, although it had been the subject of unrealised plans by Henry VIII, was, from the seventh century until 1845, part of the diocese of London. Then, however, it was incorporated into that of Rochester, despite being separated from it by the Thames estuary. In 1877 it was transferred to the new diocese of St Albans, and then finally in 1914 it became a diocese in its own right with its cathedral at Chelmsford. The perverse Henry VIII diocese of Bristol was divided in 1836, Dorset being returned to the diocese of Salisbury (whence it had come in 1542). The city and county of Bristol, augmented by some other areas taken from the dioceses of Bath and Wells, Hereford and Salisbury, were annexed to the diocese of Gloucester, now given the title 'Gloucester and Bristol'. The motivation for this change was to prevent an increase in the number of bishops in the House of Lords on the foundation in that year of the diocese of Ripon. However, in 1897 the diocese of Bristol was re-established, with its territory newly defined. A more straightforward case was the large diocese of Winchester. This was unchanged until 1905, when the new diocese of Southwark was taken from it; then in 1927 it was further reduced by the formation of the dioceses of Guildford and Portsmouth.

For the creation of the second new diocese – of Manchester in 1847 – a new mechanism was devised to avoid increasing the number of bishops who sat in the Lords. This continued with all subsequent new dioceses, and still applies today: the bishops or archbishops of Canterbury, Durham, London, Winchester and York always have a seat, but the others only on a basis of seniority. The total of twenty-six has remained unchanged since 1550 (though since 1920 it has excluded the Welsh bishops).

The establishment of a new cathedral required an Act of Parliament. From decision to implementation could take some years. For example, at Coventry the parish church of St Michael, having been chosen to be the cathedral of a new diocese, was in 1908 reconstituted as a collegiate church. A chapter was appointed. Premises to be used as a chapter-house were acquired in 1910. However, delayed by the war, it was not until 1918 that its Act was passed and the new diocese and cathedral created. In some cases a further year might pass after the founding of the diocese before the cathedral was formally established.

Though the members of the 'extended canon' – Ripon, St Albans, Southwark and Southwell – are not discussed here, we may reflect with gratitude on their survival to become cathedrals. This positive outcome runs contrary to the usual sorry story of destruction mainly in the sixteenth century. Ripon is cathedral of a diocese now called 'Ripon and Leeds', which (as also in other cases) does not imply that both places have a cathedral. The delayed realisation in 1877 of Henry VIII's unfulfilled plan for the Benedictine abbey of St Albans gave us what is, at about 547 feet, the country's second-longest cathedral. The diocese of Southwell, created in 1884 again implementing a proposal of Henry VIII, was renamed 'Southwell and Nottingham' in 2005. Last of this group is the former Augustinian priory church of Southwark.

There remain sixteen cathedrals to be considered here. All were established or provisionally established in an existing parish church (two of which, Derby and Manchester, had been collegiate). This great enlargement of the Anglican body of cathedrals has produced very varied but sometimes spectacular architectural results. At one extreme, it has given us the country's largest cathedral. At the other are two or three little-altered former parish churches of relatively modest scale and distinction.

In three places, a complete new cathedral was built as a result of the creation of the see (in all cases replacing a parish church which at first served as pro-cathedral). These are Guildford, Liverpool and Truro. A fourth, at Coventry, came as a result of the wartime destruction of its parish church predecessor. These four cathedrals were all completed essentially as planned, in the cases of Guildford and Liverpool despite the difficulties and delays caused by one or two world wars. We may be thankful for this; it contrasts with what happened at several other cathedrals where, as we will see, major extensions were curtailed as a result of the Second World War. The four new cathedrals are all major buildings, in their character and ambition at least comparable with the medieval cathedrals. Each is very different from the others.

The remaining twelve cathedrals are still based on the pre-existing parish church, of which all or almost all remains standing. At four, those of Birmingham, Leicester, Manchester and Newcastle, no significant structural extension has taken place as a result of their creation as cathedrals. Manchester and Newcastle stand out as being exceptionally large and fine by parish church standards; the other two are smaller. All have had major changes to their fittings to suit them to their new purpose. As cathedrals, they are also of course distinguished from parish churches by the life that takes place in them, including liturgical, musical and civic aspects.

The other eight cathedrals have been extended. These extensions have generally had two basic objectives. One has been to provide them with more space for their functioning as cathedrals. This means both the accommodation of larger congregations and the creation of a larger area for their liturgy. The other objective has been to give them more of the traditional character and appearance of a cathedral. In general, of course, the two objectives have been addressed together, and their implementation has produced some interesting and sometimes splendid architecture. Chelmsford, however, has been only modestly extended, and still looks very much the parish church that it was. The remaining seven enlarged cathedrals form an impressive if disparate body of buildings. Four combine work from the twentieth century with a basically medieval structure. At Portsmouth about half of the earlier work is of the late seventeenth century, while at Derby the basis is largely eighteenth century. Blackburn before enlargement was entirely of the early nineteenth century. Some have set out with the ambition of creating something seriously resembling a medieval cathedral, but probably only Bury St Edmunds may be considered to have successfully achieved this. This cathedral and that of Wakefield are the only two of the seven in which the full originally intended enlargement has been completed. At the other five, extension schemes were planned and in some cases construction was started in the 1930s, which turned out to be an inauspicious time for beginning a major cathedral project. Work in progress was stopped by the Second World War at Blackburn, Portsmouth and Sheffield. At Bradford and Derby, designs had been prepared but construction had not begun. After the war, not only had financial conditions become more difficult, but in some places aspirations had changed, affecting both the scale of what was required and the architectural style appropriate for it. At all three cathedrals where work in progress had been stopped, subsequent completion was on a reduced scale. Sheffield, by abandoning the very ambitious plan on which previous work had been based, has inevitably ended up as something of a muddle. The large-scale extension of Blackburn has obviously been curtailed, but the cathedral has arguably gained much by the distinctive modern tower it was finally given. Portsmouth was eventually completed in the spirit of the pre-war work, though to a reduced length. At Bradford, construction of the proposals of the 1930s did not begin until the 1950s, but they were then mostly implemented. In the case of Derby, instead of the pre-war design, a much-reduced version was eventually built about three decades later.

At Blackburn, Bradford, Bury St Edmunds, Derby and Wakefield, the principal extensions have been to the east end. Although realised to different degrees, the intention in all of these has been the provision of a splendid and long chancel together with one or more additional chapels and in some cases a plan enriched by the addition of transepts or an eastern ambulatory. The extension at Chelmsford is also of the chancel. By contrast, the new work at Portsmouth was principally the addition of a new nave to the west; however, as a consequence the functional chancel was much enlarged by the incorporation into it of what had previously been the nave. Sheffield, too, has ended up with an extension to the west, while the original chancel has remained unchanged; however, it has also gained an impressive array of chapels on its north side.

As we have seen, a major reason why these larger chancels were required was for the accommodation of the cathedral liturgy and its music. However, from about the 1960s a new ideal became important. Coming from what is known as the Liturgical Movement is the objective of enabling better congregational visual participation in the liturgy. By this time the new cathedrals and most of the extensions had already been designed, and its effect has been limited; but the altars at Birmingham, Chelmsford and Portsmouth have been moved forward, leaving the structural east end relatively unused. As will be seen in the next chapter, this change has had a much greater impact on many Roman Catholic cathedrals.

In all cases, new ancillary buildings have been constructed, usually attached to the cathedral. Facilities include vestries, offices and a song school, often included in one block of building. Sometimes, as at Derby and Guildford, such accommodation is incorporated into the main structure of the cathedral. Some of the earlier design schemes for new or extended cathedrals, as at Truro, followed medieval precedent in also including a large-scale octagonal chapter-house and a quadrangle of cloister walks. Nevertheless, no such chapter-house has been constructed, although there are relatively small octagonal chapter-houses at Guildford and Liverpool, while Sheffield has one built to a rectangular plan. Often, no architecturally significant structure has been created and the term 'chapter room' is more appropriate. As for cloisters, the ancillary buildings may, as at Portsmouth, include passages akin to cloisters. At Guildford, cloister-like walks form wings attached to the west end. However, except for an abortive beginning at Truro, only at Bury St Edmunds has a full cloister quadrangle been attempted; at the time of writing, two of its walks have been completed.

From the second half of the twentieth century facilities for visitors have sometimes been added, as also at the ancient cathedrals. As well as a shop, restaurant and toilets, there may be a treasury for the display of plate and other precious objects. These are often in separate buildings, but they may be connected to or inside the cathedral itself.

It is perhaps surprising that, although the process of creating twenty new cathedrals began in 1836, little of the resulting new building took place in the nineteenth century. Other than some small additions at Manchester and the extensions at Wakefield designed at the end of the century but built in the next, the new cathedral of Truro is the only case. This was designed by John Loughborough Pearson (1817–97). Some will feel grateful that it was he who was chosen to design the country's one Victorian cathedral. It is, however, interesting to speculate on what some of the other major nineteenth-century church architects might have made of a similar opportunity. Unsuccessful competitors for Truro included G.F. Bodley, William Burges, J.O. Scott and G.E. Street. R.H. Carpenter designed a new cathedral for Manchester, but it remained unexecuted. However, much of the answer to the question is to be found outside England. Sir George Gilbert Scott (1811–78), the most prolific of the church architects of the Victorian era, had his chance in Scotland with St Mary's Cathedral in Edinburgh, built in 1874–1917 for the Scottish Episcopal Church. Other English architects of the Victorian years designed cathedrals for places in the British Empire, Ireland or the United States.

Almost all the rest of the architectural harvest from this great expansion of the English cathedrals is of the twentieth century. Perhaps the most extraordinary opportunity for a young architect was for the creation of Liverpool Cathedral, given to Giles Gilbert Scott at the age of twenty-two (later knighted; 1880–1960). He was the grandson of Sir G.G. Scott. This is the first of the three complete twentieth-century Anglican cathedrals. The next is Guildford, by Sir Edward Maufe (1882–1974). Maufe also designed the enlargements at Bradford. Sir Charles Nicholson (1867–1949) was responsible for several cathedral projects in the earlier part of the century, designing extensions at Chelmsford, Portsmouth and Sheffield, though none of his greater schemes was completed. Sir Ninian Comper (1864–1960) produced the original enlargement plans for Derby. William Adam Forsyth (1872–1951) designed a massive scheme for the extension of Blackburn.

All the architects so far discussed produced designs basically of traditional character, mostly in gothic styles related to medieval precedent. In the post-war period, however, new forms appeared, most dramatically at Coventry, the century's third complete new cathedral, built in 1955–62 to the designs of Sir Basil Spence (1903–76). This cathedral has made Spence perhaps still the best known of twentieth-century cathedral architects. Other designs in comparable modern styles were produced at Blackburn by Laurence King (1907–81) and at Sheffield by Arthur Bailey (1903–79). Meanwhile, a very different path was being followed by Stephen Dykes Bower (1903–94), whose work at Bury St Edmunds from the 1960s remained firmly gothic.

Some of the unexecuted cathedral designs of the twentieth century deserve to be remembered. Particularly interesting schemes include that of Sir Giles Gilbert Scott for the rebuilding of Coventry after its wartime destruction, and Sir Charles Nicholson's first proposal at Chelmsford. Many designs were submitted unsuccessfully to the competitions held at Liverpool, Guildford, Coventry and elsewhere: altogether many hundreds of cathedral designs. Some were by well-known architects, and among them there was surely much of interest and value. However, we should remember that these were generally not finished, fully worked-out plans: as with those few that were actually built, they would probably have been considerably refined and altered before and during execution.

The twenty-first century opened with the building of the great crossing tower at Bury St Edmunds – a remarkable achievement. Following this, however, at the time of writing no further important additions seem in prospect at any of these cathedrals. The architectural consequences of the expansion of 1836–1927 have perhaps by now been worked through. So this tower could possibly prove to be the century's last as well as first major work among the Anglican cathedrals. But the story of English cathedral architecture from the nineteenth century onwards is far from complete if it considers only the activities of the established Church. The contributions from others, especially the Roman Catholic Church, will be discussed in chapter six.

Birmingham (Warwickshire, now West Midlands)

The parish church of St Philip in Birmingham was designed in 1709 by Thomas Archer and built from 1711, with the tower completed in 1725. It became the cathedral in 1905. Extension to provide a substantial chancel had already been carried out in 1883–4, and there has been

Birmingham Cathedral

no further enlargement. Its length is about 162 feet. Some may find it surprising that England's second city has so small a cathedral: but it is an important and distinguished building. Archer had travelled on the continent, and this is one of the few English churches that can be described as baroque, even if it is moderate by European standards. It stands in a large and beautiful green square, the only such oasis in the centre of the city.

The cathedral consists of a west tower, a rectangular body and a narrower chancel, all faced in ashlar. Doric pilasters articulate the bays, which have a single large round-arched window surrounded by banded rustication. Above are a frieze, a cornice, and a balustrade with urns. Rich doorcases face east and west at the ends of each side; oval windows are above them. The chancel, by J.A. Chatwin, is of full height and closely matches the rest. It appears externally as of one bay followed by a partly apsidal second bay. The most striking external feature is the splendid tower, largely engaged in the building. Its main stage has deeply concave sides containing the large round-arched belfry openings. Between these are narrow diagonal faces with paired Corinthian pilasters. Above is a short recessed stage with great pairs of scrolled brackets in the diagonals. This leads into a dome surmounted by an open cupola with dome and ball.

Inside, the nave has five bays, with arcades of square fluted pillars carrying round arches. The ceilings are flat and have little ornament. There are full-length north and south galleries with panelled oak fronts. These are original; a further gallery across the west end has been removed. Flanking the tower is another bay containing the gallery stairs. At the east end of the aisles a further bay is now separated as vestries. In the central vessel this bay now forms part of the chancel, which internally has two bays and the partly apsidal eastern bay, and is impressively rich. Flanking the east window are great fluted Corinthian pilasters. Both sides of the chancel have three further pilasters, with an enormous fluted Corinthian column, painted to resemble marble, standing forward from each. These columns, introduced by Chatwin, define the chancel and give it a most opulent effect.

The apse has rich wrought-iron rails, perhaps by Jean Tijou who did similar work at St Paul's Cathedral in London. They formerly served as communion rails, but the altar has been brought forward. Box pews were removed from the nave after 1905, but two were allowed to remain at the back. Most famous of the contents are four great windows of 1885–97 by the Pre-Raphaelite Edward Burne-Jones, made by Morris & Co. They are of fine design and gorgeous colours. Three are in the apse, a fourth at the west end. The cathedral suffered serious wartime damage, but fortunately these windows had been removed for safe keeping. In 1989 an undercroft was created at the west end to provide a song school and other facilities.

Blackburn (Lancashire)

The former parish church was built in 1820–6 to the designs of John Palmer, replacing a medieval church on a slightly different site. It was elevated to cathedral status in 1926, and now forms the nave of a cruciform cathedral. It has six bays with tall aisles and a clerestory, in a good early gothic revival style, the tracery having both Decorated and Perpendicular elements. There is a big west tower with long twin belfry openings and an openwork straight parapet with tall corner pinnacles. Internally, this nave is strikingly attractive and indeed cathedral-worthy, with an excellent tierceron vault of plaster, enhanced by modern colouring of the ribs. The aisles have flat ceilings with large coves, also given ribs like those of vaulting.

In 1938 work began on a great eastern extension to the designs of W. A. Forsyth in an attractive style related to Perpendicular. Construction ceased in 1941 but resumed in 1951; however, Forsyth's plan was never finished. Completed are the crossing and the transepts, which have narrow east and west aisles. The east bay of Palmer's nave arcades was rebuilt to cant out to Forsyth's greater width; the crossing is surrounded in all directions by a narrow bay corresponding to the aisles. This new work is on a generous scale, with the transepts extending two large bays beyond the aisles; but as the height is that of the earlier nave, it seems quite low in proportion. The transepts have good coloured timber roofs.

Forsyth's plans had included a lofty octagonal crossing tower, a long aisled chancel with apse, large flanking chapels and an octagonal chapter-house. In 1961 Laurence King took over as architect, and the cathedral was completed more modestly and in a different style. The altar is in the crossing and to its east is just an ambulatory and the short Jesus Chapel, with simple details. Striking and distinctive, however, is

Blackburn Cathedral, looking north across the transepts

King's lantern tower over the crossing. This is octagonal and quite short, with multiple ribs continuing as tapered pinnacles; it carries a thin but tall spire or flèche. Disappointingly, it suffered major structural problems and had to be rebuilt in 1998, when the original concrete cladding and ribs were replaced in sandstone.

Despite the anti-climax of the east end, this is a fine and surprisingly harmonious cathedral. It has many good fittings, including significant modern artworks. One of these is an enormous circular coloured piece on the exterior of the windowless east wall. There are eight medieval stalls with carved misericords, which probably came from nearby Whalley Abbey. Beneath the eastern parts is a large and lofty crypt, still partly unfinished but housing a gift shop and café.

Bradford (Yorkshire, WR, now West Yorkshire)

This former parish church became the cathedral in 1919. Set with much attractive green space around it on a hillside rising towards the east, it had been largely rebuilt in the fourteenth and fifteenth centuries. About the beginning of the sixteenth century it was given a big, dignified west tower, which has survived Civil War bombardment to be probably the finest feature of today's cathedral. It has twin transomed two-light belfry openings, panelled battlements and sixteen pinnacles. Battlements finish the nave and aisles too, but these parts have been much renewed.

Bradford Cathedral

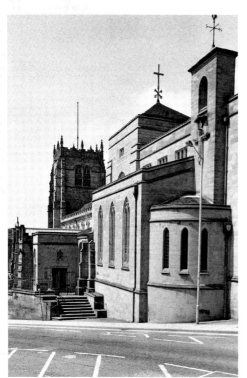

The nave has the unusual length of nine bays. Internally it is consistent in its effect though not fully uniform. The arcades are largely Decorated, with quatrefoil pillars carrying arches with two orders of sunk quadrants. Above is a Perpendicular clerestory. Flanking the east part of the nave are low chapel-like transepts added in 1899, opening from the aisles by arcades of two bays on the north and three on the south.

Plans for major cathedral extensions drawn up in 1935 by Edward Maufe (later knighted) were eventually constructed between 1951 and 1965. Most of his original proposals were executed, and there is no sense here of compromise or incompleteness. However, they continue the modest scale of the old building, and except perhaps for the medieval tower there is nothing here of traditional cathedral magnitude. The new work is in a simple gothic style related

Bradwell-on-Sea: the chapel of St Peter-on-the-Wall

Crediton church (photograph by Ed Rossmiller, by kind permission of the Governors and PCC of Crediton parish urch)

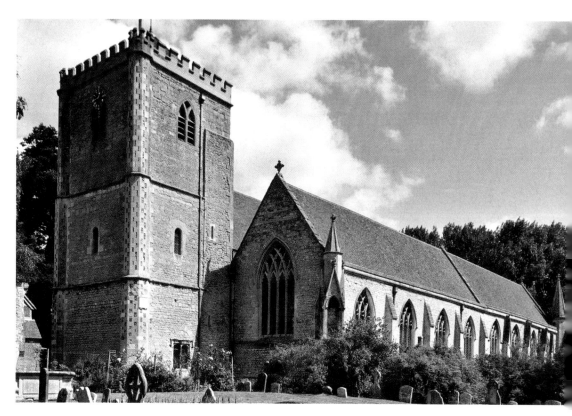

3. Dorchester Abbey

4. Dorchester Abbey: the chancel

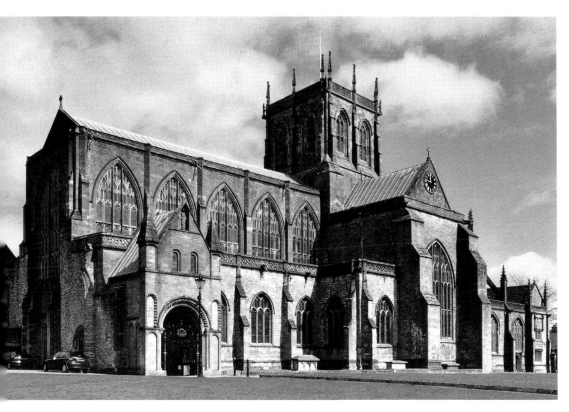

Sherborne Abbey

Sherborne Abbey

7. Bath Abbey, from the south-west

8. Bath Abbey

Glastonbury Abbey, looking west

. Bury St Edmunds Abbey, looking north across the transepts

11. Fountains Abbey, from the south-ea

12. Fountains Abbey: the west doorway

3. Guisborough Priory

14. Westminster Abbey: the nave and west towers

15. Westminster Abbey: the choir (copyright Dean and Chapter of Westminster)

16. Bury St Edmunds Cathedral, with its twenty-first-century tower

17. Coventry Cathedral, looking north-east across the ruined nave

18. Coventry Cathedral

19. Birmingham RC Cathedral

20. Liverpool RC Cathedral

21. Bayswater: Greek Orthodox Cathedral

22. Bloomsbury: Central Church of the Catholic Apostolic Church

3. Bloomsbury: Central Church of the Catholic Apostolic Church

Terrington St Clement church

25. Terrington St Clement church

26. Beverley Minster

27. Beverley Minster (by kind permission of the Vicar and Churchwardens of Beverley Minster)

28. Byland Abbey, looking west

29. Tewkesbury Abbe

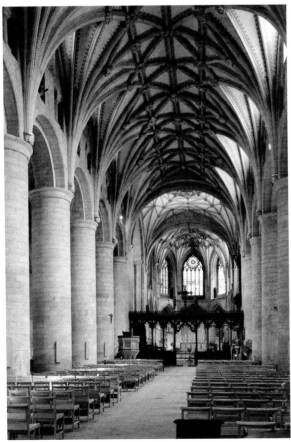

30. Tewkesbury Abbey (by kind permission of the copyright owners: the Vicar and Churchwardens of Tewkesbury Abbey)

to Perpendicular, and is recognisably by the architect of Guildford Cathedral. Arches have no capitals, and mouldings are usually no more than chamfers. Most windows are tall in proportion. There are simple groin vaults. At the west end, large two-storeyed blocks for the song school, vestries and offices were added forming wings to the tower. At the east end, the old chancel was demolished except for the side walls of its flanking chapels, and a new tower was erected here. This, with a pyramidal roof, does not attempt to compete with the west tower. Inside, it forms the first part of the chancel, with three further bays to its east, taller than the nave and with quite broad aisles. To the north and north-east is a series of attachments including two substantial chapels and the chapter-house. Behind the altar three narrow arches open to an ambulatory and, beyond a fine timber screen, the Lady Chapel with polygonal apse. It brings the length to about 230 feet. Not executed of Maufe's plans were a large west porch and an outer south aisle with at its west end a polygonal baptistery.

The new parts have timber fittings of fine quality, mostly designed by Maufe. Some excellent glass of the 1860s by Morris & Co. is now fitted into the windows of the Lady Chapel. The octagonal font is Victorian, but has an elaborate late-medieval spire-cover.

Bury St Edmunds (Suffolk) — Plate 16

This beautiful town, also known as St Edmundsbury, still has at its centre the spacious medieval walled precinct of the abbey (see chapter three). After the abortive attempts in the eleventh and sixteenth centuries, Bury finally in 1914 became the location of a see for Suffolk, with the diocesan title St Edmundsbury and Ipswich. Alas the abbey church was no more, but the precinct still contained two outstandingly fine and large parish churches. St Mary's, slightly the larger, is entirely medieval and very unspoilt. St James's has a nave comparable to that of St Mary's but had a Victorian chancel and other alterations. Also, unlike St Mary's, it was towerless. Interestingly, the church of St James was chosen to become the cathedral. A factor in this choice was probably its suitability for alteration and extension, which would not have been appropriate at St Mary's.

The splendid medieval nave was begun in 1503 and finished only in the 1550s (when destruction of the abbey had already begun). It was almost certainly designed by the great master mason John Wastell. It has nine bays, with large three-light transomed aisle windows and a clerestory of two windows to each bay. It is all battlemented, and much is ashlar-faced. The west front has a panelled plinth, panelled buttresses, an enriched doorway flanked by canopied image niches, and a main window of six lights. Internally, the arcades are especially tall and elegant, with two-centred arches on slender columns of four shafts and

Bury St Edmunds Cathedral

four broad hollows; only the shafts facing the arches have small capitals. Above is a fine hammerbeam roof, though this is Victorian, by Sir G.G. Scott. Since at least the fifteenth century, the church has used as its bell tower the adjacent great Norman tower gateway of the abbey.

The extensions here have been remarkably successful in transforming the church into something resembling a small medieval cathedral. They were designed by S.E. Dykes Bower, appointed architect in 1943, who argued passionately that enlargement must be in a style consistent with the ancient structure. The new work might be described as in a freely treated and in no way simplified Perpendicular. Although it has traditional facing of stone or flint, its basic construction is of reinforced concrete. The first phase dates from 1960–70. A new entrance porch was built at the north-west corner, opening both to the nave and to a cloister walk constructed along the north side. Scott's chancel of 1865–9 was demolished and replaced by a complete new eastern limb. Its length was determined by the ruined west front of the abbey immediately to the south-east: just a narrow gap separates the two. It brings the cathedral to about 255 feet long. There is a lofty crossing with shallow full-height transepts, and an aisled chancel of six bays. Its height is greater than that of the nave but the aisles are relatively low, with square-headed windows. Externally there is much enrichment of flint flushwork, emphasising its East Anglian character, and the parapets are battlemented. Equally rich is the internal treatment; a plane of open arcading at the base of the tall clerestory windows provides a suggestion of a triforium. The rich triple

sedilia came from the Victorian chancel. The excellent fittings of traditional design are also by Dykes Bower. Roofs are of timber; the high
roof is exquisitely coloured. Similar colour has also been applied to the
nave roof, helping to unify the building.

North of the chancel, the Cathedral Centre was completed in 1990.
A further major building campaign began in 2000, funded in part as a
National Lottery Millennium Project. This completed the south walk
of the cloisters and constructed an east walk across the front of the
Cathedral Centre. The north transept was extended by a gallery above
the cloister walk, which here has groin vaulting. A large new Chapel
of the Transfiguration was added alongside the north chancel aisle,
together with further ancillary buildings. Most spectacularly, the central tower was constructed to the designs of Hugh Mathew, continuing
the spirit of Dykes Bower's work. It was completed externally in 2005,
with other work continuing until 2010. It forms a magnificently rich
and appropriate climax to the work done here. With its rich pinnacled
outline, pairs of long, two-light transomed belfry openings and sophisticated detailing, it bears comparison with some of its great medieval
cathedral predecessors.

Chelmsford (Essex)

The cathedral occupies an attractive large churchyard in the centre of
this busy county town. It is essentially a large late-Perpendicular parish
church, much altered or renewed and also extended both before and
since its elevation to cathedral status in 1914. The finest ancient parts are
the west tower and the south porch. The tower is big, mainly of flint,
in three stages, with set-back buttresses; the plinth is panelled and the
rich west doorway has a crocketed ogee hood-mould. There are stepped
battlements with flint flushwork and eight small pinnacles. A small
octagonal cupola of 1749 carries a copper-covered needle spire. The
porch is a display piece: two-storeyed and covered in rich flushwork. It
has a triple image niche above its entrance arch; the battlements, stepped
at the front, carry pinnacles.

The nave has lofty four-bay arcades and a low clerestory: the style is
Perpendicular, but most of it dates from 1801–3, following a collapse
caused during the digging of a burial vault. Also then provided was a
beautiful ribbed, depressed plaster barrel vault; this now has exquisite
colouring of 1961. The aisles are embattled and embrace the tower,
where externally they are largely of brick and authentic. Otherwise the
south aisle and clerestory are mostly renewed, with surprising facing
of white ashlar. On the north side an outer aisle was added in 1873, in
matching style. The chancel is much rebuilt, but its three-bay southern arcade is ancient, with four-centred arches. Three arches are on the
north side too, of which the two west bays form a distinctive feature.

Chelmsford Cathedral

They are set within a large round arch, with a central spandrel of open Perpendicular tracery. Their stonework shows that there have been repairs or alterations, but it appears in a painting of 1800 and is generally accepted as medieval. Behind it is a transept added in 1873.

Sir Charles Nicholson was appointed as architect when the church became a cathedral. In 1920 he produced a splendid scheme that would have created essentially a new cathedral to which the existing church would have formed the south aisle. A second west tower would have been added to give a twin-towered front. However, none of this was executed. Instead, in 1923 the chancel was modestly extended by two dignified, aisleless bays. In 1926 there followed an attractive two-storeyed range of cathedral offices in domestic Perpendicular style, extending north from the transept.

There are striking standing wall monuments of 1571 and 1756. Most furnishings are due to re-orderings from Nicholson's time and since. They include many striking recent artworks. One is a brightly-painted Tree of Life in the blocked Perpendicular-style north transept window, of 2004 by Mark Cazalet.

Coventry (Warwickshire, now West Midlands) Plates 17 and 18

Coventry is probably the most famous and most visited building in this book: more so, indeed, than some of the cathedrals of the canon. Many factors contribute to its unique position. One is the emotive story of its wartime destruction – it was the only English cathedral to have been wrecked beyond repair in war – followed by inspirational rebuilding. Equally, it has to do with the character of that rebuilding, and of the art that is part of it. Here is something dramatically different from any previous cathedral; one that, it is felt, is a great work of our own age, a major achievement of what was and still is regarded as modern art and architecture. Moreover, what happened in 1940 remains preserved for all to see, and from this, there has been developed a particular emphasis here on reconciliation between nations and between faiths. Whatever the individual may feel about its architecture and art, for most the whole has a striking and visionary quality that makes a visit a powerful and memorable experience. Coventry Cathedral is an especially moving and significant place.

The diocese was established in 1918. As the only place to have completely lost a major medieval cathedral (see chapter two), Coventry was particularly appropriate for a new see. Of its three great late-medieval parish churches, the largest and most magnificent, St Michael's, was chosen. It needed no extension: it was an exceptionally large and rich example of a Perpendicular town church, about 280 feet long. When struck by multiple incendiary bombs in the great air raid of 14 November 1940, it was reduced to a shell. The decision that it would rise again was taken immediately. Some hoped for restoration as it had been. However, Sir Giles Gilbert Scott was engaged as architect and produced a remarkable design. This proposed a long body on a north to south axis, running across the site of the old chancel, the walls of which would have been demolished. There would have been a central altar, and projecting east was to be the medieval sanctuary, which would have been restored. The tower would have remained, and apparently the shell of the nave as at present. The new structure would have been massive and distinctive, in a style still basically gothic but utterly different from the architect's work at Liverpool. However, the design was rejected by the Royal Fine Art Commission, and in 1947 Scott resigned.

A competition was then held, not stipulating a gothic style, and in 1951 out of 219 entries the design of Basil Spence (who was later knighted) was chosen. Construction began in 1955, and the completed cathedral was consecrated in 1962. Spence was central to the whole project, and for many of the contents he commissioned some of the outstanding artists of the day. As a result, they form an exceptional collection of the art of the age. They are a major and essential part of the cathedral: there is no other in which the fittings are so important a part of the whole.

The roofless medieval shell, paved and with some modern sculptures, is an integral part of the experience of Coventry. It forms a forecourt to the new cathedral, which stands north of the old chancel with its axis running north-south. Features immediately convey emotional intensity.

On the stone altar in the ruin are the charred cross (made from two fallen roof beams) and a cross of nails (one of many made of three medieval nails from the destroyed roof). Movingly inscribed on the sanctuary wall are the words 'Father Forgive'.

The medieval plan has some surprising irregularities. Its axis changes noticeably for the chancel; the west tower is narrower than and placed asymmetrically with respect to the nave; and (like Manchester) much of the nave had double aisles as a result of the addition of guild chapels in the late fifteenth and early sixteenth centuries. The earliest feature is the late thirteenth-century south porch with trefoiled doorway; and beneath the north chancel aisle there remains in use a vaulted chapel of similar date. All else is Perpendicular, but of multiple campaigns. Apart from one short section, the arcades collapsed in the fire (probably brought down by Victorian reinforcing girders sagging in the heat). The outer walls remain complete, battlemented throughout, all of sandstone ashlar. Windows are very large, and most retain their tracery; even the side windows are of up to seven lights, some with one or more transoms. The nave had six bays and the chancel had three plus the sanctuary, which (unusually) is a polygonal apse; the walls of the sanctuary and west end now rise higher than the rest. There are some decayed memorials, tombs and coffin-lids. Fortunately, the tremendous tower and spire survived intact: the height is 295 feet, exceeded among cathedrals only by those of Norwich and Salisbury. They were much restored in about 1890. The tower is in five stages, with many enrichments. It carries battlements and corner pinnacles which launch flying buttresses to an octagonal stage, also embattled; from this rises the superb and elaborate spire.

A huge and lofty porch projects from the entrance front of the new cathedral to link to the old. Despite its 'modernity', the new cathedral relates to tradition in many aspects. It is longitudinal, with the entrance at one end and the altar at the other; it is divided into a nave and aisles by very tall, thin columns; and these columns carry something akin to a vault, with concrete ribs. Externally, it is faced in ashlared sandstone. Its external length is almost 315 feet, and 380 if the porch is included; the internal height is 80 feet. The entrance wall is entirely of glass, in panels inscribed with figures of saints and angels. Through most of the church, the side walls are of zigzag form, the enormous windows being in the sections of the zigzag angled towards the altar. They all contain abstract stained glass, by several artists. The baptistery, on the right near the entrance wall, has an even larger, brilliantly coloured window, also abstract in its design and gently outcurving. This, by John Piper, is said to be the country's largest stained-glass window. The font is memorable: a rough natural boulder from near Bethlehem, with a small basin cut in its top. Beyond the high altar, forming the dominant feature of the whole interior, is a vast tapestry of Christ in Majesty, by Graham Sutherland. From the body of the cathedral project two striking circular

chapels, tall and externally finished in slate, which contrast strongly with
the rest. The larger of these is the Chapel of Unity, devoted to the cathedral's ministry of reconciliation. In the nave are eight very large stone
'Tablets of the Word', with inscribed texts. Another particularly memorable artwork is on the exterior, near the approach from the street: a
great bronze sculpture of St Michael and Lucifer, by Jacob Epstein.

Derby

This new diocese of 1927 took as its cathedral the church of All Saints.
This, the most important parish church of the town, had been collegiate,
with the status of royal free chapel. The college was dissolved in 1548,
but the church remained a royal peculiar (exempt from the jurisdiction
of the bishop) until the nineteenth century. Although its character is
mainly that of a very large parish church, aspects make it seem a worthy
cathedral. This is true of the massive, very tall tower, built in about
1510–30 and now the only medieval part of the structure. It has three
major stages, divided by bands of panelling; angle buttresses are slightly
set back from the corners, containing large canopied image niches and
with pinnacles in relief higher up. An unusual feature is a long inscription running along the north and south sides. The large belfry openings
have four lights and a transom. Above are panelled battlements with
large corner and smaller intermediate pinnacles. The fine west doorway,
flanked by further image niches, forms the main entrance. Eighteenth-
century gallery stairs curve up elegantly inside.

Derby Cathedral

The body of the church was rebuilt in 1723–5 to the design of James Gibbs. It is of ashlar, six bays long, with a single tier of large, round-arched windows having a keystone and intermittent rustication. Externally the walls are articulated by paired pilasters, and above are a cornice and balustraded parapet. Internally, it is divided into a nave and aisles of full height by tall Tuscan columns, with round arches hardly distinguished from the plaster ceilings. Ceilings above the aisles are groin vaults while the central space has a barrel vault with restrained enrichment, exquisitely decorated in white, pink and a little gold.

Just before the Second World War, Sir Ninian Comper was commissioned to design an extension. His drawings, dated May 1939, proposed a spectacular three-bay chancel, taller and in some features even richer than the existing nave, with a large Lady Chapel on its south side. He produced a revised version in the early 1950s, but neither was executed. Eventually, in 1965–72, now under Sir Ninian's son Sebastian, a more modest chancel of two bays was constructed. This matches Gibbs's work, but with some simplification. The fall of the land was exploited to provide other accommodation beneath and to each side, including sacristies and a choir school. Internally the most spectacular feature is the great baldacchino, pedimented and resting on Corinthian columns.

The organ stands within a splendid deep west gallery on fluted Ionic columns; there have never been side galleries. Glass is clear except for two bright windows of 1965. A splendid feature is the great wrought-iron screen extending across the full width; it incorporates the Royal Arms in its centre. It is of 1730, made by the smith Robert Bakewell to Gibbs's design. Other work by Bakewell includes the altar rails and the gates outside the entrance. A timber former consistory court dates from 1634. The exquisite octagonal baluster font of white marble surprisingly only dates from 1974, but it is to a design by Gibbs. There are some notable memorials. A decayed late-medieval recumbent effigy rests on a tomb-chest with small figures along its side: unusually, both are of oak. A fifteenth-century incised slab commemorates John Lawe, sub-dean. The famous Bess of Hardwick, who died in 1608, has an appropriately enormous standing wall memorial, with her recumbent effigy.

Guildford (Surrey)

The diocese was founded in 1927, initially using the church of the Holy Trinity in the High Street. Only after some controversy was the decision made to build a new cathedral on a fresh site. A competition in 1932, entered by 183 architects, was won by Edward Maufe (who was later knighted). Building began in 1936, but ceased on the outbreak of war in 1939, resuming only in 1952. The cathedral was consecrated in 1961 and completed in 1966. The position, in a park-like setting on the summit of the east-west ridge known as Stag Hill, is splendid, though it is a long half-hour's walk from the town centre. Indeed, with its approach drive from the Guildford bypass, opened in 1934, it was expected that many people would arrive by car. Built of beautiful red brick, it is of full cathedral size and scale, about 383 feet long. In both plan and style it is broadly traditional. It is cruciform, with a massive tower over the crossing and a long Lady Chapel at the east end. The style is a simplified gothic. Arches are without capitals. Most windows are divided by mullions into two, three or four lights, and have some tracery. Some observers criticise the style as unadventurous, but most

Guildford Cathedral

Guildford Cathedral

agree on the impressive character of the exterior and the fine internal proportions. Moreover, it is very different from either a medieval or a Victorian cathedral.

The exterior is mainly plain, with a quite complicated grouping of massive, largely rectangular blocks. The low-pitched roofs are copper covered. Statuary or carved details in stone appear in various places, but seem few and small by comparison with the great areas of plain brick-work. The main windows are mostly long and narrow in proportion; some small windows are square-headed. The tower is 160 feet high and very massive. It has long twin belfry openings. Above its straight parapet it carries a 15-feet tall gilded angel that turns in the wind: this is a memorable feature, glinting in the sun by day, floodlit by night. The west end is distinctive, with north and south porches forming long cloister-like walks which turn west to flank the main front.

Internally, wall surfaces are rendered and architectural features are of Doulting limestone, both having a similar pale colour. Groin vaults of reinforced concrete cover the main spaces. The nave has very tall arcades of seven bays, with a miniature clerestory over. Its proportions are strikingly different from those of a medieval cathedral, the central space being notably wide while the aisles, though tall, are very narrow. At the west end is a narthex beneath a structural gallery. The transepts are of shallow projection, and contain galleries similar to that at the west. A chapel in the north transept has fine wrought-iron screens. The chancel is quite different from the nave. Its first three bays have low arches each side, while the remaining two have no openings at low level. The sanctuary seems austere: the east wall simply has a small circular window above a 50-feet long curtain. No obstacle divides the length of the nave and chancel. A low ambulatory round the chancel is mostly flanked by vestries and offices. It connects to the Lady Chapel, which has a polygonal apse and windows set high. With its timber roof painted with lilies and stars, it makes a richer impression than most other parts. On its south side is the modest octagonal chapter-house. The cathedral has relatively few striking fittings, and most glass is clear.

The church of the Holy Trinity served as pro-cathedral until 1961. Built in 1749–63, it is a dignified but rather staid structure of red brick, the largest eighteenth-century church in Surrey. Essentially it is a very broad undivided rectangle six bays long, with a west tower. It has quoins rusticated in brick, and long, plain round-arched windows that in 1869 were altered almost undetectably from their previous two tiers. There is a huge flat ceiling. From the previous building there remains a small late-medieval chapel, attached to the south side. In 1886–8 Sir Arthur Blomfield added a chancel with an apse and large flanking chapels, well-matched to the earlier work but with richer and grander details. The church contains some large and interesting memorials. Of eighteenth-century furnishings little more remains than the fine pulpit and some panelling.

Leicester

This large parish church of St Martin became the cathedral in 1927. It has not since been added to structurally and, as a cathedral, is with the exception of its tower modest in scale and character. The Norman central tower was demolished in 1861 and replaced by a splendid tall structure in late thirteenth-century style, carrying a broach spire with three tiers of lucarnes, reaching 220 feet. This was designed by Raphael Brandon. Much of the rest of the church, too, is of various Victorian campaigns of restoration or rebuilding; as well as Brandon, G.E. Street and J.L. Pearson have also worked here. Various medieval parts remain however, and the medieval layout is largely unaltered: originally cruciform but now irregular.

Flanking the four-bay chancel are a two-bay north chapel and one of three bays on the south, both largely rebuilt. Cathedral buildings are attached at the south-east. The north transept projects only slightly. The nave has five bays with thirteenth-century arcades on pillars of four major and four minor shafts, but the west bay is a Perpendicular extension. A short stretch of Norman billet moulding remains in the east respond of the north arcade. There is a rebuilt Perpendicular clerestory. On the south side, a wider outer aisle runs past both nave and transept, in six bays. Its arcade is taller and rather later than those of the nave, with which it does not align. Most windows are renewed. The north doorway, however, is authentic Early English work, with multiple orders of filleted mouldings. It is covered by a charming timber-framed porch, basically Perpendicular though much restored in 1880; it is memorable for having a timber tierceron vault. Even the fine doors are medieval. The rich, vaulted two-storeyed south porch is of 1897, by Pearson.

Leicester Cathedral

The interior, in excellent condition and finely decorated, is beautiful. Most furnishings date from its cathedral period, especially the striking chancel fittings designed in 1927 by Sir Charles Nicholson: they include a richly gilt gothic screen and a bishop's throne with a spire-like canopy. The excellent hexagonal pulpit, complete with its original stair, is probably late seventeenth-century. There is a fine eighteenth-century Archdeacon's Court. A long, iron-bound chest is medieval. Richard III, who was buried in Leicester, is commemorated by a modern slab in the chancel.

Liverpool (Lancashire, now Merseyside)

The diocese was founded in 1880. It initially used as pro-cathedral the town's original parish church of St Peter, an attractive classical building of 1699–1704. In 1901 a site was purchased, and in 1902 a competition was held for the design of a cathedral. Remarkably, this was won by the young Giles Gilbert Scott, grandson of Sir G.G. Scott, and a Roman Catholic. Construction began in 1904. This scheme had perhaps something of megalomania: as finally completed, with its length of 619 feet, it is by a substantial margin the country's longest cathedral. Indeed, it seems that in the world the only longer church is St Peter's in Rome. The creation in the twentieth century of such a building seems astonishing! Was Liverpool being England's most sectarian city a factor? (The Roman Catholics indeed took it as a challenge – see chapter six.) However, as well as immensity, this cathedral has sophistication, splendour and richness of detail, though everywhere its character is massive rather than light. It occupies a superb, dominating position on a sandstone ridge behind the city centre; the ridge runs north to south so this is the cathedral's axis, with the altar to the south. Directions given here are ritual. During construction, Scott made many changes to the design (even requiring demolition of some work already constructed); most dramatic was the substitution of a single, huge central tower for the originally intended twin transeptal towers. Once the Lady Chapel came into use in 1910, St Peter's lost its role as pro-cathedral; it was demolished in 1922. The eastern limb of the cathedral was consecrated in 1924; the tower was completed in 1942. Construction slowed but continued. Scott died in 1960, still working on his designs for the nave. Despite spiralling costs, the nave was finally completed in 1978.

The cathedral is largely traditional in that it is constructed of local pink sandstone, and is in a gothic style related to Decorated. However, in major respects it is unlike a medieval cathedral. Both the nave and chancel have just three great bays. They are similar in design. The rich, tall arcades open to passage aisles with ribbed transverse barrel vaults. There is no triforium, but high up small clerestory windows illuminate a gallery with a rich openwork parapet. The main vault, 116 feet above the floor, has two quadripartite bays for each main bay. Uniquely, two pairs of transepts are placed immediately east and west of the tower. Between these is the Central Space, a huge aisleless volume wider than the nave and chancel, with a lierne vault rising to 175 feet. Its great breadth gives the tower above its massiveness. Externally the tower starts square and fairly plain, but as it rises it develops a subtle and sophisticated shape and becomes steadily richer. Its summit has an openwork parapet and eight relatively small pinnacles. It is 331 feet high. The body of the cathedral has straight parapets, but there is much enrichment including pinnacles, turrets and an open gallery high along the sides. The entrance front, simpler than Scott had intended, has a huge external arch. Most

windows, though very large, are in just two lights; the great east window has four, with flame-like flowing tracery. The spaces between the pairs of transepts are treated as huge porches, though not now normally used as such; one contains a refectory.

(left:) Liverpool Cathedral

(right:) Liverpool Cathedral: the nave, looking east

No screen divides the great length of the interior; instead, between nave and western transepts, is the Bridge, a broad round arch carrying a stone balcony. Its value could perhaps be questioned. Surprisingly attached not axially but to the south-east corner of the chancel and at a much lower level is the long Lady Chapel, itself aisled and ending in a polygonal apse. Its florid style is rather different from that of the rest, this being partly attributable to the involvement of G.F. Bodley with Scott in this first phase. At the north-east corner is the small octagonal chapter-house.

The fittings are as rich as the architecture. Such features as the reredos and the canopy over the font are enormous and elaborate. Many of the contents were designed by Scott himself, but there are also more recent artworks. None, however, is abstract. They include considerable statuary. All windows have stained glass.

A consistent vision was continued here through seventy-four years of building. Inevitably, some critics in the later years of its construction called it an anachronism. However, in its magnificence and the conviction with which the whole has been executed, it surely banishes all doubts.

Manchester (Lancashire, now Greater Manchester)

Though now a great industrial city, Manchester has a history going back to Roman times. Its parish church became a major collegiate church in 1421–2. Though dissolved in 1547, the college was re-founded under Queen Mary and, despite vicissitudes, continued through most of the next three centuries with a warden, four fellows, four boy choristers and four singing men. In 1840, this establishment was altered into a dean and canons in preparation for the church becoming a cathedral in 1847. Remarkably, the medieval collegiate buildings to the north survive almost intact, though not in cathedral ownership: they are now Chetham's School of Music.

The cathedral is a large and splendid structure, entirely in Perpendicular style. The only structural addition since it became a cathedral is a large and rich west porch with flanking attachments, dating from 1898–1900. Excluding this, the external length is over 220 feet. However, it is not cruciform and its character is that of a major parish church rather than a 'great church'. In the 1870s it was proposed to build a new cathedral on a fresh site in Piccadilly Gardens. Designs were prepared by R.H. Carpenter for a magnificent building with double aisles to its nave and a central octagon clearly inspired by Ely but here carrying a lofty octagonal tower in several diminishing stages. However, the proposal came to nothing.

Both the nave and chancel are of six bays, and are closely similar in their design and proportions. Roofs are all low pitched. The chancel was

Manchester Cathedral

built under John Huntington, the first warden (1422–58); the nave followed under the third warden, of 1465–81. There is a large west tower. In the sixteenth century, ranges of chantry chapels were added outside the aisles of both nave and chancel, effectively creating double aisles. As a result, Manchester is one of the widest cathedrals in England. A small Lady Chapel was also added at the east end; this was rebuilt in 1750. Unfortunately, restoration has been extensive. Much damage was done in 1814–15, and renewal in 1885 and later included the rebuilding of the nave arcades. This Victorian work maintained the Perpendicular style but increased the external richness, including the addition of elaborate openwork parapets with pinnacles. The splendid vaulted two-storeyed north and south porches replaced earlier structures. The tower was rebuilt in 1862–8, and although the original design was partly reproduced it was increased in height. Major damage was sustained in 1940 from a land mine that fell just outside the north-east corner, flattening the Lady Chapel and some other parts. The present Lady Chapel is a post-war rebuilding to a new, rather austere design.

Nevertheless, the interior has much that is authentic. It is dark, an effect accentuated by its sombre sandstone. The arcades have pillars of a complex section, with capitals on their shafts; the spandrels are panelled, and above are large five-light clerestory windows. The tall tower arch remains original, surrounded by damaged Perpendicular panelling; the fan vault in the tower is Victorian. Most windows of the outer aisles are in four lights. These aisles are broader than the inner aisles, and have many irregularities. A single-bay chapel, the Ely Chapel, projected even further north near the east end until 1940, but this was omitted in the subsequent restoration. Towards the east end on the south side, there is a small but charming octagonal chapter-house. It has a fine entrance arrangement with two richly moulded four-centred doorways set within a larger panelled arch. Extensive cathedral attachments are at the south-east.

The chancel is magnificent, the best part of the interior. Moreover, it displays the superb medieval woodwork that is the finest feature of the cathedral. Outstanding are the thirty stalls, with excellent carved misericords and tremendously rich and lofty canopies; they date from about 1505–10. The great veranda rood screen is original though much restored. Screens of distinctive form occupy the arcades east of the stalls, with wrought-iron work below big ogee arches: these are an engaging eighteenth-century modification of medieval work. The splendid roof is panelled, with cusped braces springing from shield-bearing angels. Many other roofs, too, are authentic. Several original parclose screens are in the outer aisles, and even the medieval screen to the Lady Chapel survives, with interesting carved figures. There are some good memorials, including two medieval brasses. Much post-war stained glass has been added.

Newcastle upon Tyne (Northumberland, now Tyne and Wear)

With an external length of over 260 feet, this church of St Nicholas was one of the largest parish churches. As mentioned earlier, it nearly became a cathedral in 1553; in the event, this finally happened in 1882. Dating mainly from the fourteenth and fifteenth centuries, this is a generally uniform and consistent building. The ashlar-faced exterior is much renewed, but internally the structure is mostly very authentic. It is cruciform and of uniform height in all four limbs; there is a true full-height crossing, though it carries no tower. Windows are generally large: some are Decorated but most are Perpendicular; the east window has seven lights. The interior is unified stylistically by its arches throughout having multiple orders of chamfers (mostly three for the arcades) always dying without capitals into the pillars or responds. All parts have a clerestory of almost square-headed three-light windows. Roofs are low-pitched and mostly ancient. The aisles are wide (those of the nave wider than the nave itself), making this a very spacious building. Both nave and chancel are of four large bays (those of the chancel especially large). The south transept is of two bays while the north transept has three; both have a narrow west aisle and the north transept has a large east chapel. All this gives a real cathedral feeling; but with the moderate height, the large bay spacing and the absence of capitals or intricate mouldings, it seems spread out and of low intensity.

Newcastle Cathedral

The closely surrounding streets and buildings prevent the exterior from being anywhere visible as a whole. Easily seen, however, is its most notable feature, the massive Perpendicular west tower, famous for its crown spire. The tower has openwork battlements with very large octagonal corner pinnacles carrying spirelets. From the corners, flying buttresses rise to carry a square openwork structure which itself has pinnacles and a crocketed spirelet. It reaches 193 feet. Inside, the tower has a lierne vault. Flanking the tower are large two-storeyed porches of the 1830s; internally they effectively form western transepts. Attached to the south chancel aisle is a delightful three-storeyed vestry and library block of 1736, in Palladian style.

No structural extensions have been made for its cathedral role, though a block of offices and vestries was added at the north-east in 1926. However, in the 1880s the eastern limb was rearranged and richly fitted out in a fifteenth-century cathedral manner to the designs of R.J. Johnson.

Newly provided were the rood screen, stalls with misericords, bishop's throne with a very tall spire canopy, and a lofty reredos of alabaster with tiers of figures. Beyond the reredos is an ambulatory with three chapels against the east wall.

There are a few large standing wall memorials and an early four-teenth-century recumbent effigy of a knight. An exceptionally large early fifteenth-century brass came from elsewhere. The splendid concave octagonal font in black marble is of the early fifteenth century, with a fine spire canopy of similar date. The brass eagle lectern dates from about 1500. There are some plain medieval stalls. Largely filling the north transept, the organ still has most of its Renatus Harris case of 1676.

Portsmouth (Hampshire)

On the creation of the diocese in 1927, the parish church of St Thomas of Canterbury was initially designated pro-cathedral. It was soon decided, however, that it should itself be the cathedral, and was to be enlarged. Two phases of twentieth-century extension have followed. Not all com-mentators consider the result successful, but though idiosyncratic it is delightful and very fine at least in its parts. As it now stands, the east end is of the late twelfth century, with west of it major work of the seven-teenth century, then of the 1930s, and finally the west front completed in 1991. It stands in an attractive churchyard in the old town.

The original church was built in about 1180–8; though then only a chapel of ease, remarkably it was of 'great church' type, albeit on a small scale. Cruciform with aisles and central tower, it was clerestoried and vaulted throughout. This is one of the first buildings in the Early English style, with deep mouldings, Purbeck marble shafts (now mostly replacements), and some stiff-leaf capitals. Only its transepts and chancel survive, forming a very cathedral-worthy east end. The chancel has two double bays; its arcades are distinctive for having pairs of pointed arches set within a large round arch. Where original, windows are lancets, sometimes in pairs or triplets. Internally, the clerestory has a wall passage with triple openings. Original quadripartite vaults remain in the aisles, but the main vault is a convincing 1843 restoration in plaster.

Following Civil War damage, a new nave was constructed in 1683–93, with a west tower. It has tall round-arched arcades on Tuscan columns, in three bays with a larger fourth bay for the transepts. There are plain plaster ceilings, pierced by dormer windows. From the former eight-eenth-century galleries there remains a shallow west gallery with a beautiful curved panelled front. Externally, the tower is plain but carries a large and distinctive timber cupola with a dome, a further small cupola and a weather vane in the form of a 'golden barque'.

Enlargement began in 1935 to the designs of Sir Charles Nicholson. No doubt to harmonise with the seventeenth-century work, it employs a fairly simple round-arched style sometimes described as Byzantine. It added a new nave to the west, with the earlier nave and chancel becoming a large-scale chancel; the formerly west tower is now central. This new nave has tall arcades with cylindrical pillars, a clerestory above and roofs of barrel- or groin-vaulted form. Its larger windows have some tracery. The aisles are broad, and there are also narrow outer aisles with arcades of two bays for each nave bay. To allow some east-west

Portsmouth Cathedral: the west front of 1990–1

Portsmouth Cathedral: the medieval chancel and seventeenth-century former nave

communication, the tower was pierced with arched openings at two levels, though the upper is filled by the organ. Nicholson also added additional transepts flanking the tower and outer aisles to the seventeenth-century former nave. When work ceased in 1939, only three nave bays of an intended seven had been built. A 1960s scheme for a spectacular completion in contemporary style was not executed. Finally in 1990–1, to the designs of Michael Drury, a fourth bay of nave and a west front were constructed, continuing in the spirit of Nicholson's work. The outer aisles are returned across the front, and there are many engaging or whimsical details, including small twin towers with ogee tops. This work brings the total length to nearly 240 feet.

The interior is large and complex, with many subsidiary spaces; the tower still largely divides it into two parts. In a major re-ordering in 1991, the altar was moved into the medieval crossing. Many new furnishings were introduced, but the old box pews remain, though cut down and rearranged. The fine pulpit is of 1693. There are some good mural tablets and many naval memorials and memorabilia. On the north side, a modest enclosed cloister connects to the cathedral offices.

Sheffield (Yorkshire, WR, now South Yorkshire)

What had been a large, partly Perpendicular parish church was in 1914 raised to cathedral status. It had already suffered much rebuilding, mostly in the nineteenth century, and the following years saw major but not entirely satisfactory cathedral extensions. The basis remains the building as it stood in 1914, which is battlemented throughout. Finest is the crossing, which is unaltered fifteenth-century work with quite tall arches having good intricate mouldings. The tower above has big four-light transomed belfry openings with complicated tracery, battlements, corner pinnacles and a fine crocketed spire. Also largely of this period is the three-bay chancel; its north aisle is mainly Victorian but its south aisle, the Shrewsbury Chapel, was added in about 1520. The tall two-bay arcade to this chapel is original, with slim octagonal pillars, castellated capitals and double-chamfered arches. Its windows are of three lights and transomed. Roofs here are ancient, that over the chancel being a fine hammerbeam structure. The east wall is rebuilt, however, with Decorated-style windows. The transepts are of around 1880. The five-bay nave is in a Perpendicular style comparable to the chancel, but with a clerestory; it is a rebuilding of about 1804–5, with Victorian alterations.

In the 1930s, work began on a radical plan by Sir Charles Nicholson that was to involve the demolition of the nave and the creation across its site of a great new cathedral body on a north-south axis with the altar to the north. The original crossing and chancel would have remained, forming a very large ritual south transept to the new cathedral; they would have been balanced by a second tower and spire on its ritual north side. Work was halted by the war, after which only those parts well advanced were completed. These include a large complex of cathedral offices north of the medieval chancel, incorporating a substantial rectangular chapter-house. West of these, at a lower level, is the Chapel of the Holy Spirit, which was to have been at the ritual east end of the new cathedral. This gives the finest impression of what Nicholson's cathedral would have been: it is an exquisite vaulted room, four bays in length, in a conventional, quite rich Decorated style.

Finally, in the 1960s, the north-south axis was abandoned and the cathedral was completed on its original east-west axis. The architect was Arthur Bailey. What was to have been three of the four bays of Nicholson's high chancel became the broad, low Chapel of St George, opening from the north nave aisle. Its west side is by Bailey, but its east side has Nicholson's arcade, and behind the altar are triple arches

Sheffield Cathedral: the western crossing, looking west

opening north to an ambulatory and the chapel of the Holy Spirit. Beneath it is a beautiful vaulted crypt chapel. The most prominent aspect of Bailey's scheme was a major addition at the west end of the old nave. This provided a new western crossing, with a large narthex on its south side and an entrance porch with a tower above. West of this crossing is one further aisled bay. Bailey's style is very different from the rest, essentially of its time though still with gothic allusions. Over his crossing rises an octagonal lantern, with brightly coloured abstract stained glass. Long bars of curious form project both above and below: they are symbolic of the crown of thorns. Externally, with its strange square-topped pinnacles, some eyes find this new work assertive and not a harmonious blend with the older building. Internally it seems more successful, and the lantern is a memorable feature.

North of Bailey's west end, yet another large block of building, the Community Resources Centre, was finished in 2007.

The cathedral has some fine contents. Particularly beautiful are the screen, stalls and other fittings in the Chapel of the Holy Spirit, by Sir Ninian Comper. Two great sixteenth-century memorials with recumbent effigies are in the Shrewsbury Chapel; until 1933 this remained technically a Roman Catholic private chapel. Overall, the successive extensions have created a large and very complex cathedral. Inevitably its plan is diffuse, and its mixture of styles may be thought unconvincing; but it is a fine building, and there is much to enjoy.

Truro (Cornwall)

The diocese of Cornwall was re-established in 1876, with its first bishop, E.W. Benson, being enthroned in 1877 in the parish church of St Mary at Truro. Benson was an energetic man, intent on leading an Anglo-Catholic religious revival in the county, for which it should have a cathedral of a scale and splendour comparable to those of the Middle Ages. After a competition, J.L. Pearson was appointed as architect. The transepts and chancel were constructed in 1880–7; after Pearson's death in 1897 work continued under the direction of his son, F.L. Pearson, and the cathedral was completed in 1910. The site is constricted, limiting the length to about 300 feet, but this does not seem a small cathedral. It is especially striking for its verticality, both of its body and in its possession of three spires: the central spire rises to 244 feet while the west spires reach 204 feet. It spectacularly dominates the town as seen from almost any viewpoint.

The style is essentially Early English, with lancets and plate tracery, but there are many French touches. These are noticeable in the large rose windows of the west front and the transept ends, and in the very rich portal of the south transept. Also reminiscent of France, particularly Normandy, is the form of the towers and their spires; the spires

(left and right:)
Truro Cathedral

can seem short for their towers. Moreover the cathedral stands straight out of the street, as is typical of France. Inside, there are beautiful rib vaults throughout. The nave has eight bays, with a sophisticated triforium and a clerestory with wall passage. Unusual freestanding tall wall arcading enriches the aisles. The transepts have both east and west aisles; the north transept has three bays, while the south transept (constrained by the street) has two. West of the latter is a very rich circular baptistery. The central tower has a lofty lantern. Five bays of chancel are followed by shallow east transepts of full height. Beyond are one further bay and a complicated east wall. This limb differs considerably from the nave in its design and also has richer detailing and more elaborate vaults. Both inside and out, the design is of medieval cathedral richness, with the exquisite elegance characteristic of the architect. The walling is of ashlared granite, which makes for a rather hard appearance close up. Carved work is in limestone.

We may be grateful that though much of the medieval church was demolished to make way for the cathedral, its southern aisle was preserved (perhaps against Benson's wishes). Called St Mary's Aisle, it forms a six-bay outer south aisle alongside the chancel, with its floor at a much lower level. Between it and the chancel aisle, a further narrow aisle was required to provide adequate buttressing. St Mary's Aisle dates from 1504–18, and externally is very richly decorated with bands of stone panelling, pinnacles and panelled battlements. Internally, it still has its arcade with four-centred arches and its partly original ceiled wagon roof, to which fine modern decoration has been applied. Functionally it remains the parish church, and Pearson provided a new tower at its west end, with copper-covered pyramidal spire. Standing up against the transept, this attractively varies the external aspect of the cathedral. The incorporation of St Mary's Aisle determined the bay spacing of the chancel, and compelled its axis to incline perceptibly north from that of the nave.

Both inside and out, the medieval aisle seems very low beside Pearson's soaring building. This highlights a criticism frequently made: that the cathedral is not Cornish in character. Cornish churches are usually low and rarely have spires. However, this criticism seems unfair. Pearson has designed a 'great church', as a cathedral should be, and medieval 'great church' design was predominantly national rather than regional. Exeter Cathedral, for example, bears little resemblance to the parish churches of Devon. It is in any case hard to see how an impressive cathedral could have been based on the typical character of Cornish parish churches. Truro Cathedral must be assessed by national cathedral standards. Arguably it is the finest church created in the Victorian era.

There are some fine Victorian and later fittings. Still in St Mary's Aisle are an inlaid eighteenth-century pulpit of rather ungainly bulbous form and a beautiful organ of similar period. Many memorials from the old church are now in the north transept. Pearson intended a cloister and an octagonal chapter-house on the north side. One cloister bay was built in 1935, but such ideas were then abandoned. In this area a large chapter-house and a memorial hall were built in 1967 in an assertively contemporary style.

Wakefield (Yorkshire, WR, now West Yorkshire)

Among the parish-church cathedrals, Wakefield is unique in having a large-scale Victorian-designed cathedral extension. It was previously a very large, externally all-Perpendicular church, and became a cathedral in 1888. Most of the Perpendicular work of its exterior is due to Sir George Gilbert Scott's restoration of 1858-74, partly replacing eighteenth-century alterations. Internally, it remains largely authentic.

Dominant is the massive but relatively plain fifteenth-century west tower carrying a crocketed spire, which at 247 feet is the tallest in Yorkshire. Roofs are low-pitched throughout. There is a long nave with clerestory and wide aisles, externally very rich, with elaborate panelled parapets and pinnacles. The four-light aisle windows fill the spaces between the buttresses, and the clerestory is of almost continuous straight-headed windows. Internally, the first impression is of splendid, well-proportioned uniformity: both arcades have quite tall, slender pillars with moulded capitals and Decorated arches that have two orders of sunk quadrants. Not everyone will notice that while the north arcade has seven bays, the south arcade, which is the same length, has eight; the

Wakefield Cathedral

pillars on both sides show variations that relate to the earlier history of the church. Also Decorated is the chancel arch. The medieval chancel is entirely Perpendicular, and unusually large: in its height and width it continues almost unchanged from the nave. It has a clerestory and arcades of five bays; the walls of its aisles are in three bays.

In 1897 J.L. Pearson was commissioned to design an eastward extension, a task taken over after his death later that year by his son, F.L. Pearson. It was built in 1901–5. Unlike most Pearson work, this is Perpendicular, continuing the style of the rest but with even more richness. Windows are very large, the angles are emphasised by big, pinnacled turrets, and some external surfaces are panelled. With the fall of the land to the east, it stands very tall; beneath it are offices, vestries and the chapter room. To the medieval chancel it adds a sanctuary bay, and this is flanked by transepts of full height, which have east aisles. These parts have rich tierceron vaults. There are also sedilia with lavish canopy work. The east end is a three-bay chapel of full height, dedicated to St Mark; it is divided by very tall, slim pillars into a centre and very narrow aisles, and has a lierne vault. It all creates an impressive display of cathedral splendour.

There are medieval stalls, of which eleven have carved misericords. Some medieval work is also in the screens around the chancel. The centre part of the chancel screen is fine work of 1635. The octagonal font is boldly inscribed CR II 1661. Large attachments are north of the chancel.

6

CATHEDRALS OF OTHER DENOMINATIONS

Since the seventeenth century, the existence has been accepted in England of Christian groups – what we now call denominations – other than the Church of England. At first these were limited to the so-called Nonconformist or Free Churches, such as the Baptists, Congregationalists, Presbyterians, Quakers, Unitarians and (later) Methodists. None of these Churches, however, had an episcopal organisation, so there was no question of there being cathedrals other than those of the established Church. Matters changed in the nineteenth century with Roman Catholic emancipation, which led in time to the creation of Roman Catholic cathedrals in England. This is the most important denomination to be considered in this chapter, and it has by far the most important series of cathedrals. However, some other episcopal Churches have also established themselves in this country, sometimes with nineteenth-century or earlier beginnings but increasingly through the twentieth century, largely as a result of immigration. These are predominantly the various Orthodox Churches, led by the Greek Orthodox, and they are grouped as a second section of this chapter. They have a considerable number of cathedrals to be considered, though none is of great importance. There are also a few further denominations with buildings that should be addressed, and these are found in a third section.

At this point, we may pause more generally to consider cathedral building in England since the mid-nineteenth century. Alongside the established Church, the other denominations, predominantly the Roman Catholic, have made major contributions. We saw that in the nineteenth century only one new Anglican cathedral was constructed, at Truro, though that is of a size and character worthy of comparison with the medieval cathedrals. There are, however, arguably four cathedrals of comparable stature created by other Churches in that century.

Three are Roman Catholic: Arundel, of 1869–73; Norwich, 1882–1910; and Westminster, 1895–1903 (though, surprisingly, the first two of these were not built as cathedrals). The fourth (also not built as a cathedral by name) is Bloomsbury's Central Church of the Catholic Apostolic Church, constructed in 1850–4. There are thus five such nineteenth-century cathedrals altogether. Four are based very much on medieval precedent: in most respects they are 'great churches' that might have been built in the Middle Ages (though they may mix French with English characteristics). Only Westminster, with its Italian-Byzantine design, was and still is completely different from any other cathedral in this country. There are also many other cathedrals constructed in the nineteenth century, almost all by the Roman Catholic Church; but though far from insignificant they are on a lower level of aspiration.

Moving to the twentieth century and beyond, we have seen that this has been a time of great cathedral-building activity by the Church of England, with three major new creations at Coventry, Guildford and Liverpool, and also some important enlargements of earlier buildings. Roman Catholic contributions, too, have continued through the twentieth century, although only one, at Liverpool, is on the largest scale. For the Catholics, as for the Anglicans, the great change from traditional to modern forms came after the Second World War, with its defining monument being Liverpool (Roman Catholic), constructed in 1962–7. It is interesting to compare it with the Anglican Coventry, designed about a decade earlier. Since Coventry, the Church of England has begun nothing new, though some earlier projects have been continued. In the Roman Catholic Church, however, three further interesting though smaller new cathedrals were created in the last three decades of the century, at Brentwood, Clifton and Middlesbrough. In neither denomination have modern styles been the only ones favoured since 1960. However, while every Anglican cathedral is conventionally longitudinal (being based on a layout defined before 1960), the four Roman Catholic cathedrals created since 1960 are planned differently. As discussed earlier, it is doubtful whether further important Anglican cathedral building is to come in the foreseeable future. Is the outlook different for the Roman Catholics, or indeed for other denominations?

A: THE ROMAN CATHOLIC CHURCH

The changes in the English Church in the mid-sixteenth century, and the sorry story of the repression and persecution of those who could not accept them, are the stuff of much fascinating history. Events such as the Prayer-Book Rebellion of 1549, the Gunpowder Plot of 1603, and later the support for Bonnie Prince Charlie (the Young Pretender) helped to reinforce the intense antipathy to 'popery' of governments and the bulk of the population. This position was often more political than doctrinal, but it continued in full force for more than two centuries. Yet meanwhile, suppressed and hidden, the Catholic religion did continue in this country. Such was the tenacity of its believers that it continued despite financial penalties, civil disabilities and sometimes serious danger. It was much sustained by those gentry, the recusants, who, because of their adherence to the 'old religion', refused to take part in the services of the Church of England. Practising their religion had to be in secret, and the priests of that religion had to be hidden.

It was only in the second half of the eighteenth century that it became evident to governments that Roman Catholics were not politically dangerous and could be accepted as loyal citizens. The first Catholic Relief Act of 1778 made only modest concessions, but it meant that Roman Catholics could at last openly acknowledge their faith, and that Roman Catholic priests could celebrate mass in private without fear of penalties. Nevertheless, such was the strength of popular feeling that this move was sufficient to spark the Gordon Riots of 1780. A second Catholic Relief Act in 1791 removed further disabilities such as the prohibition of Roman Catholics from practising law. It also permitted the construction of Roman Catholic places of worship, though subject to a restriction preventing them from having steeples or bells. In the years following the French Revolution of 1789, many thousands of French Catholics, including priests and monks, came to England to escape the anarchy in their home country. They were made welcome. They included a few English Roman Catholic institutions that had been functioning on continental soil. As a result several monasteries and Roman Catholic schools were established or re-established in England in the 1790s. So by the end of the eighteenth century, toleration of Roman Catholics was well established, although this did not mean that all fear of and discrimination against them was ended. Further freedoms, including the right for a Roman Catholic to hold a seat in parliament, were granted in the Catholic Emancipation Act of 1829, which is usually taken as the date of true emancipation.

By this time a flowering of Roman Catholic church building had begun. However, there were still no bishops. During the years of persecution, Rome had arranged for an underground organisation of the Church in England by the creation of vicars apostolic. The first was appointed in 1623, and covered the whole of England and Wales. From 1688 there were four, corresponding to four districts into which England and Wales were divided. In 1840, the number was increased to eight. Vicars apostolic were titular bishops, their titles being taken from abroad, and so had episcopal status; but they had no cathedrals or diocesan organisation. The number of Roman Catholics in England was steadily increasing, partly as a result of mass immigration from Ireland in consequence of the Potato Famine. In 1850, following encouragement by leading Catholic clergy including Nicholas Wiseman and William Ullathorne, Pope Pius IX announced the restoration of a Roman Catholic hierarchy in England and Wales.

The 1829 Act had anticipated the possibility of Catholic dioceses being established, and specified that they could not use the titles of existing Anglican dioceses. Even had this not been the case, the Catholic leaders were aware of Anglican sensibilities on this point. In the discussions, it is interesting that Charles Acton, from 1842 until his death in 1847 the only English cardinal, favoured the use of titles taken from defunct Anglo-Saxon sees such as Elmham and Lindisfarne. In the event, however, the choice was largely dictated by the foundation of cathedrals in places that had a substantial Catholic population, and if possible where there was already a suitable major church in existence. The new organisation comprised one metropolitan see, at Westminster, and twelve suffragan[1] sees. The latter were of Beverley, Birmingham, Clifton, Hexham, Liverpool, Newport and Menevia (Wales), Northampton, Nottingham, Plymouth, Salford, Shrewsbury and Southwark. As will be seen, in order to conform with the 1829 Act, the cathedrals in the conurbations of Bristol and Manchester, which both by this time possessed an Anglican cathedral, were given the titles respectively of Clifton and Salford, the names of the localities in which they stood. A surprising inclusion is Hexham, a country town that was once an Anglo-Saxon see but which in the event never received a new Roman Catholic cathedral. Was it a survivor from Acton's proposal?

The restoration of the hierarchy came with the appointment of Wiseman both as cardinal and archbishop of Westminster. When summoned to Rome in July 1850 on his nomination as cardinal, he had not realised that the restoration of the hierarchy was imminent, and had supposed that he was to spend the rest of his life as a cardinal in Rome. When he arrived and learned what was happening, in his excitement he immediately issued a pastoral letter, which, perhaps naturally, had a triumphalist note. This was widely publicised in England, and produced a remarkable furore. Wiseman was shocked. However, to his credit, after his return to England in November, he wrote an 'appeal to the English people', pleading for fair play. This, too, was widely distributed, and did much to recover the position and secure popular acceptance. Nevertheless, the restoration of the hierarchy was seen as provocative by many, including the government of Lord John Russell, which in 1851 enacted the Ecclesiastical Titles measure. This prohibited any person outside the Church of England from using an episcopal territorial title, meaning that the bishops created in 1850 could not use their titles. In fact, however, the law was never enforced: this was the last major fling of prejudice against Roman Catholics. The Act was repealed by Gladstone's government in 1871.

Some of the churches that became cathedrals in 1850 – those of Birmingham, Newcastle, Nottingham, Salford and Southwark – had already been built with future elevation to cathedral status in mind. In other places, such as Northampton and Shrewsbury, plans were now brought forward for the construction of a cathedral. As happened with some of the new Anglican dioceses, several Catholic sees initially used an existing church that was designated as pro-cathedral, pending the construction of a permanent replacement. Liverpool and Clifton made do with a pro-cathedral until the later twentieth century. The dioceses of Hexham and Beverley never had a cathedral in those towns. The cathedral of the diocese of Hexham was always in Newcastle, a fact that was recognised in 1861 by changing the diocesan title to Hexham and Newcastle. In 1878 the diocese of Beverley ceased, being divided to create the two new dioceses of Leeds and Middlesbrough.

Many other changes have been made since 1850; there are now nineteen Roman Catholic sees in England. In 1882 a new diocese of Portsmouth was taken out of that of Southwark. A major structural change in 1911 was the division of the country into three provinces, with archbishops in Birmingham, Liverpool and Westminster, while maintaining the supremacy of Westminster. Care was taken here to avoid the rivalries that there had been in the medieval Church with its division of the country into the two provinces of Canterbury and York. Later, Wales was made into a separate province, and in 1965 a further province of Southwark was created. Other new dioceses established were Brentwood in 1917; Lancaster in 1924; Arundel and Brighton in 1965 with its cathedral at Arundel; East Anglia in 1976 with its cathedral at Norwich; and most recently Hallam in 1980 at Sheffield. It is interesting to note that the last two are in places possessing an Anglican cathedral, and that they were given titles such that they still conformed to the 1829 restriction. It seems unlikely, however, that there would have been any objection had it been otherwise. There are now five places that possess both a Roman Catholic and an Anglican cathedral of the same title, distinguished only by their dedications. These are at Birmingham, Liverpool, Newcastle, Portsmouth and Southwark. In all of these, the Anglican see arrived later, the first being Liverpool in 1880.

The Roman Catholic cathedrals, all established in the nineteenth or twentieth century, are mostly very different in their architectural character from the Anglican cathedrals created through the same period. This is so despite both denominations having similar architectural ideals and inspiration, taken largely from the medieval cathedrals. One reason for the difference of course is that in most cases the Anglicans were starting from an existing parish church, whereas the Roman Catholics usually started from scratch. Another major distinction is that many of the Roman Catholic cathedrals were built in about the middle of the nineteenth century whereas, as we have seen, Anglican cathedral building or extension generally took place much later. Moreover, for the Roman Catholics, although now freed from legal restrictions on building, finance was often a problem. Most of the growth of the Roman Catholic population in the cities was poor. Major financial support for the great nineteenth-century wave of Roman Catholic building came from members of the great Catholic aristocratic families. Particularly notable among these was John Talbot, sixteenth Earl of Shrewsbury (1791–1852), whose patronage included support for building the cathedrals of Birmingham, Nottingham and Shrewsbury. Rather later, another major patron was Henry Fitzalan Howard, fifteenth Duke of Norfolk (1847–1917). Nevertheless, most Roman Catholic cathedrals were wanted quickly, and money was a determining limitation on what could be built. An incidental point concerning finance is that the consecration of a Roman Catholic church or cathedral sometimes did not take place until many years after its completion: this is because it could not happen until all debts incurred had been fully paid off.

Of the nineteenth-century architects of the Roman Catholic cathedrals, first both in time and stature is Augustus Welby Northmore Pugin (1812–52). He was a man of tremendous energy, who unfortunately ended his days insane. His importance is not limited to his buildings for the Roman Catholic Church: he is probably best known for his pioneering contribution to the course of the English gothic revival, and for his part in the rebuilding of the Houses of Parliament. As well as a remarkable number of churches (some of them Anglican) and other buildings, he designed four Roman Catholic cathedrals: those of Birmingham, Newcastle upon Tyne, Nottingham and Southwark. He began with the highest ambitions for his cathedrals, and was frustrated by the necessity of tempering these because of financial realities. He was also often responsible for decoration and fittings, including stained glass. He had converted to the Catholic faith in 1835, and most of the other architects of Roman Catholic churches and cathedrals in the nineteenth century were also Roman Catholics. Edward Welby Pugin (1834–75) was a son of the elder Pugin and to some extent his successor, but he did not have his father's brilliance. Matthew Ellison Hadfield (1812–85), a friend and follower of A.W.N. Pugin, worked in partnership with John Gray Weightman (1801–72) and designed the cathedrals of Salford and Sheffield. Perhaps the most prolific Catholic architects were the Hansom family, most prominently Joseph Aloysius Hansom (1803–82). He is probably best known for the unlikely distinction of having been the designer of the Hansom cab, much used through the Victorian era. For some years he worked in partnership with his brother Charles Francis Hansom (1817–88), who was also active separately for much of his career. To be encountered at Portsmouth is his son Joseph Stanislaus Hansom (1845–1931). Edward Joseph Hansom (1842–1900), son of Charles Francis, practised in partnership with Archibald Matthias Dunn (1832–1917); their principal cathedral work was the tower and spire at Newcastle. Another prominent architect who designed buildings that appear in this chapter was George Goldie (1828–87). Unfortunately, many critics consider that, after A.W.N. Pugin, none of these was in the front rank of the architects of the age. Thus the preference for using Catholic architects had its consequence in the character of the nineteenth-century Roman Catholic cathedrals. This perhaps makes it the more interesting to consider the cathedral of Lancaster, built 1857–9, which unlike the others is by an Anglican architect, Edward Graham Paley (1823–95).

All of the Roman Catholic cathedrals of the middle years of the nineteenth century are, then, moderate in character: fine as they are, they are not particularly large. Probably the most notable are Birmingham, Lancaster and Salford, but none of them are usually considered to be among the finest of the country's Victorian church buildings. The cathedrals of Arundel and Norwich, built later in the century and under patronage that allowed architectural ambition to be given almost free rein, are as already discussed a different matter. That at Norwich was largely designed by George Gilbert Scott Junior (1839-97), a son of the famous Sir G.G. Scott and a convert to Catholicism. For different reasons, a similar freedom to design on the largest scale also applied with the cathedral of the metropolitan archdiocese of Westminster. It was not until nearly the end of the century that this project went ahead, but what was then created was worth waiting for. Its designer, John Francis Bentley (1839–1902), was another convert.

Several of the new sees created since 1850 used, without extension, buildings that had been erected in the nineteenth century as parish churches. Arundel and Norwich are special cases but Lancaster and Sheffield, too, are neither smaller than nor inferior to the generality of the Catholic cathedrals that were built as such. This points out the relatively moderate scale of the latter. Unlike the position with the Anglican parish-church cathedrals, the Roman Catholic cathedrals, whether they had been built as cathedrals or had originated as parish churches, have usually not subsequently been significantly enlarged. Those that have been are Brentwood (where the old cathedral was effectively replaced rather than merely extended) and Northampton. That of Middlesbrough has been completely replaced.

New Roman Catholic cathedral building continued in the twentieth century. In the first decade, that of Leeds was built on much the same scale as those of the previous century; it is notable for its excellence as an example of the Arts and Crafts style. Later in the century a large extension was constructed at Northampton. The most important project by far was the creation of a cathedral for Liverpool. Though begun in the 1930s to designs by Sir Edwin Lutyens (1869–1944), the cathedral as now seen is of 1962–7, designed by Sir Frederick Gibberd (1908–84). Neither of these architects was a Roman Catholic, and both had a varied practice (among the buildings designed by Gibberd is London's

Regent's Park Mosque!). As well as being of innovative modern character, Liverpool is (as previously mentioned) the first to have been planned quite differently from hitherto. It was designed to meet the new objective coming from the Liturgical Movement of better participation by the laity in the liturgy, an objective that was formalised by the Second Vatican Council of 1962–5 ('Vatican II'). In consequence, traditional longitudinal planning was abandoned, and this cathedral is basically circular.

The requirements of Vatican II were also fundamental to the designs of the three further cathedrals of the late years of the century: all are centrally planned. Though they are much smaller in size than Liverpool, all three are striking and interesting buildings. Clifton, built in 1970–3, in materials and style might be said to follow the bold and challenging path forged by the Anglican Coventry and by Liverpool's Catholic cathedral. Middlesbrough, of 1985–7, also follows this direction, but much more quietly. It is Brentwood of 1989–91 that is the big surprise, for except in plan its design has nothing 'modern' at all: it is in a mature and sophisticated classical style that in most ways might have been built in the time of Wren.

Attached or close to most of the Catholic cathedrals is a large block of ancillary buildings, frequently called 'Cathedral House'. There may also be a separate bishop's house. These buildings are often large and in Victorian gothic styles, but they are not built around a cloister and do not follow any medieval precedent in their layout.

We may give a thought to a few of the cathedral designs that were never realised. Earliest was A.W.N. Pugin's first proposal for a cathedral at Southwark, which, while it ignored practical limitations, would potentially have been spectacular. Much the same might be said about E.W. Pugin's cathedral begun in 1853 at Everton, in Liverpool. Further proposals on the largest and most splendid scale were those of Henry Clutton from 1867 for Westminster. But what must be the most magnificent entry of all in the catalogue of unbuilt English cathedrals, of any denomination, is Sir Edwin Lutyens's ultimately abortive project of the 1930s for Liverpool. At least we can see a small part of it.

A particular circumstance concerns the contents and decoration of the Roman Catholic cathedrals. Most of those built in the nineteenth century were given elaborate fittings, which complemented their architecture and were often an important part of their overall effect. We have seen that Vatican II demanded changes to increase the involvement of the congregation in the liturgy, which for new churches meant central planning. For existing buildings with their traditional longitudinal plan, it often meant major changes of layout. In most, the altar was moved forward to be in front of the structural chancel. Obstructions such as screens were removed. These changes have usually been implemented as part of a general re-ordering, or sometimes more than one.

The consequences have usually been a great change to the atmosphere and appearance of the interior, and the destruction of many important Victorian furnishings. An example of the latter is A.W.N. Pugin's great rood screen at Birmingham. Original decorative schemes have also often been removed or painted over. Sometimes the chancel is left as an almost unused and apparently unwanted appendix to the cathedral. This destruction, and the loss of the appearance intended by the original creators of the buildings, may be considered an artistic tragedy. On the other hand, the replacement of dark and oppressive Victorian interiors by the light and open appearance of the refitted cathedrals is viewed favourably by many. Modern fittings of high quality have often been introduced. It may be argued that the removal of massive Victorian furnishings has shown the architecture to better effect. Some will consider that the relevance of these cathedrals to the modern world has been enhanced. From around 1990, however, realisation has grown of the losses that have been suffered. As a result, some restoration or reinstatement of earlier decorations and furnishings has taken place, notably at Lancaster.

This destruction of old furnishings and wall paintings has parallels with what happened in the medieval churches and cathedrals at the Reformation. It has made the Roman Catholic cathedrals more similar in atmosphere to their Anglican counterparts. Indeed, there has perhaps even been some crossing over. At the Anglican cathedral of Derby, a splendid new baldacchino was introduced in the same years as a comparable baldacchino was demolished in the Roman Catholic cathedral of Portsmouth. However, there of course remain differences between the buildings of the two denominations. One may be commented on. Many ancient Anglican cathedrals and churches contain, as dusty relics of a distant past, features such as chantry chapels and the sites or remains of shrines and reliquaries. Those accustomed to seeing these may be surprised on visiting a Roman Catholic cathedral to find that it contains similar elements, but created in the nineteenth or twentieth century; moreover, here they usually still serve their original function.

Aldershot (Hampshire): Cathedral of the Forces

Built in 1892–3, this was originally one of three Anglican garrison churches here. In 1972 it became the Roman Catholic garrison church, and in 1987 it became the cathedral of the Bishop of the Forces. Externally it is of red brick, quite large but austere. All windows are lancets. There is a nave with aisles and clerestory; transepts that do not project on plan; a chancel with flanking chapels; and a west tower with big twin lancet belfry openings and a quite tall timber spire. The interior, by contrast, is faced in yellow brick with some stone dressings. This church has one rare distinction: its foundation stone was laid by Queen Victoria. A case set in the tower contains the mallet and silver trowel used on that occasion.

Arundel (West Sussex)

This is one of the most spectacular of the Roman Catholic cathedrals. Built in 1869–73 at the expense of Henry, fifteenth Duke of Norfolk (of Arundel Castle) and marking his coming of age, it was designed by J.A. Hansom. The Howard family, dukes of Norfolk, is probably the most wealthy and powerful of the great English families that remained loyal to the Catholic faith; the fifteenth duke was interested in architecture and became a notable patron of church building. Surprisingly, Arundel was built as a parish church and became a cathedral only in 1965 on the establishment of the diocese of Arundel and Brighton. In its scale and manner, it is fully of cathedral stature. It is strongly French in inspiration, probably influenced mainly by Bourges; being lofty and set on the highest point of the town, it is remarkably spectacular in distant views. There is, however, little open space immediately around it. It is cruciform and is vaulted throughout; the high vaults are 72 feet from the floor. Only in its length, just under 200 feet, does it fall short of medieval cathedral standards. It is faced inside and out in ashlared Bath stone, though the core is of brick.

This cathedral has been criticised by some architectural writers: but this seems unjust, for however much it may be derived from medieval precedent, this is a splendid and inspiring building. The exterior is very elaborate, with openwork parapets, flying buttresses, many pinnacles and some statuary (though there are also empty niches). Windows are traceried, many in a style close to the Decorated. There are several rose windows, notably that in the west front. The transepts project one bay

The Arundel skyline, with the cathedral (left) and castle (right)

beyond the aisles. A giant north porch stands on three tall arches: this was to have become a tower with a lofty spire, but was never carried up. A tall flèche is set on the roof just east of the crossing. The interior is very beautiful. The main space seems tremendously broad as well as lofty; however, the aisles are comparatively narrow. There are six bays of nave; the arcades have very tall multi-shafted pillars and richly carved capitals, and their spandrels contain roundels with busts of English saints. Above a band of trefoils, the tall clerestory is of paired two-light windows with their tracery internally doubled. The chancel has a narrower bay spacing; there are three bays with flanking chapels, and then a polygonal apse with only a tall, very narrow passage outside the arcade. A full ambulatory with radiating chapels and eastern Lady Chapel was at first intended. The west end has a big stone gallery that

Arundel Cathedral: the nave, looking north-west

contains the organ. A polygonal baptistery projects at the south-west corner. There is much fine stained glass, mostly by Hardman. Although the main altar is now under the east arch of the crossing, modern re-ordering has not had a great effect here. Following the canonisation of an Elizabethan member of the Howard family in 1970, the cathedral was rededicated to Our Lady and St Philip Howard, and the saint's remains were transferred from the castle to a new shrine in the north transept.

Belmont (Herefordshire)

Now simply a Benedictine abbey church, this served from 1859 as the pro-cathedral of the diocese of Newport and Menevia, which covered the whole of Wales together with Herefordshire. From 1895 the diocese was smaller, and then in 1916–20 the see was moved to Cardiff. As mentioned earlier, Belmont carries particular interest as it is the only case of a monastic cathedral to have existed since 1539. It has a rural setting just outside Hereford. Built in 1854–7 to the designs of E. W. Pugin, it was later extended, but remains shorter than its scale might imply. It is cruciform with a crossing tower, and is an impressive and upstanding building in an attractive and sophisticated Decorated style. It is built of ashlared Bath stone. The nave, of only three bays, has lean-to aisles with arcades having pillars of filleted quatrefoil form, rich foliage capitals and arches with two orders of sunk quadrants. Each bay has a clerestory of

*Belmont
Abbey, from the
north-west*

two two-light windows. The transepts are much lower than the nave. Similarly lower is the crossing, which has rich, acutely pointed arches and a lierne vault. It carries a tower completed in 1882; it is quite tall, with long twin two-light belfry openings and stepped battlements.

The eastern limb, gradually completed in the 1860s and 1870s, is longer than the nave and of almost the same height. It has two dissimilar sections. First are four small but rich bays, with dormer windows serving as clerestory and flanking chapels under pitched roofs. Two larger aisleless bays forming the east end (now the Blessed Sacrament chapel) have a lavish internal treatment with very tall arcades opening only to shallow recesses. Fine fittings include traceried stone screens to an outer chapel at the south-east. The monastic buildings stand on the south side, attached to the transept, where there is also a modern glass porch for the entry of lay people.

Beverley (Yorkshire, ER)

Curiously, although this was one of the dioceses created in 1850, Beverley has never had a cathedral. Indeed, there may never have been a serious intention of building one. Instead, the diocese was served by two successive pro-cathedrals at York. The presence of the Anglican cathedral in that city meant, of course, that the new diocese could not take York as its name. This anomalous situation was resolved in 1878 when the diocese was divided to become the dioceses of Leeds and Middlesbrough, with a cathedral in both of those places. The churches in York remain in use as parish churches.

The first pro-cathedral was the church of St George, in Peel Street, designed by J.A. Hansom and built in 1849–50. It is a pleasant but unremarkable building in a quiet Decorated style, with aisles under pitched roofs. It has no clerestory or tower; a stone belfry is above the chancel arch. By contrast, the second pro-cathedral is anything but quiet. This is the church of St Wilfrid, built in 1862–4 and becoming the pro-cathedral in 1864; its architect was George Goldie. The style, both inside and out, is a harsh and assertive gothic, with heavy and ornate details. Moreover, its materials are out of place in York: yellow stone with dressings of an almost black stone and shafts of a dirty red. It is tall and quite large: a nave of five bays with lean-to aisles and a clerestory, and a chancel of two bays with polygonal apse. The ritual west front facing the street has a large and heavily ornamented portal in four orders. To one side stands the tower, 147 feet high with a tall pyramidal roof carrying ornamental ironwork. The church stands only 100 yards from the west front of the minster, in some views of which it is prominent. It is not for sectarian reasons that some consider its presence regrettable!

Birmingham (Warwickshire, now West Midlands) Plate 19

Built in 1839–41, this was the earliest of the cathedrals designed by A.W.N. Pugin in anticipation of the re-establishment of the hierarchy. It has been a cathedral since 1850, and the seat of an archbishop from 1911. This is an impressive building, one of Pugin's finest achievements. It is only moderately large, but it is tall. Surprisingly, the design takes inspiration from fourteenth-century Baltic Germany. The exterior is of red brick, mostly plain and unadorned. However, the west front (which actually faces south; ritual directions are used here) makes a fine show. It has a richly treated portal, a large six-light window, six niches with statues, and striking twin towers carrying tall, slender timber spires. Behind it are an aisled nave of five bays, a crossing with full-height transepts not projecting on plan, and a chancel of two bays with polygonal apse.

Internally, it is striking and beautiful. The arcades are startlingly tall; they have cylindrical pillars with four attached shafts, and carry the lofty timber roof without a clerestory. The roof slopes continue across the aisles, which also are tall. Most windows are long, in two lights. Colour has been applied to the roofs, to good effect; those of the transepts and chancel are panelled and have even richer colour. Gilded texts are painted in spiral form on the east crossing pillars. A small but tall Lady Chapel flanks the chancel on its north side. Projecting north from the north aisle are a long chapel with polygonal end (added in 1931–3), and a projection containing the baptistery. There is an extensive vaulted crypt, in Norman style, containing several memorials and chantry chapels.

A major re-ordering that took place in 1967 is sometimes considered the worst case of the destruction of an original interior among the Roman Catholic cathedrals. Many notable Pugin fittings were ejected, and much mural decoration was painted over. The altar is now under the crossing, raised by several steps. Some striking old furnishings still remain, however, both by Pugin and some ancient work brought in mostly in his time. The very fine carved pulpit, concave hexagonal in form, is late-medieval Flemish work. Also in part medieval are the stalls, with carved misericords, from Cologne. There are several medieval oak statues, though painted in the nineteenth century. The canopy of 2003 over the archbishop's throne is based on the original, which was destroyed in 1967. In the north transept, railings surround Pugin's monument to Bishop Walsh, under whom the cathedral was built; it has a recumbent effigy under a rich pinnacled ogee canopy.

The cathedral survived the Second World War unscathed, but only by a very fortunate circumstance. A painted 'Deo Gratias' marks the place where an incendiary bomb fell through the roof in November 1940. It struck a radiator, which burst. This extinguished the bomb!

Brentwood (Essex)

This is a unique and most remarkable building. When the diocese was established in 1917, it used as cathedral a church of 1860–1 designed by Gilbert Blount; it was no bigger than an ordinary parish church and of indifferent quality. Most of this still stands: faced in Kentish rag, it has a nave of four bays with a lean-to south aisle (and originally also a north aisle), south porch, chancel and vestries. At its south-west corner a small tower rises, with a recessed octagonal belfry and a stone spire.

This was the smallest of the Roman Catholic cathedrals, and more space was needed. In 1972–4 its north aisle wall and north arcade were removed and a very large extension was constructed to the designs of John Newton; the interior was completely re-planned. Startlingly (but compare Blackburn and Liverpool (Roman Catholic)), this new building

Brentwood Cathedral, from the north

soon developed major structural problems, and urgent action was necessary. With the use of large anonymous gifts, it was demolished and replaced in 1989–91 by what is essentially a new cathedral. So Newton's building, which had much the same footprint as its successor, probably has the unfortunate distinction of being England's shortest-lived major cathedral structure.

The new building is classical, in a gently baroque style influenced by Wren and the early Italian Renaissance. Its architect was Quinlan Terry. Under the guidelines of Vatican II, it is centrally planned, and is a rectangle with wide aisles on all four sides. Most of the 1861 church remains, and stands in place of the south aisle of the new building. Architectural detail inside and out is of Portland stone; external walling is partly of ragstone (matching the Victorian church) and partly of yellow brick. Most windows are round-arched in moulded surrounds, but one each to east and west is Venetian. The walls are articulated by Doric pilasters, and above have a frieze, cornice and straight parapet with ball finials. There is a clerestory of round-arched windows carrying a low-pitched roof crowned by a large octagonal cupola. The main front is on the north, with three entrance doorways. Two of its bays are pedimented, and the principal doorway in the centre has a large part-circular portico on four Doric columns, inspired by the transept porticos of St Paul's Cathedral in London.

Brentwood Cathedral, looking east

Internally there are arcades of three bays to east and west and five to north and south. They have Tuscan columns carrying round arches; above are a frieze and cornice. The aisle ceilings are plain, but the high ceiling is enriched with beams carrying gilt patterns. The cupola opens as a lantern. Beneath is the altar, of white Italian stone in classical style, as are the other main furnishings; they form a fine ensemble. The seating is of chairs. There is a multiplicity of brass chandeliers.

This is a sophisticated and beautiful building. Its employment of a classical style may be surprising but it is delightful. Perhaps the only aesthetic criticism that might be made is that the retention of the Victorian gothic structure, though justified in historical and practical terms, inevitably creates a grinding stylistic clash.

Clifton (Bristol)

Clifton, a suburb of Bristol, was one of the sees established in 1850. It now has a cathedral designed in 1965 and constructed on a fresh site in 1970–3. The architects were the Percy Thomas Partnership. Its bold architecture forms a startling contrast to the elegant nineteenth-century residential area in which it is set. It is of reinforced concrete, internally all exposed though textured by the grain of the shuttering used in its construction, and externally partly exposed but mostly faced with panels of crushed pink granite. Designed during Vatican II, it is centrally planned, with a subtle layout based on an irregular hexagon. From the hexagonal sanctuary, the nave or congregational space extends out on three sides. At the back is a low ambulatory with a beamed concrete ceiling, resting on concrete pillars. The rest forms an impressively large unsupported span. Above the nave are complex concrete beams, still fairly low, with concealed natural lighting and timber tetrahedrons for acoustic purposes. Over the sanctuary, the roof rises into a great lantern with sloping sides and large areas of glass, illuminating the area below. Alongside the nave are the baptistery and a chapel. A narthex and a further large chapel are on the perimeter of the building. Seating is of moveable chairs. Fittings are stylistically all of their time, including the Stations of the Cross modelled in concrete. Almost the only colour is bright abstract glass in the narthex. Externally, the lantern carries three lofty concrete pylons incorporating a cross: they form, however, an accent that is jagged and strange rather than beautiful. Surprisingly, a low-level car park extends under much of the cathedral.

The story of the preceding pro-cathedral of the Apostles is interesting but unfortunate. It was begun in 1834 to a very ambitious Grecian design by H.E. Goodridge. However, construction was abandoned incomplete after difficulty with the foundations on the hillside site, compounded by

Clifton Cathedral

financial problems. An attempt in 1843 to resolve the difficulties failed. In 1847–8, what had been built was patched up under C.F. Hansom to provide a usable building at minimum cost. This became the pro-cathedral in 1850 and served as such for 123 years, though it was never consecrated. A scheme in 1876 proposed to complete and remodel it in Italian Romanesque style, with a tower of 200 feet: but only a new entrance front with a schoolroom behind was executed. Finally, the decision was made in the 1960s to build a new cathedral; on its opening the pro-cathedral was closed. More than three decades of increasing dereliction followed, but at the time of writing a major scheme of conversion into apartments and offices has just been completed.

The pro-cathedral is large. The entrance section of 1876 is low but quite elaborate. Behind it, the nave has six bays and continues with three bays of chancel flanked by broad, shallow transepts. The walls are of stone with banded rustication, with around them a series of immense cylindrical pillars. Hansom's completion ignored architectural proprieties, and these pillars, intended to be Corinthian, end ignominiously without capitals under the eaves. Aesthetically this is a disaster; no impression is conveyed of the character originally intended. Internally, the body was divided into a central space and aisles by tall, thin timber pillars and arches carrying the low-pitched roof. The conversion scheme includes a large additional block beyond the east end.

Ipswich (Suffolk)

This church, built in 1860–1 to the designs of George Goldie, deserves mention, though it has never been a cathedral. It stands in Orwell Place, in central Ipswich. When begun it was proposed that it would become the cathedral for East Anglia. What was built was intended as only the chancel. It is externally of red brick: a lofty aisled body of four large bays plus a further bay with polygonal apse. Windows have Decorated tracery; there is a clerestory. Inside, the unmoulded pointed arches are boldly striped in red and white, giving a distinctive character. The scale is quite impressive.

Lancaster (Lancashire)

This was built in 1857–9 to the designs of the Lancaster Anglican architect E.G. Paley. Though originally only a parish church, being raised to cathedral status in 1924, it is a fine cathedral. Its scale and loftiness combine with the sophisticated beauty of its Decorated-style architecture to make an impressive whole. It has a nave of five bays with lean-to aisles, their arcades having tall circular pillars with elaborate foliage capitals and arches with Decorated mouldings. A clerestory of two windows per bay is externally set in enriched blank arcading. The coloured timber roof reaches 74 feet from the floor. In the north-west corner stands the

Lancaster Cathedral

great tower, which has fine detailing and carries a spire with three tiers of lucarnes, 240 feet high. In its hillside position above the town, it forms a fine landmark.

There are lower transepts and no crossing. The chancel is lofty, with two bays and a three-sided apse. It has a clerestory of circular windows and a tierceron vault of timber; the apse has large three-light windows. Of the two-bay flanking chapels, that on the south is divided, part being accessible only from the adjoining cathedral buildings. From the north transept, a short link opens to a lovely vaulted octagonal baptistery that was added in 1901 and looks like a small chapter-house. Attached to the south aisle are two fine chantry chapels, both with quadripartite vaults in two bays.

The interior was enhanced by a major re-ordering in 1995, which reversed many losses caused previously. With help from English Heritage, most original fittings of the chancel were reinstated; it is now the Blessed Sacrament chapel. Most striking is the magnificent, enormous 1909 reredos in the form of a triptych, by Giles Gilbert Scott. The vault is splendidly coloured and the walls are covered in paintings. The stalls, of 1899, have rich canopies and even carved misericords. Introduced in 1995 behind the brought-forward altar is a splendid screen of iron, black and gilt. A west gallery contains the organ.

Leeds (Yorkshire, WR, now West Yorkshire)

The town's principal Roman Catholic church, a gothic building of 1836–8, was raised to cathedral status in 1878. This must be the only cathedral to have been demolished for a road-widening scheme: notice of compulsory purchase was served in 1899. Its replacement on a new site was built in 1902–4 to the designs of J.H. Eastwood and S.K. Greenslade. Its position is unfortunate: a city-centre block with streets on three sides, commercial buildings all around and scarcely any green to be seen. It is not large, and the plan is constrained by the site to be short and wide. However, this is a fine and distinctive building in the Arts and Crafts gothic style, the best example of this style among the country's cathedrals. It is constructed of good pale-coloured ashlar, and especially internally is very attractive.

Leeds Cathedral, from the south-east

Most windows are recessed under well-moulded segmental arches. The west front has a main window of seven lights and octagonal flanking turrets with pretty concave octagonal tops. There is some stone panelling. The width of the interior is striking. The aisles of the three-bay nave are of full height, making this a hall church; it also has low outer chapels. There are transepts but no crossing. West of the north transept stands the tower, which is sheer and quite tall, with twin two-light belfry openings, corner turrets and a tall pyramidal roof. The chancel has four-bay arcades opening to low passage aisles. Above these are galleries with tall windows; parts are occupied by the organ. On the south side is the Lady Chapel, containing the very rich altar and reredos from the earlier cathedral, of 1842 by A.W.N. Pugin. The main spaces have pointed barrel ceilings of timber and steel, transverse over the aisles. There are many enjoyable details. Major re-orderings took place in 1963 and 2005–6.

Liverpool (Lancashire, now Merseyside)   Plate 20

The cathedral story of this, one of the new dioceses created in 1850, is probably the most remarkable of all of the Roman Catholic sees. In 1853, building began in Everton, just north of the city centre, of a cathedral to the designs of E.W. Pugin. This was to have been on a magnificent scale, with a tremendous crossing tower and spire. Unfortunately, no financial provision existed to match this vision, and construction was abandoned in 1856 with just the eastern Lady Chapel complete. This then became the parish church of Our Lady Immaculate, a career that unfortunately ended in demolition in the 1980s. Meanwhile, the church of St Nicholas, Hawke Street, was used as pro-cathedral. This had been built in 1813–15, a substantial structure in an early gothic revival style typical of its time. It served in its elevated role for over a century until 1967, but it too was finally demolished, in 1973.

In 1911, Liverpool became an archdiocese, and in the 1920s consideration was again given to building a cathedral. A site was purchased in 1930, less than a mile from the Anglican cathedral and on the same prominent north-south ridge. Catching the force that was driving the Anglicans, and in an undoubted spirit of inter-denominational competition, the design commissioned from Sir Edwin Lutyens was of staggering ambition. The length was to be 680 feet, with a dome reaching a height of 510 feet. Not only was this considerably longer than the Anglican building, it would be only slightly shorter than the world's greatest church, St Peter's in Rome, and its dome would be even larger than that of St Peter's. It was to be in a distinctive Byzantine classical style, with a massive but essentially conventional cruciform plan. The transepts and nave would have double aisles, and the chancel would end in an apse. All this can be visualised both from pictures created at the time and from a splendid model. Construction began in 1933, but was brought to a halt by the Second World War, when only the crypt beneath the intended chancel (at the

Liverpool RC Cathedral, with the exterior of the Lutyens crypt in the foreground

north) was largely built. After the war, completion had become financially impossible. In 1953, with Lutyens now dead, Adrian Gilbert Scott (brother of the architect of the Anglican cathedral) produced a design for completion on a reduced scale. But this idea too was abandoned; however, in 1956–8 the crypt was completed. The space above it is now a great raised piazza. The crypt gives an evocative impression of what Lutyens's cathedral, sometimes dubbed 'the greatest building never built', would have been. Constructed mainly of granite and brick, it has great tunnel vaults and some fine architectural features inside and out. Its massive scale is obvious, and it is not low. A memorable feature is the rolling-stone gate of the archbishops' burial chapel.

In 1960 a competition was opened for a fresh design to a much smaller budget. This had now to meet the liturgical requirements soon to be formalised by Vatican II. From 298 entries, that of Frederick

Gibberd (who was later knighted) was chosen. It was constructed in the short period of 1962–7. It stands immediately south of the crypt on a platform (containing a car park) continuing the level of the crypt's piazza, so occupying the site intended for the Lutyens nave. In style it is entirely of its time, structurally based on reinforced concrete. Basically it is circular, 195 feet in diameter, with sixteen great concrete beams set at an angle to form the framework of a conical roof. Near the centre, the beams turn skyward as a huge, slightly tapering cylindrical tower. This rises to a crown of sixteen slender, lofty pinnacles of stainless steel, with complex filigree work, reaching 282 feet. The external aspect is distinctive and powerful, and forms a feature of the city's skyline that is almost as prominent as the Anglican cathedral.

Projecting far on the south side is the entrance porch, with its front rising as a huge rectangular slab, pierced at the top by four openings containing the bells. Prominent carving relieves the front face. The great, lofty circular interior has the altar at its centre, around which the seating is laid out radially. Above is the tower, entirely glazed with brilliantly coloured abstract glass by John Piper and Patrick Reyntiens. Around the perimeter, projecting between vertical lower sections of the sixteen beams, is a series of chapels and porches, differing from each other in both their forms and their treatment. Externally they are faced in Portland ashlar. Between and above the chapels is further coloured glazing. All this glass makes the glowing colour of the light a memorable aspect of the interior. The variety of the chapels forms an attractive contrast to the uniform, centralised main space. There are many striking fittings and art-works, largely consistent in their abstract forms.

With its non-traditional and dramatically bold form, this cathedral is an extreme contrast to the Anglican cathedral; yet it may well be thought a worthy companion to it. Perhaps because of its innovative character, soon after completion it was beset by severe leakage and structural problems. So bad were these that demolition became a serious possibility. However, it was secured by a great restoration and modification programme in 1992–2003, which also resolved problems with the crypt. The cost was over £8 million. In 2007–8 a glazed rotunda was added, containing stairs that give direct access from the cathedral to the crypt.

Middlesbrough (Yorkshire, NR, now North Yorkshire)

This diocese was established in 1878, and its cathedral was built in 1876–8 to the designs of George Goldie. It was an aisled building on a substantial scale, nine bays long, though a planned tower of 160 feet was never built. Externally it was of red brick. By the time it reached its centenary, the area was run-down: most of the Roman Catholic population had moved away from central Middlesbrough, and the fabric was in poor condition. So it was decided to move: a new cathedral was built

in 1985–7, surprisingly set 5 miles away in the new satellite town of
Coulby Newham. Following this, the old cathedral deteriorated; it was
gutted in 2000 as a result of arson, and was demolished.

The new cathedral was designed by Frank Swainston and Peter
Fenton. It is a polygonal, fan-shaped building; its walls are low and faced
inside and out in light brown brick. The layout has many variations, as
has the tent-like roof, which is slated and fairly low in pitch. Windows
are simple, narrow rectangles of varying lengths. Externally the tallest
accent is the campanile, a brick pylon nearly 60 feet high carrying three
bells. The interior has gently raked pews, radiating from the sanctuary at
the base of the fan. Added to the main space is a large narthex, a service
section including a spacious meeting room, and, to one side, the Blessed
Sacrament chapel.

This is a pleasant building with a quiet dignity, but it is low-key. All
is of good quality but fairly simple. There are (as yet) few artworks;
probably the most significant is the large abstract painting forming
the reredos.

Newcastle upon Tyne (Northumberland, now Tyne and Wear)

Dedicated to St Mary, this was built in 1842–4 to the designs of A. W. N.
Pugin, and attained cathedral status in 1850. Although the diocese was
originally named Hexham, there was apparently never any intention
that its cathedral should be anywhere other than here. This is an attractive building, listed Grade I, and one of Pugin's finest churches. It is a
large, uniform, aisled rectangle of ashlar in a good-quality Decorated
style, of seven bays without lengthwise division. There are three parallel
pitched roofs and no clerestory. The main east window has seven lights,

with rich tracery; the west window has
five. The arcades have pillars of four major
and four minor shafts and arches of complex mouldings. Colour has been applied
to the rather thin roof timbers.

A tower was added in 1870–2 to the
designs of A.M. Dunn and E.J. Hansom,
attached to the south aisle and originally
also serving as porch. It is slender and tall,
and carries a strikingly lofty spire reaching 222 feet. Just west of this an octagonal
baptistery was added in 1901–2. In 2002–3,
the baptistery became the porch, attached
to a new entrance and visitor building. The
interior of the cathedral was re-ordered
in 1982 and again in 2010. It is quite light
despite much stained glass. Cathedral
buildings are attached at the south-east.

Northampton

When it became a see in 1850, Northampton's Roman Catholics were
served only by a modest chapel of 1844 designed by A.W.N. Pugin. In
1863–4 this was greatly enlarged by the addition of an aisled structure
running west from it, designed by E.W. Pugin. This reversed the orientation and had the altar at its west end, set in a polygonal apse. However, in
1955–9 the building of 1844 was demolished and replaced by a new crossing, transepts and chancel to the designs of A.S. Herbert. This returned the
cathedral to an eastward orientation and gave it a largely conventional plan.

*Newcastle RC
Cathedral*

Herbert's eastern limb is in a simple gothic style with mostly lancet
windows, externally of pale-brown brick with a few stone dressings and
a little enrichment. Internally the tower forms a lantern, with a surprising circular stair turret of stone suspended in one corner. E.W. Pugin's
nave, in Decorated style, has a quite attractive and distinctive character.
It is of five bays, with short pillars of quatrefoil form, elaborate foliage
capitals and arches with two orders of sunk quadrant mouldings. Above
are quite large two-light clerestory windows, externally with their
tops amusingly just projecting through the eaves. The timber roof is of
attractive, complex design. Hardman stained glass fills the three-light
windows of the west-facing apse; a gallery and a doorway have been
inserted here. The generally simple furnishings, with the altar under the
crossing, seem appropriate to the architecture.

Surviving as a sacristy attached to the north transept is the first
Catholic chapel built here in 1825. Only its windowless east wall, of
ashlared local ironstone, is visible.

*Northampton
Cathedral*

Norwich

This is the cathedral of the diocese of East Anglia, which was only created in 1976. Like Arundel, its building is due to Henry, fifteenth Duke of
Norfolk. It stands in a prominent position just outside the walled city. Site
preparation began in 1882, and the church was built in 1884–1910; unusually, work started with the nave. The original architect was G.G. Scott the
Younger, but his brother J.O. Scott later took over. This is an extraordinary
creation: a building of the character and quality of a medieval cathedral,
and almost the size of one with a length of about 280 feet. Unlike the
duke's earlier church at Arundel, this is firmly English in manner, in Early
English style. It is cruciform with central tower. The aisled nave has the
great length of ten bays. There is a north porch. The transepts project two
bays beyond the aisles and have both an east aisle and a chapel projecting
beyond that. Only the chancel is short by cathedral standards, having four
aisled bays and ending straight. It deviates slightly to the north.

The exterior is all of ashlar, with many fine, typically Early English
details. The aisles and the clerestory both have a single large lancet
window in each bay. There are flying buttresses. The west front has a
great triplet of lancets and a rich gabled projection for the portal, which
is of the most lavish Early English design. Flanking square turrets rise
to arcaded tops and spirelets. The other fronts have similarly rich treatment. There is a particularly sumptuous double portal on the west side
of the north transept. The tower has three stages, with battlements; its
belfry has two pairs of large lancets. The east chapel of the north transept
contrasts surprisingly with the rest, being in French style, two-storeyed,

with a polygonal apse. It dates from 1909 and was designed by J.O. Scott.

The internal design is heavy but impressive. It is vaulted throughout. The nave arcades have thick cylindrical pillars with richly moulded arches and capitals alternately moulded or having stiff leaf. Above is a triforium of two arches per bay, with flanking blank arches. The aisles have lavish wall arcading employing black Frosterley marble for its shafts and imposts. This treatment differs north from south: the latter has deep internal buttresses, no doubt in anticipation of cloisters that were never built. An outer chapel stands alongside four bays on the south side. Even more enrichment is applied to the transepts and chancel, which are also a little higher and, unlike the nave, have vaults with tiercerons. The triforium here has the richer form of two subdivided arches per bay. In the chancel, the clerestory lancets have flanking blank arches. The crossing forms an impressive lantern.

The altar was brought forward in the 1970s to a position under the crossing, and at the time of writing the east end was unused and

(above:) Norwich RC Cathedral

(below:) Norwich RC Cathedral, from the north-east

curtained off. There is much fine stained glass; some was remade after damage in the Second World War. Cathedral House and other offices are attached on the south side, and there is a new complex of visitor buildings at the south-west. It is interesting to consider which of the duke's two cathedrals is the finer.

Nottingham

This was built in 1841–4 to the designs of A.W.N. Pugin and was intended to be a cathedral, which it became in 1850–1. It has a full cruciform plan with central tower and is uniform throughout, externally of yellow ashlar. The style is Early English, with predominantly lancet windows. The nave has five bays, with lean-to aisles, north and south porches and a clerestory of two cusped lancets per bay. There are full-height transepts, which like the west front have in their end walls a graduated triplet of long, slender lancets. The high chancel has three aisled bays, similar to the nave but slightly richer; the east window is a rose. On the south side is the three-bay Blessed Sacrament chapel, opening to the south chancel aisle by a low arcade. East of the chancel is an ambulatory with three chapels, of which that in the centre is a two-bay Lady Chapel.

Nottingham Cathedral, from the north-west

This is a substantial and quite impressive structure, about 200 feet long. However, much of it is rather austere. Finest is the tower, with twin two-light belfry openings, carrying a stone spire with at its base lucarnes and big pinnacles with niches containing images. The internal impression is cool and low-key, in part as a result of re-orderings and the fact that most surfaces have been painted pale grey. In dramatic contrast is Pugin's decorative scheme in the Blessed Sacrament chapel, which was restored (largely though not entirely authentically) in 1933. It is of vivid patterns in dark red and blue, with some gold: it may be considered magnificent, but some will think it garish and vulgar. There is extensive stained glass, much of it designed by Pugin. Large cathedral buildings stand to the south.

Plymouth (Devon)

This was one of the sees created in 1850. A church of St Mary initially served as pro-cathedral. A cathedral was built on a new site in 1856–8 to the designs of J.A. and C.F. Hansom. It is cruciform, externally of irregular white stone, and fairly modest. The nave has five bays and the chancel has four plus a polygonal apse. Both have lean-to aisles and a clerestory; the transepts are lower, and each has an east chapel. Windows are mostly lancets, often in pairs or triplets; just the windows of the apse have bar tracery. The interior is attractively light and quite lofty. The arcades have tall, slim octagonal pillars. At the north-west is the tower, originally a porch tower but now internally a chapel. It carries a spire added in 1866–7 which is externally by far the most striking feature: it is very tall and slim and rises to 205 feet.

The internal effect is dominated by a re-ordering of 1994: most fittings are new, with good benches of hardwood; the altar is under the crossing. A further new feature is a glazed narthex outside the west doorway. This continues as a covered way connecting to the Cathedral Centre, a modern building erected within the walls of the former Notre Dame convent, which was gutted by bombing in 1941. The former pro-cathedral of St Mary has been demolished.

Portsmouth (Hampshire)

Construction began here in 1879 to the designs of John Crawley; he died in 1880, after which J.S. Hansom took over. The diocese was created in 1882 when the first part of the cathedral, comprising just five bays of the nave, was opened. Construction continued in stages, and was completed in 1906 with the west narthex and porch. An apsidal chapel projecting from the north aisle was added in 1924. The cathedral

Portsmouth RC Cathedral

is cruciform, with an aisled nave of six bays. The transepts are of full height, though shallow in projection; the chancel has a polygonal apse. Windows are in Decorated style. Externally it is of bright red brick with stone dressings and parapets enriched with pinnacles. There is no tower, but attractive octagonal turrets with spirelet tops flank the west end. A striking rose window with leaf-like flowing tracery in the south transept, called the Dean's Window, was probably inspired by the 'Bishop's Eye' at Lincoln.

It is the interior that is finer here. The nave arcades have pillars of quatrefoil form carrying leaf capitals; above is a clerestory of large three-light windows. The high timber roofs are distinctive, with large ribbed coves suggestive of vaulting. Successive reorderings since 1970 have included demolition of a large baldacchino and erasure of many elaborate wall paintings by Nathaniel Westlake in the eastern limb. The nave has a beautiful light and glowing quality, probably helped by the destruction of much stained glass in 1941. However, the east end, now St John's chapel, with its walls largely blank below clerestory level, seems disappointingly bland. Its shorter flanking chapels, by contrast, both have a gorgeous reredos and retain their rich wall paintings.

Salford (Lancashire, now Greater Manchester)

This stands in the city of Salford, separated from Manchester by the River Irwell, but is less than a mile from Manchester Cathedral. It was built in 1844–8 and became a cathedral in 1850. The designer was M.E. Hadfield. This is one of the finest of the early Roman Catholic cathedrals. It is of cream-coloured ashlar, finely detailed externally and shown to good effect since being cleaned of industrial soot. The plan is cruciform; its length is about 185 feet, and it is dominated by its splendid crossing tower and spire, which is 240 feet in height. This splendid sight stands in startling contrast to the sordid post-industrial surroundings: at the time of writing much of the area is still wasteland, and many of the standing buildings are derelict.

To the experienced lover of old churches, Salford Cathedral may seem unexpectedly familiar. Hadfield followed a procedure not uncommon in the 1840s of copying from authentic medieval originals, here reproduced exactly except for some reductions or simplifications. The style is a rich Decorated, with the nave and west front based on those of the collegiate church of Howden and the chancel reproducing that of Selby Abbey. They make a well-unified whole. Both nave and chancel here have four bays. For the tower and spire, Newark was the model, though with one stage of tower omitted. This too is Decorated. There are large twin two-light belfry openings under a crocketed gable and a panelled straight parapet with corner pinnacles; the spire has four tiers of lucarnes.

The west front (actually facing south: directions given here are ritual) has a four-light window, panelling, and four large octagonal turrets of openwork with spirelets. Inside, the nave has tall arcades on pillars of four filleted principal shafts and a small clerestory of twin two-light windows. Roofs are of timber. For the chancel there is greater richness, including stone vaults, with tiercerons for the high vault. The arcades have leaf capitals, above which corbels carry large statues under canopies; the clerestory has three-light arched windows. Especially splendid is the tracery of the great seven-light east window.

This is a light and attractive interior. However, some will regret the extensive destruction of Victorian woodwork that took place mainly in re-orderings of 1972 and 1988. The altar is under the crossing, and the architecturally splendid chancel is largely bare. Traceried stone screens still separate chapels in the east bays of the aisles. In contrast to the rest, rich furnishings, largely of 1884 by P.P. Pugin, remain in the south transept. The west window has striking glass of 1990.

Salford Cathedral

Sheffield (Yorkshire, WR, now South Yorkshire)

This impressive church, built in 1847–50, became the cathedral of the Roman Catholic diocese of Hallam in 1980. It is in Decorated style, designed largely by M.E. Hadfield. As at Salford, he took inspiration from existing medieval architecture, here mainly the church of Heckington (Lincolnshire) and confined to individual features, such as the east window. The cathedral stands straight up from the street on its south side and is otherwise hemmed in by other buildings. It is of ashlar and is cruciform in plan, with transepts lower than the main body. The nave has five bays, with aisles and a clerestory of almost continuous three-light windows. A narrow outer chapel is alongside part of the north nave aisle. In the south-west corner stands the tower, which is internally vaulted. It is large and tall, in three stages, with quite rich detailing; above a straight parapet with large crocketed corner pinnacles rises a lofty spire with three tiers of lucarnes.

The chancel has an elaborate composition of piscina and triple sedilia. It is flanked by chapels: on the south there are two under a north-south roof. The outer of these contains the unusual Lady Chapel at an upper level, reached by a curving staircase in a projection. Its eastern half is an octagonal structure, richly gothic and resting on marble columns; externally this structure forms a broad turret with a short leaded spire.

As usual, there is a brought-forward altar, and significant nineteenth-century fittings including a rood screen by A.W.N. Pugin have been removed. Two tall, rich shrines are in the north transept.

Shrewsbury (Shropshire)

This diocese was one of those established in 1850. The sixteenth Earl of Shrewsbury was ready to finance building a cathedral, and went to A.W.N. Pugin for its design. However, Pugin died shortly afterwards, in 1852; his son E.W. Pugin, then aged only eighteen, continued the commission and was largely responsible for the design. The cathedral has a striking position with its ritual west front (actually facing south) on the elevated street called Town Walls. It is pleasant but towerless and quite small, hardly larger than an average parish church. The style is Decorated. It has a nave of five bays with lean-to aisles; the arcades have octagonal pillars with foliage capitals, and the clerestory windows are distinctive by being spherical triangles. There is a large stone belfry above the front. An elaborate porch at the ritual south-west was added in 1906. The chancel is short, in two bays; it has an elaborate seven-light east window and a coloured hammerbeam roof. It is flanked by chapels. That on the right was added in 1890–1 to the design of Edmund Kirby; it is small but has a tierceron vault, much marble shafting, and lavish enrichment.

The principal distinction of the cathedral is its stained glass. Some is by Hardman, but much is excellent early twentieth-century work in the Arts and Crafts style by the Shrewsbury-born Margaret Rope.

Southwark (London)

Built in 1840–8, this was designed by A.W.N. Pugin and became a cathedral in 1850. It is dedicated to St George. In 1965 it was made the seat of an archbishop. Pugin's first proposals of 1838 were impossibly ambitious, and had to be much curtailed by the financial realities. The building as executed is nevertheless large, with a length of about 250 feet. Externally it is of yellow brick and, standing straight up from the busy street, is not attractive. It runs north-west to south-east, and surprisingly the altar is at the north-west end; directions in this account are ritual. As built, it had a chancel of two bays, an aisled nave of eight bays, and the entrance in the massive base of an intended but unexecuted lofty west tower with spire. There was no clerestory and roofs were of timber. In 1941 it was hit by an incendiary bomb and gutted. The adjacent Amigo Hall served as pro-cathedral until rebuilding in 1953–8 to the designs of R.B. Craze. The outer walls were re-used with little alteration, but the arcades were

replaced and a new and much loftier clerestoried structure created. The new work is firmly and richly gothic; it has been criticised by some architectural observers, but it harmonises with Pugin's work, and has produced a dignified and beautiful interior. Large complex pillars carry arcades of richly moulded arches; above, the clerestory has four-light windows and a big wall passage. The roof, 57 feet from the floor, is of painted, panelled timber between stone transverse arches. Attractive vaults of flying ribs cover the aisles. In the seventh bay from the west, Craze raised the aisles to form small pseudo-transepts: this ingenious introduction also effectively lengthened the chancel by one bay. Completion of the tower and spire was again hoped for but not implemented.

Pugin's east window, with its striking post-war glass, is in nine lights. The aisle windows have five lights. Chapels flank the chancel: that on the north is the Blessed Sacrament chapel, and contains some original furnishings. On the south side is a complex space connecting to the very large Day Chapel, which was added in 1963 and has enormous five-light square-headed windows in sixteenth-century style. The Lady Chapel is to its east. Along the south side of the nave is a series of vaulted chapels forming a narrow outer aisle: these escaped the fire. Also surviving are the attractive Petre and Knill chantries: vaulted stone cages resembling those of the late Middle Ages. Beside the tower base is an octagonal baptistery, Craze's final addition, of 1966. There are several tomb-chests with recumbent effigies.

Westminster (London)

By common consent, this, the country's principal and largest Roman Catholic cathedral, is also its finest. It is fully of cathedral scale and power, and is unique in its character. From 1867, Henry Clutton made several gothic designs for a cathedral on a different site, which would have been splendid; but they remained unexecuted. The present site was bought in 1884; however, it was only the third archbishop, Herbert Vaughan, enthroned in 1892, who was determined to go ahead with construction of a cathedral. The architect chosen was J.F. Bentley. Archbishop and architect agreed that the style should be Byzantine (or Early Christian): Vaughan did not want a gothic cathedral that might appear to compete with Westminster Abbey. As implemented, the style is Byzantine with Italian elements and is treated originally. It was constructed in 1895–1903. The style is without parallel on a large scale in England, so the cathedral seems startlingly unfamiliar to English eyes. Nevertheless it is traditional in being longitudinal and having transepts (though these do not appear on its plan). The external length is 360 feet. Its axis is to the south-south-east (directions used here are ritual). The covering is by domes: the nave has three, of which the third is flanked by the transepts. A slightly taller dome covers the chancel, with windows around its base; beyond it is a lower apse. Externally the impression is tremendously massive but not lofty. The exception to this is the strikingly tall and slender campanile, 285 feet high, rising near the north-west corner. This is the most Italianate feature, and is crowned by a complex, cupola-like structure. Walling is of bright orange brick with extensive use of contrasting white Portland stone, much of it in stripes (again an Italian characteristic). The whole is complicated and varied.

Westminster Cathedral

A high open arcade runs around the apse. Turrets and secondary towers appear in several places, including twin towers flanking the apse. The west facade has a huge round-arched portal containing the three entrance doorways, with a tympanum of mosaic. Originally facing only a narrow street, it now appears splendidly from Victoria Street across a piazza created as part of a redevelopment in 1976.

If the external character is unfamiliar, a first sight of the interior must be even more startling. The main arches rise to 90 feet, and the highest dome to 117 feet. The main space is exceptionally wide at 60 feet. Outside this are aisles and then a series of large chapels. Each nave bay is divided into two by massive rectangular pillars rising to the dome base. These half-bays are further subdivided at low level by two arches, carrying a broad gallery with balustrade. Above are pairs of round-arched windows,

Westminster Cathedral: the east end

and then large lunettes (semi-circular windows) with strange tracery. Further long chapels flank the chancel. The aisles and other spaces have tunnel or groin vaults. Dominating the effect of the whole, however, is the fact that it is unfinished. All walls are intended to be covered by a veneer of marble, and the upper parts and vaults to be covered by mosaics. In the chapels flanking the chancel, and some others, the treatment is complete, to gorgeous effect. In the main space, the lower parts are largely covered by marbles with striking patterns and colours. Higher up, all is bare, plain brick, almost black in colour and disappearing into the darkness. It is reminiscent of railway architecture. However, its strange and mysterious effect is part of the character and power of the building. The addition of marbles and mosaics slowly continues. Will it ever be completed? Should it be?

An impressive baldacchino stands over the main altar; there has been no major re-ordering here. On the nave piers are the Stations of the Cross of 1913–18 by Eric Gill, which are considered the finest artwork here. There are other excellent and varied contents

The archdiocese was established in 1850. Initially, St Mary Moorfields, a large classical church opened in 1820, served as pro-cathedral. In 1869, it was replaced as pro-cathedral by the newly built church of Our Lady of Victories, Kensington. This was designed by George Goldie and was an impressive structure in French style, with triforium and clerestory; its chancel was apsidal. However, it was gutted by incendiary bombs in 1940, and was subsequently completely demolished to make way for its replacement. Meanwhile, St Mary Moorfields had moved to a new site, and the old church was demolished in 1900.

B: ORTHODOX CHURCHES

The Orthodox Churches, commonly referred to collectively as the Eastern Orthodox Church, form the principal further group possessing an episcopal organisation. Today, Orthodoxy is, along with Pentecostalism, the country's fastest-growing Christian denomination. Most prominent are the Greek Orthodox and the Russian Orthodox, but many other Orthodox Churches also have a presence. These Churches have come to exist in this country largely as a result of immigration, but it is startling to realise that the first Greek Orthodox church building in London was established in the later seventeenth century, with the Russian Orthodox following not far behind. As well as many Orthodox church buildings, there are also now Orthodox cathedrals. A few of these cathedrals have been purpose built but most originated as churches or chapels built by the Church of England or other denominations, usually in the nineteenth century. Though redecorated and refurnished to varying degrees, none has been structurally enlarged for its new role. Architecturally most of the Orthodox cathedrals are of minor interest, but several are worthy of more attention. The fittings and atmosphere of Orthodox churches and cathedrals are strikingly different from those of the Western Churches. There are often many candles, incense is much used, and icons or holy pictures are prominent. The altar is normally concealed from the congregation by the iconostasis or screen, which has central doors through which only priests may pass. Some Orthodox churches, including those of the Russian Orthodox, have no pews: the congregation stands throughout services, though a few chairs are provided at the sides for the infirm.

The Greek Orthodox is by far the largest of the Orthodox Churches in this country; across the United Kingdom it has about 125 church buildings at present. Much of the increase in its adherents through the twentieth century came from the immigration of Greek Cypriots, who settled mainly in the largest cities and particularly in London. However, immigration is not the only factor in its growth. Aspects of Orthodoxy, perhaps particularly its conservatism, have made it attractive to some among the indigenous population. Many of those who have left their previous denominations for Orthodoxy have joined the Greek Orthodox, with its widespread presence across the country.

Great Britain and Ireland form the Greek Orthodox Archdiocese of Thyateira and Great Britain. There are eight cathedrals in England: seven in London and one in Birmingham. (A further church in Leicester, sometimes referred to as a cathedral, does not formally have this status.) This distribution may seem baffling: but the country is not divided by the Greek Orthodox Church into dioceses or even parishes, so a cathedral does not have a diocese. The status of cathedral is effectively honorary, although the designation of these churches as cathedrals is unequivocal. A bishop is associated with some of the cathedrals, but the status of these bishops again is essentially honorary: their jurisdiction and authority are the same as for normal parish priests. The Church in this country has an archbishop, who has authority throughout the archdiocese; however, he has no throne in any particular cathedral or church. Nevertheless, the Cathedral of St Sophia in Bayswater has seniority among the cathedrals, and is where the present archbishop was enthroned. The special position of this cathedral is reflected in its history and architecture. Of the eight cathedrals, St Sophia and that of All Saints in Camden Town are architecturally the two of principal interest.

Second in size among the Orthodox Churches in this country, though much smaller than the Greek Orthodox, is the Russian Orthodox. Unfortunately it has suffered division. For many years there were two separate Russian Orthodox Churches in parts of the world outside Russia: that of the Patriarchate of Moscow, and the Russian Orthodox Church Abroad (also known as the Russian Orthodox Church Outside Russia), of which the headquarters is in New York. Under Communist rule in Russia, the Russian Orthodox Church there was obliged to make compromises with the state. As a consequence, in 1927 the Russian Orthodox Church Abroad broke away in order to remain uncontaminated. The two Churches were not in communion with each other. The Russian Orthodox Church, Moscow Patriarchate was and is the larger in this country, but both eventually established a cathedral here. Happily, the two Churches were reconciled in 2007, though the Russian Orthodox Church Abroad remains semi-autonomous.

Many other Orthodox Churches have some adherents and a few church buildings in England. These include the Antiochan, Armenian, Belarussian Autocephalous, Bulgarian, Coptic, Serbian and Ukrainian Orthodox Churches.[2] Several have a church that is sometimes referred to as a cathedral, though some seem to have no formal status as such and are also regarded simply as churches. Noticed here are only those of the Antiochan and Coptic Orthodox Churches. The dedications of Orthodox churches are sometimes distinctive, and are given here.

Bayswater (London): Greek Orthodox Cathedral   Plate 21

This is the Cathedral of St Sophia, also referred to as the Cathedral of the Divine Wisdom. Located in Moscow Road, it is the successor of the first Greek Orthodox church built in Soho in 1677; reset within it is a stone inscription from that church. Its design, in a Byzantine style, was commissioned from J.O. Scott; it was built in 1877–9, consecrated in 1882 and elevated to cathedral status in 1922. In plan it is a Greek cross with a dome. The exterior is fairly plain, but the entrance facade (ritual west, actually facing south) has some enrichment. The opposite side has a polygonal apse. Externally it does not look large, though the length is about 115 feet.

The interior is a startling contrast: the scale is big and the decorations and fittings make a magnificently rich effect. Most surfaces have mosaics, marble panelling or painted decoration. The dome is large and, with its paintings, very impressive. There is a narthex on the entrance side, with a gallery above. Three graduated arches open to the apsidal chancel, in front of which is the splendid iconostasis of walnut with round arches, fluted pilasters and exquisite inlay. Many of the furnishings have gilding.

Birmingham (Warwickshire, now West Midlands): Greek Orthodox Cathedral

The Cathedral of the Dormition of the Mother of God and St Andrew stands in Arthur Place, Summer Hill. It was designed by the prominent local architect J.A. Chatwin for the Catholic Apostolic Church and opened in 1873; it became Greek Orthodox in 1958. It is quite large, externally of red brick with some bands of blue; internally it is of white brick elaborately banded or patterned everywhere with red and blue. There is no tower. Windows are in early Decorated style. A long, lofty nave has heavy arcades opening to passage aisles passing through the boldly projecting buttresses. There are apses at both east and west, and further attachments especially at the west end. The setting is not fortunate, with little green to be seen.

Camberwell (London): Greek Orthodox Cathedral

What has since 1977 been the Cathedral of the Nativity of the Mother of God was originally a church of 1873 by J. and J. Belcher for the Catholic Apostolic Church. It stands in Camberwell New Road, near Camberwell Green. It is towerless, low and quite small scale, with an austere red brick exterior; it is the humblest of the Greek Orthodox cathedrals. Its chancel is apsidal, with flanking chapels and a larger outer south chapel; there are transepts and a nave with lean-to aisles. Twin three-bay cloister-like porches come forward from the west front towards the street. An interesting curiosity is that, following war damage, most of the nave has remained roofless, treated as a garden, with the intact aisles open to it like cloister walks.

Camden Town (London): Greek Orthodox Cathedral

This Cathedral of All Saints was an Anglican church, built as Camden Chapel in 1822–4 to the designs of the father-and-son team William and Henry Inwood. It stands in Camden Street. It became Greek Orthodox in 1948 and a cathedral in 1991. Appropriately, it is in Grecian style. Standing in a green churchyard, this is a large and stately building, listed Grade I. Its rectangular body is of yellow brick with long round-arched windows, and the east end has an apsidal sanctuary of full height. The west front is of Portland stone and has a great semi-circular portico of four fluted Ionic columns. Behind this stands the circular tower, its tall belfry stage surrounded by Ionic columns.

The spacious interior has deep galleries on three sides. There is a broad flat ceiling. Ionic pilasters and some plasterwork enrich the sanctuary. The chancel has rich Greek Orthodox fittings; however, much furniture remains from Anglican days, and the decoration (restored in 2009–10) is largely white, with gilding.

Camden Town: Greek Orthodox Cathedral

Chiswick (Middlesex, now London): Russian Orthodox Cathedral

Standing in Harvard Road, this belongs to the Russian Orthodox Church Abroad. It is dedicated to the Dormition of the Most Holy Mother of God and Holy Royal Martyrs. After many years using a leased London church, a site for a cathedral was purchased in Chiswick in 1992. Constructed in 1997–9, the main upper church was only ready for use in 2007. In terms of area, it is small. It is in traditional Russian Orthodox style: a tall, centrally planned building with shallow projections in the cardinal directions and low-pitched

Chiswick: Russian Orthodox Cathedral

roofs with prominent eaves. The eastern projection has an apse; the west side has the entrance and is at present unfinished; addition of a belfry is planned. Arches are round and windows are small. Most of the exterior is white and simple, but the centre rises in a circular tower carrying a great blue onion dome with gold stars, surmounted by a small ball and a large and rich gold cross. The interior is bare and white at the time of writing except for the recently installed iconostasis with three tiers of richly gilt icons; wall paintings and other enrichments are planned.

Golders Green (London): Greek Orthodox Cathedral

This was an Anglican church of St Michael, built as recently as 1913–14 to the designs of J.T. Lee. It was extended to the west in 1924–5, and further additions in 1960 included a north-west porch tower. From 1970 it was shared with the Greek Orthodox community, and in 1979 it became wholly Greek Orthodox, dedicated to the Holy Cross and St Michael. It stands at the junction of Golders Green Road and The Riding. It is quite large, of brick, in a fairly simple but attractive gothic style. Many of its windows are lancets. Both nave and chancel have a clerestory and, surprisingly, the nave is vaulted. The porch tower is distinctive, with simple three-light mullioned windows of seventeenth-century type; it has a straight top, but carries a tall, thin classical cupola.

Kensington (London): Russian Orthodox Cathedral

This is the cathedral of the Diocese of Sourozh (covering Great Britain) in the Patriarchate of Moscow. Originating as the Anglican All Saints, Ennismore Gardens, it became the Russian Orthodox Cathedral of the Dormition and All Saints in 1956. It was built in 1848–9 to the designs of L. Vulliamy, and is a fine building in Italian Romanesque style. The west front of ashlared limestone has panelling of shallow pilasters, many small shafted windows, and a large wheel window. There is a porch with a round arch carried on shafts, some twisted, with characteristic foliage capitals. At the south-west is a tall campanile added in 1870 in the same style.

Like the exterior, the interior is distinctive and beautiful. The nave has six bays with tall red-painted Corinthian columns carrying round arches and a clerestory. Galleries run along the aisles, and there is another at the west. The east end has a semi-circular apse, with a half dome. Surfaces above the arcades and the apse arch have beautiful decoration by Heywood Sumner. The iconostasis has rich doors that came from the pre-Revolutionary Russian embassy. With the floor unencumbered by chairs and with numerous icons and paintings in gold frames glinting in the light of the many lamps and candles, it is very atmospheric.

Kentish Town (London): Greek Orthodox Cathedral

This cathedral in Kentish Town Road originated as an Anglican church of St Barnabas, built in 1884–5 to the designs of Ewan Christian. It became Greek Orthodox in 1957 and is dedicated to St Andrew. Externally it is uninspiring, built of yellow brick and standing straight up from the street, with windows of lancets or plate tracery. It is short and wide, with a broad nave, aisles under pitched roofs and a wide apsidal chancel. Surprisingly, the north aisle has an apsidal west end projecting beyond the nave; in the angle is an octagonal turret carrying a short spire. The beautiful interior comes as a surprise. All of its surfaces, including the plastered barrel ceilings, have colourful paintings in traditional Byzantine style, and the furnishings are almost entirely Greek Orthodox work of fine quality.

Kensington: Russian Orthodox Cathedral

Regent's Park (London): Antiochan Orthodox Cathedral

Located in Albany Street, this was built in 1836–7 to the designs of James Pennethorne as the Anglican Christ Church. It became the Antiochan Orthodox Cathedral of St George in 1989. It is quite substantial, in a convinced Grecian-Egyptian style. The broad rectangular body of yellow-grey brick has corner sections standing slightly forward and higher than the rest; there is a shallow projecting sanctuary. The side doorways are large and pedimented, and windows are tall, plain and round-arched. Above the entrance front is a slender, columned tower rising to a short spire. The interior has galleries, but was much altered in later Victorian times by William Butterfield. At the time of writing, its structural condition is not excellent.

Shepherds Bush (London): Greek Orthodox Cathedral

Standing in Godolphin Road, this was an Anglican church of St Thomas, designed by A. W. Blomfield and built in 1882–7. Following redundancy in the 1960s, it became Greek Orthodox, dedicated to St Nicholas. It is substantial but of little distinction. There is no tower; the exterior is mainly of yellow brick and is quite plain, with mostly lancet windows. The nave is quite tall, with a clerestory; the chancel is only a little lower. There are many icons and much Greek Orthodox painted decoration. Most striking is the magnificent, richly carved pulpit, in baroque style, which came from Belgium.

Stevenage (Hertfordshire): Coptic Orthodox Cathedral

The Coptic Orthodox is the Church of Egypt; it considers its founder to have been the evangelist St Mark, in succession to whom its leader at the time of writing, Pope Shenouda III, is the 117th Patriarch. It has a significant presence in Britain. In Stevenage, a Victorian mansion houses the Coptic Orthodox Church Centre; alongside it, their first purpose-built church, dedicated to St George, was opened in 2006 and is sometimes described as a cathedral. Its style is a mixture of modern and traditional. The exterior is of red brick, incorporating large white crosses. It is cruciform, with a long nave, a short chancel with a shallow apse, and a thin campanile with a domed top. Inside, a moveable partition separates most of the nave for social or sporting uses.

Wood Green (London): Greek Orthodox Cathedral

This cathedral, in Trinity Road, was built as Trinity Methodist church in 1871, to the designs of the Revd J.N. Johnson. It has been Greek Orthodox since 1970, dedicated to the Dormition of the Mother of God. To the street and the attractive park opposite, it presents a tall gothic facade of brown brick with a tower and spire at the ritual northwest. A modern entrance porch has been added, but the building still looks very much the large Nonconformist chapel that it was. The body has aisles with galleries, and terminates in an apse. Much has been redone following a fire in 1986. Greek Orthodox painting covers many wall surfaces.

C: FURTHER DENOMINATIONS

Some further Churches should also be considered. Three, each with a character very different from the others, have a church building deserving treatment here. Two of these buildings are not strictly cathedrals by name, but in their different ways justify consideration as such. Both are important architecturally and historically, and rank highly among the cathedrals considered in this chapter.

There also exist various small Churches that have at some time broken away from the 'mainstream' episcopal denominations. An example is the Free Church of England. Some are international, with a body in the United States or elsewhere. Several have one or more church buildings in England sometimes referred to as a cathedral or pro-cathedral; but none of these has sufficient architectural significance to warrant attention here.

Cathedrals are limited to the Christian religion. However, the Jewish faith has a long history in this country, and we may notice that three very large Victorian synagogues are sometimes called the 'Cathedral Synagogues'. They are the Singers Hill Synagogue of 1856 in Birmingham; the Princes Road Synagogue in Liverpool, dating from 1874; and the Middle Street Synagogue in Brighton, built in 1874–5.

Bloomsbury (London): Central Church of the Catholic Apostolic Church   *Plates 22 and 23*

Today, this church is often referred to as Christ the King, Gordon Square. It belongs to the Catholic Apostolic Church, also sometimes known as the Irvingites. This Church originated in the early nineteenth century and has an extraordinary and very interesting history. Reflecting a reaction to the horrors of the French Revolution, it was Adventist: believing the Second Coming of Christ to be imminent. It accepted charismatic phenomena or prophesy ('speaking in tongues'). Moreover, it believed that twelve new apostles had been sent from God, and had been identified among its leaders. Rich liturgical practices were employed, with elements derived from the Eastern Orthodox, Anglican and Roman Catholic Churches. The traditional three orders of ministry were adopted – deacons, priests and bishops (here known as angels) – but all under the authority of the additional order of the apostles, to whom ordination was reserved. The Church came to have many congregations both in Britain and overseas.

The apostles were identified between 1832 and 1836. In 1855 three died. It was decided that there was no warrant for their replacement. This decision guaranteed the eventual demise of the Church as an active institution. The last apostle died in 1901, and ordinations ceased. As clergy died, their churches were closed. The last priest died in 1971, and all services came to an end. Despite possessing no clergy or active adherents, the Church still exists and retains a core of property, which includes the Central Church. Between 1963 and 1994 this was leased to the Anglican Chaplaincy of the University of London. It was during this time that it acquired its alternative name of Christ the King.

The Catholic Apostolic Church did not designate this church as a cathedral. However, it was its principal church, and it contains a throne for its angel (bishop), although the function of angels in the Catholic Apostolic Church differed from that of bishops in other Churches. Physically it is of cathedral scale, character and quality. However, it was never completed. It was built in 1850–4 to the designs of Raphael Brandon, in Early English style. It is cruciform with a crossing tower. The nave and chancel have a lofty elevation with arcade, triforium and clerestory; the internal height of the nave is nearly 90 feet. It is faced inside and out in ashlared Bath stone. The design is sophisticated, with much good external detail including elegant turrets and pinnacles and finely shafted lancet windows. The high chancel is three bays long, with a clerestory of single lancets; to the east is a large group of three. Aisles flank the chancel, of which that on the south is broader; these aisles differ from the rest in having windows of plate or bar tracery. A lower chapel stands at the east end and is known as the English Chapel. The transepts are of shallow projection; their end walls have two tiers of great triple lancets and a rose window above. The north transept has an east chapel. Though intended to be lofty and to carry a spire reaching over 300 feet, the crossing tower was built only to the level of the roof ridges. In the nave, the aisles have single large lancet windows, but the clerestory has lancet pairs. It is of five bays; two more were planned, so there is a massively buttressed temporary west wall of brick.

A separate two-storeyed porch to the north-east gives access to a cloister-like passage along the north side, connecting to the church and to a building called The Cloisters, which contained accommodation for the clergy. Internally, the chancel is tremendously rich, with lavish stiff-leaf capitals and much dog-tooth; one order of the arcade arches is of foliage, and the spandrels are ornamented with a diaper pattern. The triforium has twin two-light openings, and the clerestory has an arcade of five arches in each bay. Above is a rich tierceron vault of stone. Surprisingly, however, the chancel aisles, and the rest of the church, have timber roofs without vaulting. Behind the altar, the east wall opens to the English Chapel through a three-light screen or window with Decorated tracery. The English Chapel has paired lancet windows and lavish internal treatment including trefoiled blank arcading and a fine timber roof with coloured decoration. The nave resembles the chancel and is only a little less rich; it has a fine hammerbeam roof with large angels. Fittings are elaborate, especially in the chancel for the many clergy involved in the Church's liturgy.

The site is cramped and, with large institutional buildings all round it, the church, despite its size, does not dominate. At the time of writing, the main part is not regularly used and is normally inaccessible except for a monthly organ recital to keep the instrument in good condition. The English Chapel, leased to the Anglican Forward in Faith movement, has services and is open on weekdays for private prayer.

Finsbury (London): Wesley's Chapel

As with all Nonconformist denominations, the Methodist Church is not episcopal and so has no cathedrals. This chapel, however, built under the founder of Methodism, John Wesley, is of special importance to Methodists around the world; it is widely referred to by both Methodists and others as the 'Cathedral of Methodism'. It stands on City Road, just north of the City. It was constructed in 1777–8; though its first importance is its historical associations, it is also a fine building. The architect was George Dance the Younger. It is of brown brick, rectangular and strikingly broad. Its dignified entrance facade (facing west) is five bays wide, with the central three brought slightly forward and pedimented; the angles and other parts have rusticated brickwork. Standing on fluted Doric columns is an open porch of stone, added in 1815. All sides of the chapel have two tiers of uniform large round-arched windows. At the east is a shallow apsidal projection of Portland stone, and this has three larger windows.

Structurally the chapel remains largely original, but there have been many nineteenth- or twentieth-century modifications, especially inside. The ceiling, of impressively large unsupported span, has fine restrained enrichment, re-created following a fire in 1879. A deep gallery, which

Finsbury: Wesley's Chapel

has been altered several times, runs round three sides; its west side contains the organ. Below, a modern glass screen separates the west end as a vestibule. Wesley's original fine mahogany pulpit remains: it is square with chamfered corners on an open arcaded base, however, it was once a three-decker and has been cut down. Behind it are the original communion rail and table; these were supplemented in 1978 by a communion area in front. There are many mural memorials.

Later wings have been added. That on the south leads to the very small Foundery chapel, of 1899: this has modest fittings that were originally in the first chapel established by Wesley on a different site in 1740. Beneath the main chapel is a crypt, which is now the Museum of Methodism. The chapel stands back behind an attractive forecourt, with the house where Wesley lived for the last eleven years of his life to one side.

Mayfair (London): Ukrainian Catholic Cathedral

The Ukrainian Catholic Church is one of a number of Eastern Rite Catholic Churches that are in communion with Rome. The cathedral, which acquired this status in 1968, stands on Binney Street and is also known as the King's Weigh House Chapel. This name comes from a predecessor, at several removes, which, after the Great Fire of 1666, occupied a site in the City where foreign goods entering London had previously been weighed. Descent from an even earlier chapel of 1148 is claimed. The present building is of 1889–91 by the architect Alfred Waterhouse: it was Congregational. It is impressive: built of brick, terracotta and stone in an elaborate but attractive round-arched style. The west facade opens by three large arches into a vaulted entrance porch, and is flanked by towers of which that to the south is tall and carries a tiled spire. The spacious auditorium is oval, with a gallery running around it.

Notes

1. The term 'suffragan' has a usage in the Roman Catholic Church that is different from that in the Church of England. It is not used for a bishop (the equivalent term is auxiliary bishop). The word is applied to dioceses: a suffragan diocese is a diocese within a province, and has a bishop. Thus most dioceses are suffragan, subject to the archiepiscopal or metropolitan see of the province in which they lie, which is presided over by an archbishop.
2. Strictly, the Armenian and Coptic Orthodox Churches are Oriental Orthodox, not Eastern Orthodox.

7

CHURCHES WITH CATHEDRAL NICKNAMES

To adopt a musical analogy, this chapter might be styled an inter-mezzo: a lightweight interlude. The word 'cathedral' is indeed used for the churches discussed here, but it is applied as part of a nickname, identifying a church as 'the cathedral' of a geographical area. So these churches have no historical validity as cathedrals: none has ever contained a bishop's throne or been proposed for one. Almost all were built as parish churches, and remain of that status. As would be expected, by parish church standards they are large and of fine quality, often the largest church in their area. But the nickname does not, of course, imply that they are really of cathedral stature in either size or character. There is nothing here of the massive splendour of 'great church' architecture.

These are not the only churches with nicknames. Two memorable other examples are the 'King of Holderness' (Hedon) and 'Queen of Holderness' (Patrington, both Yorkshire, ER). Cathedral nicknames, however, are the most numerous. How and when the nicknames came about are interesting questions. One would like to think that they became established by some process of popular attribution. Some have certainly been used for a century, and perhaps for much longer. Nicknames with such longevity may be considered well established and to have the authority of tradition. The number of churches for which cathedral nicknames may be encountered is considerable: over twenty. Occasionally, however, the cathedral word is used in a way that is not really a nickname. For example, Holy Trinity in Sloane Square, Chelsea (London) has been referred to as the 'Cathedral of the Arts and Crafts Movement': but this is a description rather than a nickname.[1] Much the same applies to St Bartholomew, Brighton (East Sussex), the 'Cathedral of Anglo-Catholicism'. Most, however, are indeed nicknames: but even so not all can be accepted as based on an authentic tradition. Some perhaps originated in a flight of fancy by a mid-twentieth-century incumbent or guidebook writer, or they may be 'marketing hype', created in the hope of increasing local awareness or visitor numbers. Only churches with nicknames that appear to possess traditional authenticity are treated here.[2] Even those nicknames accepted as authentic quite often have varying forms.[3]

The churches discussed here are predominantly medieval. They form a fine collection of rural parish churches: for it is noticeable that none is in a large town or city. Almost all appear in the selections by Simon Jenkins, Sir John Betjeman and others of churches most worth visiting.[4] Nevertheless, impressive as they are, as a group they cannot be claimed to be the very finest of the English parish churches. Some, such as Altarnun and Tideswell, are indeed among the most splendid of their region; but on the other hand, a few seem surprisingly modest for possession of such an exalted nickname. This perhaps shows that the cathedral nickname indicates, rather than the utmost in size and splendour, something subtly different. As much as with the intrinsic qualities of the church itself, it has to do with the setting, the circumstances, and the contrast with the other churches of the immediate neighbourhood. It may sometimes reflect a popular response to a relatively large and impressive church in unexpected or moving contrast to remote or deeply rural surroundings.

A few churches of which the nicknames are regarded as of doubtful authenticity nevertheless deserve mention. Several are magnificent buildings, and were size and splendour the criteria for selection they would certainly displace some that are included. One such is Blythburgh (Suffolk), occasionally referred to as the 'Cathedral of the Marshes'. It is one of the most splendid of the fifteenth-century churches of East Anglia, and also has fine furnishings of the same period. Similarly outstanding is Ludlow (Shropshire), which has been called the 'Cathedral of the Marches'. It is a very large cruciform building over 200 feet long, mainly but not entirely Perpendicular; arguably it is indeed the most splendid church in the Welsh Marches. The former church of St Alban at Teddington (Middlesex) has occasionally been entitled 'Cathedral of the Thames Valley'. This very ambitious though unfinished late-Victorian church became redundant in the early 1970s, but after long controversy was saved by becoming the Landmark Arts Centre. Uffington (Berkshire, now Oxfordshire), sometimes claimed as the 'Cathedral of the Vale', is a splendid Early English building, cruciform with a crossing tower. Another church sometimes given the same nickname (but for a different vale) is Whitchurch Canonicorum (Dorset). It is especially memorable for possessing the shrine of St Wite, an Early English structure remarkably still containing its saint's bones.

Very different from all these is what is sometimes called the 'Cathedral of the Potteries': the Bethesda Methodist Chapel at Hanley (part of Stoke-on-Trent, Staffordshire). Dating from 1819–20, with a front of 1859, this exceptionally large chapel became redundant in 1985. However, it has been saved by the Historic Chapels Trust, and at the time of writing is the subject of a multi-million pound restoration campaign.

Alfriston (East Sussex)

This is a village popular with tourists. Close to the church stands the thatched medieval Clergy House, which was the first property of the National Trust. Set on a considerable mound, the church is the 'Cathedral of the Downs' or 'Cathedral of the South Downs'. At first this sobriquet seems surprising, since the church appears rustic and not obviously large: only inside do its scale and spaciousness become more evident. It is cruciform with a central tower; its nave and chancel are aisleless and of equal length. It was entirely rebuilt in about 1360; some windows have Decorated tracery, some Perpendicular, and others something between the two. Externally it is largely of squared flint. The crossing tower is low and ineloquent, with small rectangular openings and a straight parapet; it carries a shingled timber spire.

Most impressive in the interior is the large and lofty crossing: the responds and their moulded capitals are concave octagonal, characteristically Perpendicular, while the arches have fine mouldings dying into vertical pieces above the capitals, as is typical of Decorated work. There are fine and distinctive triple sedilia: they are large, divided by octagonal shafts and with round arches carrying big ogee finials that rise through a square enclosing moulding. The adjacent piscina is of similar form. Also fine is the Easter Sepulchre, with a plain tomb-chest and a depressed arch below a big, elegant ogee moulding.

The roofs are partly ancient. Entry through the west doorway is to a lobby between timber vestries; a spacious gallery was constructed above in 1995. The font has a plain square bowl on a square stem with attached octagonal shafts, a form characteristic of the area. A large Royal Arms on canvas is of 1725.

Altarnun (Cornwall)

The stress in pronunciation is on the second syllable. Situated at the edge of Bodmin Moor, this is the 'Cathedral of the Moors'. It is large and entirely characteristic of Cornwall: Perpendicular, quite low, without clerestory, undivided east-west and with its aisles and central vessel under equal pitched roofs. Most of the walling is of irregular stone. It is stately, though other than in its fittings its character is austere rather than rich. At 109 feet the west tower is tall, though being set in a steep valley it is nowhere seen from afar. It has three stages, with set-back buttresses, battlements and tall corner pinnacles. Windows throughout the church are of four lights and arched, with granite tracery of uniform

Altarnun church

pattern. Just the west window of the north aisle must be earlier, having three-light intersecting tracery. There are north and south porches, their arches almost round within a square hood-mould.

It is a pity that most of the interior is stripped of plaster. The arcades have five large bays, again typical in their mono-lithic granite pillars of four shafts and four hollows, carrying capitals with moulded bands. On the north side the arches are firmly pointed, but on the south side the pillars are a little higher and the arches approximately segmental. The rood stair projection in the north wall is now a cup-board. There are wagon roofs throughout, mainly ancient. All glass is clear.

Seventy-nine of the bench ends form a fine and enjoyable set, carved between 1510 and 1530, illustrating widely varied subjects both sacred and secular and showing some Renaissance influence. One tells us the name of their maker, Robert Daye. Running right across is the screen, largely ancient though reconstructed in the 1880s; it lacks its loft, except that two short sections have been reinstated at the ends. Unusually, the baluster communion rails also run right across, leaving only cramped spaces for the aisle altars; they are dated 1684 and have a long inscrip-tion. Two charming boards of 1620 flanking the east window have paintings, with texts, illustrating Communion and the Crucifixion. Two later text boards are oval. Probably the finest thing here is the large and excellently preserved Norman font. On an octagonal stem with a cable moulding at its top, the square bowl has a big rosette on each face and a bold, bearded head at each corner. It is a striking example of Norman primitive power combined with sophistication.

Brailes (Warwickshire)

Now only a village, Brailes was much more important in medieval times. The principal visible evidence of this is its large and stately church, which stands at Lower Brailes. It is known as the 'Cathedral of the Feldon', the Feldon being the area of Warwickshire south of the River Avon. The west tower is Perpendicular and over 120 feet high. It is of ashlar, in three stages, with diagonal buttresses, battlements and corner pinnacles; it has twin two-light belfry openings and a west window in five lights. Also Perpendicular is the broad south porch with pinnacles

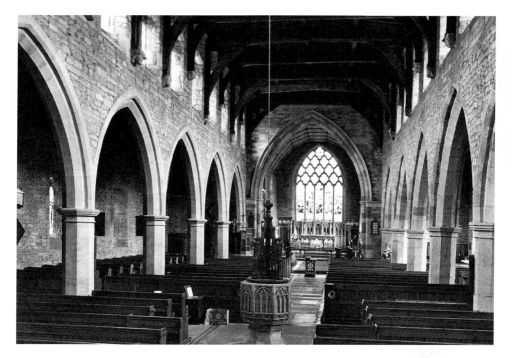

Brailes church

and side windows. The body of the church, though large, is not lofty. The nave has six bays, with arcades of octagonal pillars, moulded capitals and double-chamfered arches; they have irregularities, especially on the south side. There is a fine clerestory of two square-headed windows per bay. Windows in the north aisle are square headed too. Earlier than the rest is the east part of the south aisle, which has elegant lancet-triplet windows. This aisle has a rich later parapet with pinnacles and elegant openwork. An elaborate pinnacled sanctus bell turret is above the chancel arch.

The chancel is of striking Decorated work, with a noble five-light reticulated east window and good side windows. There are stepped triple ogee-trefoiled sedilia, unusually divided by stone armrests, and an ogee-trefoiled piscina recess with shelf. On the north side, the organ chamber with vestry is partly of 1649, constructed during extensive repairs probably occasioned by Civil War damage. Much work took place in 1879, including stripping the interior of plaster and enlarging the chancel arch.

The excellent large octagonal font has a different three-light Decorated tracery design on each face. Of two interesting chests, one is perhaps fifteenth century, its front busily decorated with tracery patterns, fleurons and other motifs. An attractive benefaction board of lozenge form is dated 1704; three other benefaction boards are probably later. There is a 1722 Royal Arms. A tomb-chest has Perpendicular panelling and a terribly defaced recumbent effigy: it was brought in from the churchyard in 1933.

Cranbrook (Kent)

This pleasant country town became a centre for cloth manufacture in the late medieval period. Wealth from this enabled the extensive rebuilding of its large church, which has become known as the 'Cathedral of the Weald'. It is of attractive ashlared sandstone. The big west tower is in three stages, with angle buttresses, battlements and a higher south-east stair turret. An empty image niche is above the west doorway, but otherwise the only enrichment is a large eighteenth-century baroque clock surround on the south side. Roofs other than that of the chancel are low-pitched. The nave and its aisles date from the early sixteenth century. They are battlemented and have aisle windows that are uniform and large, in three lights, but different north from south. Also of three lights are the clerestory windows. The arcades have six bays, with pillars of four shafts and four double waves, big capitals on the shafts, and four-centred arches. Shafts rise to the roof from angels in the arcade spandrels. Surprisingly, following a collapse in 1725, much of the south aisle and arcade were rebuilt as an accurate copy of the original. Covering the large Perpendicular south doorway is a two-storeyed Decorated porch with a vault, the large central boss of which has a green man. The porch arch contains a late-medieval timber framework with door.

On the north side, a battlemented polygonal turret contains the rood stair. Both aisles continue as two-bay chapels flanking the chancel. The rather small chancel arch is earlier than the nave, and the chapel arcades are Decorated, with moulded arches on quatrefoil pillars. Both the chancel and the south chapel have piscina recesses of straight-shanked

Cranbrook church

form. In the west wall near the tower is visible part of a blocked round arch, presumably a Norman relic.

The room over the porch is approached from the aisle by a stair on a large block of masonry, its top having attractive baluster railings. This arrangement is of about 1710 and surprisingly contains an immersion font, which is only once recorded as having been used. The fine communion rails with slender twisted balusters are eighteenth-century work. There are two plain medieval tomb-chests, a late-medieval brass and a huge marble memorial of 1736; its top is a freestanding pyramid. Also of interest are ten hatchments and a splendid brass chandelier acquired in 1736. Mounted on the stone tower screen are four splendid large timber roof bosses, probably of the fourteenth century, three of which are in the form of a green man, and a very large moulded Royal Arms of 1736. One window is filled with sixteenth-century glass.

Ivychurch (Kent)

Serving a very small village, this church bears the nickname 'Cathedral of Romney Marsh', despite Lydd, only 4 miles away, being similarly named. Especially inside, it is very unrestored, and it is this that makes it outstanding. The ragstone surfaces of the exterior are rough but attractive. There are regular buttresses and straight parapets. Inside, most floors are of old clay tiles, especially rough in the north aisle. Almost

Ivychurch church

all glass is clear. The structure seems largely Decorated, though studies show a complex building history. The west tower is bulky but not tall; it is in three stages with big angle buttresses, battlements and a polygonal north-east stair turret. Its west doorway and modest belfry openings are Perpendicular, but the excellent three-light west window is Decorated.

The church is of seven aisled bays, without east-west division. All roofs have extensive ancient timbers and are low-pitched, though a high-pitched external roof has been added to the west half of the north aisle, perhaps in a seventeenth-century repair. This aisle is strikingly broad, more so than its partner; it also has a surprising round stair turret at its north-west corner. There is a massive battlemented south porch with a quadripartite vault and an upper room. Some windows have good Decorated tracery; others are

Perpendicular. The five-light Perpendicular east window of the north aisle has been blocked, probably in the eighteenth century (such a condition was common before Victorian restorers set to work). The arcades have octagonal pillars, moulded capitals and arches of two hollow chamfers. Above is a clerestory of quatrefoiled square openings, which, however, are blocked.

The plain base of the ancient chancel screen remains in position. Parclose screens occupy one bay each side, with simple Perpendicular tracery, and there are traceried stall fronts and ends. The good, plain hexagonal pulpit is Georgian. Much of the nave is without furnishings. Dated 1686, the tower screen has balusters in its upper part and iron spikes along the top. The octagonal Perpendicular font is plain. A hudd (portable shelter for use by a priest at funerals) stands at the back. The very large Royal Arms of 1775 has a pilastered frame. Displays, mostly of farm equipment, occupy the north aisle. Set in the arcade spandrels is a set of oval boards of 1775–6, with text in gold on black. Just a little wall painting survives in the north chapel.

Lydd (Kent)

This church on Romney Marsh is referred to as the 'Cathedral of the Marsh', despite the competing claims of Ivychurch. It is indeed large (much larger than its rival), being about 200 feet long with a tower 132 feet high, and is a landmark from afar. The tower dates from the 1440s. It has angle buttresses, quite small two-light belfry openings, and battlements with big corner pinnacles; the stair turret at the south-west corner carries a crocketed spirelet. Most unusually there are twin west doorways, forming a composition with the four-light window immediately above. Inside, it has a fine lierne vault. The body of the church

Lydd church

has aisles under pitched roofs, but no clerestory. Windows are mostly Decorated or Perpendicular and large, though not regular. The arcades, however, are Early English, in seven large bays, with cylindrical pillars, moulded capitals and double-chamfered arches. There is a very large chancel arch. The aisles continue as chapels of a single bay; that on the south has a damaged trefoiled double piscina and a lancet with trefoiled rere-arch. A Decorated tomb-recess in the north chapel contains a fine effigy of a praying knight. Roofs throughout are plain but mainly old.

The chancel extends beyond the chapels, and is noble and spacious, in Early English style. An internal string-course runs round, and the three lancets on each side have trefoiled rere-arches. All this is actually an excellent re-creation of 1958, the original having been completely flattened by a bomb in 1940. That it was rebuilt seems creditable: it was carried out at great expense despite the contrary recommendation of a diocesan committee. Old materials were re-used where possible. Interestingly, three east lancets were provided instead of the former large Perpendicular window.

This church has a further remarkably interesting element. The north and west walls at the north-west corner are pre-Conquest work. Their date has been much discussed, but could be very early. They are built of especially rough small stones. Internally the plaster has been stripped to expose the features. The north wall shows three blocked round arches with imposts, turned without any dressed stonework; above is a blocked, slightly tapering double-splayed window. A larger blocked arch is in the west wall. These must have been part of an aisled church, but its complete plan remains conjectural.

The font is of the eighteenth century, with a delicate, enriched marble bowl on a stone baluster. A plain tomb-chest carries a brass of 1608, and there are several medieval and later brasses, some now mounted murally. In the chancel is an eighteenth-century brass chandelier. A very large Royal Arms of 1732 is painted on canvas.

Newland (Gloucestershire)

This stately and very large church standing in a small Forest of Dean village is nicknamed the 'Cathedral of the Forest'. It has a beautiful position. Unusually, the village and its church did not exist until the early thirteenth century; the first rector was appointed in 1216. Much of the building seems to be of the later thirteenth or early fourteenth century. Windows are varied, though mostly large. The ashlar-built west tower is Decorated, and is big and impressive, in three stages, with clasping buttresses that turn diagonal higher up. A polygonal stair turret near the south-east corner carries a big spirelet with subsidiary pinnacles, and there are openwork parapets with further attractive pinnacles. The fine west window has four lights; the belfry openings are small, but repeated

Newland church

at two levels. Inside, the thick tower arch has three pairs of continuous sunk quadrant mouldings.

The nave is notably broad and so are its aisles, which have pitched roofs. The arcades are of five bays, with double-chamfered arches on octagonal pillars and moulded capitals. Considerable changes and rebuilding took place in William White's restoration of 1861–2, including introduction of the clerestory (externally invisible), the broad chancel arch and several windows. In the north respond of the chancel arch is the rood stair. There is a big, attractive south porch, which once had an upper floor; set here are some architectural fragments found in the restoration. Immediately east of this is a projecting chapel built for a chantry founded in about 1305. Broad two-bay chapels flank the chancel. That on the north is the Lady Chapel, with characteristic Perpendicular features and externally a fine openwork parapet with pinnacles.

Interesting contents include recumbent effigies of the thirteenth, fourteenth and fifteenth centuries, some on their original tomb-chests but others set on modern pillared bases. A brass of about 1445 has mounted with it the remarkable 'miner's brass', an effigy of a traditional Forest of Dean miner: its date and provenance are unknown. Some of the many mural memorials are fine. The large octagonal font is of 1661, with busy, enjoyable decoration. A brass chandelier dates from 1724. The communion rails with twisted balusters are probably seventeenth-century work. Colourful glass of 1999 is in the east window of the south chapel.

Terrington St Clement (Norfolk)   *Plates 24 and 25*

The relatively small area of the Norfolk fens west and south-west of King's Lynn is famous for the size and splendour of its churches. Two have nicknames: Walpole St Peter is the 'Queen of the Marshlands', while Terrington St Clement is the 'Cathedral of the Marshes' or 'Cathedral of the Fens'. This is a very impressive and gracious church, seeming more than most to warrant its nickname. It is almost all Perpendicular, 180 feet long, very large but not entirely uniform. It is mostly faced in ashlar. There are panelled parapets throughout, mainly battlemented, some with pinnacles. It is cruciform with a crossing but has no crossing tower, perhaps because of mistrust of the marshy ground. Instead, a tower stands free, immediately north of the west end. This has four stages, with diagonal buttresses, a quatrefoil frieze on the plinth, and battlements with corner and intermediate pinnacles.

The west front is fine; its main window has five lights with two transoms. There are two rich image niches, turrets carrying spirelets flanking the central section, and similar turrets with especially tall spirelets flanking the aisles. The nave has seven bays, with a clerestory having twice that number of three-light windows. Entry is by a south porch with a richly panelled front. The arcades are relatively simple, with slim octagonal pillars; grotesque beasts support the shafts rising to the roof. Above the west crossing arch are seven image niches, and over the chancel arch a shallow five-light window. The clerestory continues along the side walls of the transepts, which project only slightly beyond the aisles. Blocked arcading in their west walls perhaps implies a plan to add chapels here. The south transept has a striking set of six south windows, all of three lights: three are at the lowest level, two above, and one at the top. Spirelet-crowned stair turrets flank the chancel arch. The chancel is aisleless, in three long bays with three-light side windows; above is a clerestory that is immediately shown to be a later addition by being externally of brick. Surprisingly, there are noble thirteenth-century stepped sedilia, with trefoiled arches having dog-tooth enrichment and stiff-leaf hood stops. With them goes a double piscina. Notwithstanding their authentic appearance, they are said to have been reconstructed from fragments.

The interior is very light. Two bays from the west end is a fine eighteenth-century screen of solid panelling, with Corinthian pilasters and gates with openwork foliage. Curiously, behind its centre is a gallery one bay deep, with no means of access: until 1910 it held the organ. There are a Queen Anne Royal Arms and two very large text boards dated 1635. The octagonal font with its simply panelled faces is remarkable for its cover: its lower part is clearly of the seventeenth century, externally painted and opening to reveal an interior with painted scenes. The upper part is a gothic spire, painted to match the rest: is this medieval?

Theddlethorpe All Saints (Lincolnshire)

Set in the flat lands near the coast, this is a redundant church in the care
of the Churches Conservation Trust. It is attractive and interesting, but
that it has warranted the nickname 'Cathedral of the Marsh' is perhaps
surprising. It is Perpendicular with some Decorated reminiscences, and
was probably largely built in the last decades of the fourteenth century.
Earlier, however, are the triple sedilia, which have flat leaf capitals showing a late twelfth-century date.

Much of the exterior is of ashlar, but parts of the tower and south
porch have brickwork that is probably original late fourteenth-century
work, very early for brick in England. Most of the church is embattled; the east wall of the nave has a fine openwork parapet. The west
tower has angle buttresses, battlements, a west window of four lights and
belfry openings of three. The tower carries a small lead-covered spike.
The nave has five bays, with arcades of octagonal pillars and arches of
two hollow chamfers. Above is a modest clerestory. Aisle windows are in
three lights, but are not uniform. Covered by a broad, plain porch, the
south doorway of continuous mouldings unusually is ogee in form. In
the east wall of the south aisle is a much-enriched recess for a reredos.
The chancel is quite short, and its east window has only three lights.

Roofs are mainly ancient, with some moulded timbers and bosses.
The octagonal font is a good Perpendicular piece, with generous
enrichments. Some pews are partly or wholly ancient, with traceried
fronts and backs and varied ends. A medieval *prie-dieu* (prayer desk) is
decayed but usable. The rood screen is excellent, probably fifteenth-
century work; it preserves some original colour. The east bays of the
aisles form chapels and have good screens with pretty tracery and some
Renaissance motifs, dating probably from the 1530s. Both chapels have
an ancient mensa (stone altar slab), and the south chapel has an interesting brass of 1424 and a medieval ledger with inscribed text. In the
chancel are a good standing wall memorial, oak altar rails and an altar
table of marble on slim baluster legs, all of the early eighteenth century.

Tideswell (Derbyshire)

This, the 'Cathedral of the Peak' is, at 178 feet long, not the largest
church discussed here, but it is one of the most deserving of its nickname. Dominating the little town of Tideswell, it is on a magnificent
scale and is distinguished by its gracious quality, harmoniousness and
excellent proportions. Built entirely in the fourteenth century, the nave
and transepts came first, perhaps in the 1340s, in a rich Decorated style;
the chancel that followed, perhaps in the 1360s, is also largely Decorated
in style, while the west tower alone is fully Perpendicular. The church
is faced externally and internally in ashlar. All is battlemented; the east
parts also have pinnacles and enriched or panelled buttresses. Above the

chancel arch is a large pinnacled sanctus bell turret. The nave has aisles with low-pitched lean-to roofs and fine three-light windows of flowing tracery; the clerestory windows also have tracery. Covering a very rich entrance doorway, the south porch is vaulted and has a room over. The arcades have four bays and then a much broader bay for the transepts; tall pillars of quatrefoil form carry arches with two sunk quadrant mouldings. Windows in the transepts are large, especially their spectacular five-light end windows.

Tideswell church

The chancel has four large bays; its tall three-light side windows are straight headed and have tracery of an unusual design combining Decorated and Perpendicular character, but the five-light east window is entirely Decorated. There are superb triple sedilia, richly ogee cinquefoiled and with tracery, and a similarly rich piscina. Unusually, the east end of the chancel is separated as sacristy by a wall that also serves as reredos, with miniature battlements and two very large image niches with octagonal battlemented tops. Two further large canopied niches are on the east wall. All four niches have statues of 1950.

Equally splendid is the tower, which is massive, tall and distinctive. It begins with angle buttresses that become polygonal at belfry level: these rise high above the battlements to their own battlemented tops, from which crocketed spirelets rise; there are also tall intermediate pinnacles. The belfry has twin two-light openings. Internally there is a rich tierceron vault.

Structurally almost everything is original; this includes most of the roofs, some of which are of distinctive design. There are also good contents. The chancel screen, except for its coving, is original and contemporary with the structure. There are several large ancient brasses, and in the centre of the chancel is a great tomb-chest of 1462; its open sides revealing a cadaver effigy inside are much restored, but its top with brass is authentic. Other memorials include two remarkable effigies of ladies, which are of the thirteenth and fourteenth centuries. Ten ancient stalls with mostly plain misericords are now in the north transept. The extensive nineteenth-century fittings, including oak pews, stalls and screens, are also good.

Widecombe-in-the-Moor (Devon)

This much-visited village is beautifully set in a deep valley surrounded by moorland. By the churchyard gate is the charming early sixteenth-century Church House, now cared for by the National Trust. The church is large and striking, and is known as the 'Cathedral of Dartmoor' or 'Cathedral of the Moor'. Much of it is of granite, sometimes in impressively massive blocks. Its large and stately west tower was built in the early sixteenth century, in three tall stages with set-back buttresses enriched by pinnacles on their offsets. There are three-light arched belfry openings, battlements with big octagonal corner pinnacles carrying spirelets, and a large west window of four lights. The height is about 130 feet.

Widecombe-in-the-Moor church

In many ways the church is of characteristic West Country type: low, with aisles under pitched roofs. There are also transepts; the aisles

continue one bay further east as chapels. The interior has six-bay arcades and is undivided east to west, but surprisingly, three bays from the west, the roofs step down to a lower level. Most aisle windows are square headed, in three lights. The large south porch covers a surprisingly small and low entrance doorway. All features of the walls seem to be Perpendicular but the arcades are earlier, with monolithic octagonal pillars, simple capitals, and slightly pointed double-chamfered arches. There are attractive ceiled wagon roofs with bosses, and they incorporate moulded timber arches to the transepts. East of the north transept is the rood stair. Plain rectangular recesses form the chancel piscina and sedilia.

This is a spacious, simple but beautiful interior. Most walls are whitewashed and almost all glass is clear. The western half is without any seating. Running right across is the base of the rood screen, its panels containing quite well-preserved paintings, mostly of saints. There are several granite ledgers with rustic inscriptions. The octagonal font is Perpendicular. Two perhaps seventeenth-century paintings depict Moses and Aaron. Of special interest are four boards in the tower, carrying verses describing the catastrophic lightning strike that took place during Sunday afternoon service on 21 October 1638. The verses are by Richard Hill, then the village schoolmaster, but the boards were renewed in 1786.

Notes

1. Apparently originating with the writer of the entry in Betjeman (ed.) (1958).
2. Many sources have been consulted to identify churches possessing cathedral nicknames. The selection of nicknames for which traditional authenticity is accepted is inevitably to some degree arbitrary. It is partly based on the number of sources in which they appear. Additional weight has been given to earlier sources, in particular the *Little Guides* (various authors; Methuen, original editions about 1900–16) and *The King's England* series (Mee, A.; Hodder & Stoughton, mainly of the 1930s). The subject could bear further research, which might throw light on the origin of the nicknames and refine or enlarge the list.
3. The author was reprimanded by an elderly rustic mowing the churchyard at Terrington St Clement for referring to it as the 'Cathedral of the Marshes': 'You've got it all wrong: it's always been called the "Cathedral of the Fens"!'.
4. Jenkins (1999); Betjeman (ed.) (1958).

8

OTHER CHURCHES OF CATHEDRAL STATURE

All earlier chapters of this book consider churches for which the word 'cathedral' is, was, or might have been used. This final chapter is different: it is based on physical character. It considers churches that are or were physically of cathedral stature, though they have never even been considered for becoming cathedrals. Its objective is to address all churches that, regardless of their current state of preservation or destruction, were of the scale, splendour and quality of the medieval cathedrals.

In medieval England, cathedrals had no monopoly as the country's greatest churches. There were many other churches that in their size, the beauty of their architecture and the magnificence of their contents, were fully the equal of the cathedrals. As we have seen, some became cathedrals in the sixteenth, nineteenth or twentieth century; others appeared in chapters two and three. This chapter has many more. Alas, this corpus of architectural wealth has suffered extensive destruction: some of it we know only by inference from limited remains or indications, or do not know at all. But a good deal remains to be seen and enjoyed.

A difficult problem must be addressed: what does it mean for a church to be of cathedral stature? The basis must be the cathedrals of the canon: what do they have in common? What defines the quality of a cathedral? Probably the first thing the 'man in the street' would say is that a cathedral is large. The simplest measure of the size of a cathedral is its length. Winchester, at 556 feet externally, is today the country's longest medieval cathedral. But other more subtle measures of size are possible: York Minster, though about 45 feet shorter than Winchester, is variously reported as England's largest when measured by floor area[1] or by volume enclosed. Most are also tall, both in their internal spaces and externally in their towers. A typical internal height is of the order of 70 feet. All have at least one tower, which in many is the dominant external feature. The tallest to survive into our era is the 404-feet high tower and spire of Salisbury Cathedral. Other relevant measures might be the width across nave and aisles or the bay spacing.

Equally essential is their character. Without exception these cathedrals are of 'great church' type, though that is a term easier to illustrate by examples than to define exactly. They all have a cruciform plan, with a nave and a usually long chancel, both with aisles. Often the transepts have one or two aisles. A central tower stands over the crossing (but Exeter is an exception). Some have a complex plan, perhaps with a second pair of transepts, large or small. Additional chapels may project at the east end or elsewhere. Their internal elevations are usually in three stages, having a triforium and clerestory above the arcade (but sometimes the triforium is omitted, and at Bristol both are absent). Usually, all four arms (nave, chancel and transepts) are of the same height (but Carlisle and Norwich depart from this). Every cathedral has stone vaulting covering at least some parts, and many have it throughout. An architecturally splendid west front is a frequent feature, often with twin towers. All have a generous massiveness of construction, whatever the period of the work. They display a very high standard of sophistication and perfection, with fine mouldings and extensive architectural and sculptural enrichment (though an exception must be made for some plain or even crude early Norman work, as at Winchester and St Albans).

Ultimately a cathedral is a work of art. Each one is different, and its quality is a matter of judgement. That judgement is not simple even for buildings that exist complete and in good condition. Where a building is mutilated or ruined it is harder, and where it is a complete loss above ground, as with some considered here, it is impossible. In any case, most of the factors identified cannot be used as criteria, even in a complete building.

The only practicable criterion is the simplest: that of length. A little has already been said about cathedral dimensions. Of the medieval cathedrals of the canon, a length of 500 feet is exceeded by Canterbury, Ely, Lincoln, London (both Old St Paul's and the present cathedral), Winchester and York. Old St Paul's was longest of all at about 585 feet. Many of the others are between 400 and 500 feet. Hereford (if we include the west end destroyed by the fall of its tower in 1786) and Lichfield lie between 350 and 400 feet. Less than 350 feet, however, are Carlisle (probably about 320 feet before most of its nave was destroyed in the seventeenth century) and Rochester (323 feet). (Bath, not now a cathedral, is, as we have seen, only about 230 feet; but it lacks its intended eastern attachments, and it was longer before the sixteenth century.) Also less than 350 feet are several cathedrals created under Henry VIII or of the 'extended canon'. Without suggesting that these shorter cathedrals are unworthy of their status, the criterion adopted here for cathedral stature is a minimum length of 350 feet (107 metres).

More will be said later about this criterion. First, however, the different types of church in England must be surveyed for their potential for offering examples of cathedral stature. They may include one or two surprises.

Medieval monastic churches

Unsurprisingly, monastic churches form the great majority of those worthy to be cathedrals. The architectural wealth once presented by the medieval monasteries of England is astonishing. At their height in the mid-fourteenth century, there were over 800 of them. Through the following almost two centuries, although there were a few further new foundations, for various reasons the total declined. Nevertheless, as remarked upon earlier there were still well over 600 monasteries as the dissolution of 1536–40 approached, and these included all of the largest. Because so many have been destroyed, it is easy to forget just how numerous they were.

Medieval monasteries ranged widely in size. Many were small, with typically only half a dozen or a dozen monks or nuns. Especially numerous were small Augustinian priories. Even these small monasteries often had a substantial church possessing a monumental character different from that of a parish church. Larger than these were the 200 or 300 monasteries that could be described as of medium size. Almost all of these had a large and splendid church of 'great church' character, typically perhaps 200 or 250 feet in length. Examples might be those of Hexham and Sherborne, which appeared in chapter one as successors to Anglo-Saxon cathedrals. Finally there were perhaps 50 to 100 great monasteries, some of which had a church meeting our criterion for cathedral stature. The largest number of such cathedral-worthy churches was among the Benedictine abbeys. Four of them were elevated to cathedral status in the sixteenth or nineteenth century, and three more have already appeared in chapters two and three; a further seven are discussed in this chapter. Other churches meeting the criterion belonged to the Augustinians, the Cistercians and the Cluniacs; several were priories rather than abbeys.

Other medieval religious houses

Friaries formed another major group of religious houses, numerous in the larger towns though rare elsewhere. Friary churches in general were large. They were dissolved in 1538, and the comprehensiveness of their destruction makes us forget what a prominent presence they must have been in the medieval towns and cities. Many were of the order of 200 feet in length; the Franciscan church in London, 314 feet long, is said to have been the largest. Thus, none reached cathedral dimensions. Moreover, the character of a friary church was quite different from that of a cathedral.

Much the same applies to the churches of the Trinitarians and those of the Military Orders: the Knights Templar and the Knights Hospitaller.

Medieval collegiate churches

Most collegiate churches and chapels[2] still exist today, but in general they do not approach cathedral size. However, as we have seen, in the large diocese of York there was an outstanding group of three that were effectively subsidiary cathedrals serving their regions. Ripon and Southwell have become members of the 'extended canon'. The third and greatest is Beverley, fully of cathedral length and stature yet today only parochial in status.

One other collegiate church may be mentioned. The college of Ottery St Mary (Devon) was founded in 1337 by Bishop John de Grandisson of Exeter. For it, the pre-existing parish church was greatly remodelled and enlarged. Although only 185 feet in length, it is in some ways a miniature copy of Exeter Cathedral, which was then approaching the completion of its great rebuilding campaign. This is most obvious in that, like the cathedral, Ottery has transeptal towers: an arrangement found in this country only in these two churches. Remarkably, it is vaulted throughout, with vaults of comparable richness to those of Exeter, although their form is quite different. It possesses an eastern Lady Chapel, as does the cathedral. It even has two-storeyed sacristy blocks flanking the chancel in positions similar to the small secondary transepts of the cathedral. (Both also possess the rarity of a medieval astronomical clock!)

The academic college was a new type that first appeared in the late thirteenth century. Some academic colleges have an important chapel. The largest is that of King's College, Cambridge, one of the country's greatest and most famous ecclesiastical buildings. However, at about 320 feet it is not of cathedral length. Moreover, as basically a great aisleless rectangle, its character is completely unlike that of a cathedral.

Medieval parish churches

Many of the thousands of parish churches are of course modest, but some are of very impressive size and quality. Holy Trinity, Hull (Yorkshire, ER), with a length of 288 feet, is a claimant for the position of largest. Another is St Nicholas, Great Yarmouth (Norfolk). Others close to this length include Coventry St Michael, which as we have seen became a cathedral in 1918. As well as falling short of cathedral size, none of these is of 'great church' character. With only a few exceptions, parish churches are relatively broad and low in their proportions, have main roofs of timber, and lack the monumentality of a cathedral. Many do not have a cruciform plan.

Bristol: St Mary Redcliffe

One parish church, however, is so exceptional that it cannot be overlooked. St Mary Redcliffe, Bristol, is unique among parish churches. Often quoted is the declaration of Queen Elizabeth I in 1574 that it is the 'fairest, goodliest and most famous parish church in England'. Many authors refer to its cathedral-like character. With a length of only a little over 250 feet, it is well short of true cathedral size. However, it is magnificent inside and out and is indeed of 'great church' character. Largely of the Decorated and Perpendicular periods, it is very uniform in style and has a particular sense of graciousness. It is cruciform, and even the transepts have twin aisles. The east end has an ambulatory and Lady Chapel. Most impressively, it is vaulted throughout, with rich fifteenth-century vaults of exquisite quality. Outside, there are flying buttresses between its very large clerestory windows. Another exceptional feature is the lavish hexagonal early fourteenth-century north porch, which is of a character unique in England. Its extraordinary ornamentation was probably influenced by foreign architecture (even that of India has been suggested) through Bristol's maritime trade. Only in its lack of a crossing tower does the church seem other than of cathedral type: the tower stands at the north-west corner. However, it carries a spire of 292 feet, which is a cathedral height. In this city where the true cathedral is not externally dominating, St Mary Redcliffe sometimes deludes visitors into supposing it to be that building.

Post-medieval churches

Churches built since the medieval era must also be considered. As already mentioned, for two and a half centuries after the Reformation, church building was at a relatively low ebb; and of course no churches were built for religious houses. Nothing created in this period warrants discussion here. The great expansion of church building in the nineteenth and early twentieth centuries by the Church of England and other denominations, however, produced some churches of great size and splendour. A few include features that in themselves might be considered cathedral-worthy. The previously mentioned church of St Bartholomew in Brighton (East Sussex), by the local architect Edmund Scott, has a timber roof reaching a height of 135 feet, making this the country's loftiest church interior. The Roman Catholic church of

St Walburge in Preston (Lancashire), built in 1850–4 to the designs of J.A. Hansom, has a spire 309 feet high, the tallest in England after the cathedral spires of Salisbury and Norwich. Some Victorian Anglican parish churches, especially among those designed by J.L. Pearson such as St Augustine, Kilburn (London), are vaulted throughout. Nevertheless, large as some of these churches are, none approaches cathedral size.

Many church buildings were also created for institutions. Some of the schools and academic colleges were given an impressively large chapel, the greatest being the stupendous structure at Lancing College (West Sussex). This is neither of cathedral type nor of cathedral length, however. More relevant here was the reappearance of religious houses of the types extinguished in 1536–40. One that may be mentioned is the Franciscan friary at Gorton, near Manchester, the church of which, built in 1866–72, is of amazing height and scale (but no longer used as a church). However, like Lancing, it is not of cathedral type or dimensions. The majority of newly established monasteries, both Anglican and Roman Catholic, are of the Benedictine order like many of their medieval predecessors. Some of these have built a substantial church of 'great church' type. Nevertheless, they do not generally approach cathedral dimensions. One, however, stands out from the rest: Downside Abbey is the unique post-medieval monastic church of cathedral stature.

Churches selected

The use of a minimum length as criterion for cathedral stature, although it only indirectly addresses the question of cathedral-worthy quality and character, seems broadly valid. Observation shows that generally the longer a 'great church' is, the larger is its scale and the more splendid its architecture. Nevertheless, because it is inevitably arbitrary and rigid, the churches so identified should perhaps be regarded as a selection. As already noted, the criterion would exclude several of the cathedrals of the canon, such as Rochester and Southwell. Some other consequences of its employment may be noticed. Churches possessing an eastern chapel (usually a Lady Chapel), which in some cases may add 60 feet or more to the length, are more likely to be included. At a disadvantage, then, are those that have no such Lady Chapel (as in all Cistercian churches, which were themselves dedicated to Our Lady), or that have their Lady Chapel attached elsewhere. Also making inclusion more probable is the attachment of a porch or tower at the west end.

In consideration of this, certain deserving churches excluded by the criterion are briefly surveyed in the following paragraph. These are all medieval monastic churches. Some are no more than excavated foundations, but others remain partly or completely in use. Though not attempting to be exhaustive, most of the obvious examples are mentioned. All exceed 300 feet in length.

Barking Abbey (Essex, now London) was a very important house of Benedictine nuns; little remains, but the church and other parts have been rediscovered by excavation. William the Conqueror founded the Benedictine Battle Abbey (East Sussex) to commemorate the Battle of Hastings. Impressive monastic buildings can still be seen there, but the church is no more than foundations. The church of the Augustinian Christchurch Priory (Hampshire, now Dorset) is remarkable for its complete and unmutilated survival. It is a splendid mainly Norman and Perpendicular structure. Crowland (or Croyland) Abbey (Lincolnshire) was one of the great Benedictine monasteries of the Fenland. Its largely ruined, mostly Perpendicular nave is convincingly of cathedral quality, especially in the splendid north aisle, which alone remains in use. Evesham Abbey (Worcestershire) was another major Benedictine house. Hardly anything is visible of the church, but the superb freestanding early sixteenth-century bell-tower is still perfect. Among the many monastic ruins of Yorkshire is the Augustinian Kirkham Priory (ER); just enough stands of the church to hint at its quality. Of the church of the Augustinian priory of St Bartholomew the Great in London, the very large apsidal Norman chancel is complete, and other mutilated parts survive. It falls only 2 feet short of the criterion. The great Benedictine abbey of Malmesbury (Wiltshire) also comes close. It possessed a spire that is said to have been taller than that of Salisbury Cathedral. Most of the splendid Norman nave survives, with exceptionally fine carvings in its south porch. Merton Priory (Surrey, now London) was a major Augustinian house; many of the footings of its destroyed church have been exposed in recent years. Another major Benedictine abbey was that of Pershore (Worcestershire). Much of the very fine chancel and crossing survive. Its destroyed nave shared with Gloucester and Tewkesbury the regional Norman design having cylindrical pillars of exceptional height. Selby Abbey (Yorkshire, WR, now North Yorkshire) was another important Benedictine house. Its magnificent largely Norman and Decorated church, with three towers, is a further complete survival. Sempringham Abbey (Lincolnshire) was the greatest house of the Gilbertines (the only medieval monastic order to originate in England, with double houses containing both monks and nuns). Though completely destroyed, the church has been excavated; it was divided by a longitudinal wall to separate the sexes. One of the most famous of monastic ruins is that of the Benedictine Whitby Abbey (Yorkshire, NR, now North Yorkshire). Much remains of the mainly thirteenth-century church, in a spectacular cliff-top position.

In a second sense, too, the contents of this chapter are only a selection: inclusion of a medieval monastic church depends on what has happened to it since the dissolution. Where it has been destroyed and its physical nature is unknown, it cannot be included. Although the dimensions of most monastic churches are known, those of a substantial minority are not. These are usually cases where the church has been completely destroyed above ground, and archaeological investigations have either never taken place or have been too limited to reveal its full extent. There may also be cases where information exists but has not been found in research for this book. In one or two places, the site has been obliterated by earth moving. It seems certain that among these churches are some that were of cathedral stature.

Something can nevertheless be said about them. For this, a further examination is necessary of the subject of monastic income, previously touched on in chapter three. As a result of the *Valor Ecclesiasticus*, it is something that we know for almost every monastery, regardless of its state of physical survival. (For most, we also know the value in 1291, from the taxation valuation ordered by Pope Nicholas IV.) The annual value of a religious house is a measure of its size as an institution and, with qualifications, is usually reflected in the size and character of its church. Monastic income in 1535 ranged from under £50 for some small houses to over £1,000 in many of the great establishments. The annual values of the Benedictine abbeys of Chester, Gloucester, Peterborough and St Albans, which have all become cathedrals, were respectively £1,003, £1,430, £1,679 and £2,102. All exceed 350 feet in length; the smallest is Chester, which had the smallest income. Three other monasteries, all Augustinian, have become cathedrals, but all are smaller. Bristol had an income of £670, Southwark had £626, while Oxford, by far the smallest cathedral of the canon, had only £220. The correlation is obvious.

However, caveats must be introduced. The dimensions of monastic churches are by no means always in proportion to the incomes of their monasteries. For example, the Augustinian Bridlington Priory, with a church over 400 feet long, had an annual income of £547. Yet Cirencester Abbey, the country's wealthiest Augustinian house with an annual value of £1,051, had a church of only about 288 feet. Moreover, the nature of monastic income is a complicated subject. The correlation as described applies most clearly to the monasteries of the Benedictine order. This was the wealthiest in England, and many of its houses were of pre-Conquest foundation. Much of their endowment income was usually in the form of rental, derived from cultivated land, villages and the property of appropriated parish churches. Such rental income was stable and easily recorded by the *Valor* commissioners. Monasteries of other orders, usually founded later, seem often to have had endowments in other forms that were recorded less effectively in the *Valor*. This was most marked with Cistercian houses, usually in remote areas and endowed with large estates of land that they worked themselves, originally using lay brothers and, later, often by employing servants. There would therefore be little rental income to be recorded in 1535. Most major Cistercian abbeys (Fountains is an exception) are shown in the *Valor* with surprisingly small incomes: Hailes for example, which had a church of cathedral size, had an annual income given as £357. Another reason for low income in 1535 might be the impoverishment of a once-wealthy monastery. This could be a result of financial mismanagement, the effects of war, an over-ambitious programme of enlargement or remodelling, or the need for major reconstruction following a collapse or fire. A consequent financial crisis could oblige a house to sell some of its endowment property in order to pay off its debts.

Despite these reservations, our knowledge of the incomes of the monasteries is useful. For the majority, we know both their income and the size of their church. From this information, for monasteries with a church of unknown dimensions, their incomes enable the number that exceeded 350 feet in length to be estimated. It is suggested that there may have been a further five to ten cathedral-worthy churches.[3]

Among these unknown churches possibly of cathedral stature are two particularly tantalising examples. The Bridgettine Syon Abbey (Middlesex, now London) was founded in 1415 by Henry V; it moved to its present site in 1431 and in 1535 had an income of £1,731. Following the dissolution, the large mansion of Syon House was built on the site, and still exists today. Houses of the Bridgettine order had both nuns and a community of religious men; the order originated in 1346 in Sweden, and Syon was its only English house. This was a very prestigious abbey, and of houses containing women was by far the country's wealthiest; many of the nuns came from London society. Its church is likely to have been important, and its character may well have been very different from anything else. Archaeological investigations beginning in 2003 have found the eastern part of the church and shown that it was indeed on a very large scale; but its full extent has not yet been determined.

Also especially interesting is Ramsey Abbey (Huntingdonshire, now Cambridgeshire). This was one of the great Benedictine abbeys of the Fenland, with an income given in 1535 as £1,761. Considering its historical importance, its large income, and the scale of other Fenland abbeys, it seems likely to have had a church of cathedral stature. However, even the exact location of the church is uncertain. After the dissolution, a mansion was built on the site, which has been part of a school (now Ramsey Abbey College, a state secondary school) since 1931. Deeply buried in it at basement level is a large rectangular room, much divided by later walling, with exquisite, high-quality Early English blank arcading. Many original buttresses also remain, but all other features at higher level have been obliterated. It has been suggested that this was the Lady Chapel, standing east of one of the transepts as at Ely and Peterborough. Others, however, doubt this and propose other interpretations, such as that it was the chapter-house.[4]

Discussed in the following pages are eighteen churches, all but one of which are medieval. Several have been utterly destroyed and others are in ruin. Beverley Minster and Tewkesbury Abbey, however, stand almost complete. Both would no doubt have been promoted to cathedral rank in the nineteenth or twentieth century had not their locations been unsuitable as the centre for a new diocese. The survival of these two vast buildings serving as parish churches in country towns gives us a hint of what might have been if the dissolution of the monasteries had gone differently.

An interesting fact emerging in this chapter is that the three great medieval cities of Canterbury, Winchester and York all possessed not one but two churches of cathedral stature. This also applied, of course, to London. In all cases, the cathedral stood within the walled city, while the second major church was outside. Also in all four places, the cathedral church was the larger.

Finally, it may be of interest to compare the medieval churches of this chapter with the cathedrals of the canon. Considering the extent of the destruction of the former, a full assessment of their character is impossible, but some generalisations can be made. Monastic churches of the orders represented here (and also the greatest collegiate churches) shared very much the same architectural ideals and liturgical requirements as the cathedrals. There is essentially no difference in character between a major Benedictine, Cluniac or Augustinian monastic church and a medieval cathedral. Perhaps the only significant dissimilarity concerns the Cistercians, whose earlier churches were, as remarked previously, deliberately austere in character. They also employed only a two-storeyed elevation. In this chapter this applies to the nave and transepts of Rievaulx, as it does to those of Fountains in chapter three. A further similarity is that, as with the cathedrals, most churches discussed here began with a building constructed in the Norman period. Also like the cathedrals, the churches in this chapter usually ended up as a mixture of styles. However, there are several here that appear to have possessed stylistic uniformity, though we should remember that we may sometimes be ignorant of remodelling that affected their upper parts.

In summary, most of the ancient churches in this chapter would probably be comparable in character to the smaller or medium-sized cathedrals of the canon. However, it would appear that none could match the largest and finest cathedrals such as Durham, Lincoln or Canterbury. The seventeen medieval churches here are also fewer than the twenty-six of the complete canon. But both of these shortfalls are largely made up if we also consider those churches that, by the accidents of their histories, have already appeared in chapters two or three. They would add a further seven to those meeting our criterion for cathedral stature: Bury St Edmunds Abbey, Dunstable Priory, Fountains Abbey, Glastonbury Abbey, Guisborough Priory, Waltham Abbey and Westminster Abbey. It has previously been suggested that Bury, Glastonbury and Westminster stand alongside the very finest of the cathedrals. So we may assert that this body of churches, were they all intact, would in both number and quality be broadly the equal of today's canon of the English cathedrals.

Abingdon Abbey (Berkshire, now Oxfordshire)

This was an early foundation; the date usually given is 675. The Norman rebuilding of the church and buildings was begun under the abbot Fabritius, appointed in 1100, and the complete church was consecrated in 1239. Abingdon became one of the greatest of Benedictine abbeys, with an annual income stated in 1535 as £1,876. Nothing remains of the main buildings; most of the site is now a public garden. The plan of the church was established by excavations in 1922, and confirmed by resistivity surveys in 1998 and 2001; its outline is marked in the grass. It had a length close to 400 feet. Rebuilding in the fourteenth and fifteenth centuries is thought to have included the central tower and the nave with its two west towers. Display panels on the site, suggesting that with its similar dimensions it may have resembled Wells Cathedral, evocatively show an imaginary picture of that cathedral rising from the Abingdon lawns. Within the gardens are some architectural fragments and a standing ruin, including a pair of small-scale two-bay Perpendicular arcades. However, the ruin ('Trendell's Folly') was created in the 1870s, and most or all of its material came from elsewhere.

Two intact groups of buildings remain from the abbey. West of the church site, the main gatehouse is a beautiful late-Perpendicular structure in two storeys, light and elegant, with a depressed vault covering its interior space. One side connects to the church of St Nicholas and the other to the former hospitium of St John, which attractively flank the approach. South-east of this is a group of outer buildings. Part is known as the Long Gallery, the upper storey of which is timber framed; it was perhaps a guest house. The Chequer is a fine thirteenth-century block, its lower storey vaulted. It has a memorable feature in its large, square thirteenth-century chimney, which has openings in its gabled top in the form of little lancet triplets.

Beaulieu Abbey (Hampshire)

Established at this site in 1204 and consecrated in 1246, this was the only religious foundation of King John. It was one of the most important of Cistercian abbeys, and its church is said to have been the largest in area. Its annual income was given in 1535 as £327. The church had an aisled nave of nine bays. The north transept possessed both east and west aisles; it had four bays and then extended a further bay north in a structure known as the galilee, which may have been of full height. In the south transept, the cloister walk replaced the west aisle. The chancel had three bays and an apse, with an ambulatory and chapels which here formed a continuous ring separated by radial walls. The chapels continued outside the straight part of the chancel, giving a total of ten. Three other relatively late Cistercian foundations (Croxden, Hailes and Vale Royal) also had apsidal chancels, at a period when the straight east end was

otherwise almost universal in England. Interestingly, this represents a reversal of practice in Norman times, when apsidal east ends were much employed, but not by the Cistercians.

Beaulieu Abbey: the south wall of the nave from the chapter-house

The church is mostly only an outline of its foundations, laid out in the grass. The site was thoroughly excavated in the first years of the twentieth century. A timber cross marks the high altar, and the west end is indicated by a low modern wall with a plain arched opening in the place of the doorway. Just the walls of the south aisle and parts of the south transept stand up, though not to full height. On the cloister side, the aisle wall retains its ashlar facing and has the two entrance doorways, finely moulded and with respectively two and three orders of (missing) shafts. This wall unusually contains a series of large, plain arched recesses towards the cloister: they have stone benches and may have been used as study carrels. Internally the wall is much ruined, but sufficient traces remain of the window recesses to indicate that there were pairs of lancets. The transept still preserves the night stairs descending in its thick west wall; externally this wall contains a large rib-vaulted recess. Part of its south side stands, too, with a compartment beyond it said to have been a book room and vestry, of which part retains its vault. These perhaps stood within the transept, which at an upper level would have matched the possible length of its partner.

The cloister quadrangle remains enclosed. On its east side, the beautiful triple arches of the chapter-house, though re-erected in 1909, appear authentic. The west range is still roofed and is now partly a museum.

Most notable is the refectory in the south range, which remarkably after the dissolution became the parish church (confusingly, it is now often called the abbey church). It too is of the early thirteenth century; its exquisite details, especially the stair rising in the thickness of the wall to the refectory pulpit, probably give a good idea of the character of the monastic church.

The site is open to the public along with Palace House and the National Motor Museum. The core of the house is the great gatehouse, which was splendidly rebuilt in the early fourteenth century.

Beverley Minster (Yorkshire, ER)   *Plates 26 and 27*

This is the largest and finest of all the country's collegiate churches. Its early origins are unclear, but it may be that a monastery was established here by Bishop John of York in about 700; in 1037 he was canonised as St John of Beverley. It had become collegiate before the Conquest. Beverley's annual income in 1535, as already mentioned, was £724. It made two appearances in the documents of the Henry VIII cathedral schemes, but neither identified it as a prospective cathedral. Its college was dissolved in 1548. Unlike the other two great collegiate churches of the diocese of York, its college was not subsequently re-established, nor was it later made a cathedral. It remains in status simply a parish church.

Although with its length of 361 feet it is shorter than many cathedrals of the canon, its richness, splendour and generosity of scale are such that beside them it stands high. It has double transepts; the main transepts are of four bays and have east and west aisles, whereas the eastern transepts have just an east aisle. The nave is of eleven bays; the chancel has four bays to the eastern crossing, beyond which are two further bays, the east of which is aisleless. Construction of the present church began in about 1225 at the east end, and at first proceeded rapidly, reaching the first bay of the nave by about 1260–70. There was then a pause. Work resumed in about 1311, and the church was completed with the west front and north porch in about the beginning of the fifteenth century. The whole is wonderfully homogeneous in effect; this is partly because the nave, though Decorated, continues the main features of the earlier design without alteration. (Something comparable was done rather later at Westminster Abbey.) The whole is of beautiful cream-coloured magnesian limestone, excellently preserved and mostly very authentic. A major repair campaign was carried out in the unusual period of 1716–31, under the architect Nicholas Hawksmoor and his collaborator William Thornton. In this the north transept front, which had overhung its base by 4 feet and threatened collapse, amazingly was pushed back to the vertical using an immense timber frame. Other work included the insertion of several new windows that accurately copied the Decorated style of their neighbours. Most obviously designed by Hawksmoor is the low central tower, which has windows with ogee hood-moulds of gothick character. Until 1824, it carried an ogee dome of timber. The lack of a significant central tower is the only obvious aesthetic criticism of the minster.

The eastern limb is of uniform Early English work. Mouldings are deep, dog-tooth ornament is used, there are both stiff-leaf and moulded capitals, and much contrasting Purbeck marble is employed. The pillars are of four major and four lesser shafts, the latter keeled. A lavish feature of the triforium is that its arcading, of four arches per bay, is repeated in two planes. The clerestory has single large lancets set internally and externally in blank arcading. Vaults are quadripartite. Trefoiled blank arcading runs round the aisles. An especially lovely feature is the great double staircase set into the wall of the north chancel aisle; it is of the utmost Early English sophistication. It led to an octagonal chapter-house, which was demolished in 1550. Both transepts have an impressive portal. Some Perpendicular windows have been inserted in the aisles, and the east wall has a great Perpendicular window of nine lights. In the nave not only does the Early English system continue, but surprisingly even dog-tooth ornament is still employed. Vaults remain quadripartite. Other aspects, however, change to Decorated: in particular the windows are large and have flowing tracery. Capitals have lush foliage, and Purbeck marble is largely abandoned. There is a lavish two-storeyed Perpendicular north porch. The west front is entirely Perpendicular, with a wonderful pair of tall towers: so perfect is its design that it is sometimes considered the finest of all English twin-towered fronts.

The minster also has some outstanding contents. Probably finest is the great Percy tomb, just north of the high altar: this is a crowning achievement of the Decorated style, its lofty canopy having nodding-ogee arches and retaining undamaged much outstanding figure sculpture. The quadruple sedilia are also excellent Decorated work, in timber. There are several fine Perpendicular timber screens. Of the early sixteenth century are the splendid stalls with canopies and sixty-eight carved misericords. A remarkable relic is the Frith Stool, a pre-Conquest stone chair or throne. One fine Norman piece remains: the very large circular font of black Frosterley marble, with elegant fluting or scallops. Suspended above it is a splendid early eighteenth-century cover, one of a number of fine fittings from this period. Most of the glass of the great east window is medieval.

Bridlington Priory (Yorkshire, ER)

Founded in about 1114, the nave remains from this major Augustinian priory. It is on a majestic scale, in ten bays with twin west towers. Destroyed after the dissolution were a crossing with a central tower thought to have carried a crown spire, transepts with east aisles and a straight-ended chancel of nine bays. Most of the nave is early Decorated work of the late thirteenth century; it is of the highest sophistication, yet it has many surprising irregularities. The fifth bay from the east is narrower than the rest. The eastern limb deviated markedly to the north, causing disparities still evident in the nave's east bay. The south aisle, which externally shows many signs of the former cloister and west range, is narrower than its partner. Most remarkably, the elevations of the nave differ north from south, yet they cannot be much separated in time. Their arcades are almost identical, with pillars having four major and eight lesser shafts, moulded capitals and arches of many fine mouldings. The north side has a normal triforium, with twin two-light openings having sophisticated details, and a clerestory of four-light windows. On the south, however, the aisle roof is low-pitched and the whole height above has a clerestory of large transomed windows. Above the transom, these match the north clerestory windows; below it, they are internally doubled, giving walkways at both triforium and clerestory levels.

Roofs are of timber, but both aisles have springers for absent vaults. The north aisle wall is of high-quality Early English work, with single or paired lancet windows. There is a noble Early English north porch, though its upper storey has been partly rebuilt. The Early English work continues in the north-west tower, which has exquisite arcading and a round-arched west doorway. Higher up, its style becomes geometrical. However, the rest of the west front and the three western bays of the south side are fifteenth-century Perpendicular work: perhaps a

(below left:)
Bridlington Priory

(below right:)
Bridlington Priory,
looking west

previous south-west tower collapsed. The front is richly panelled and has a huge nine-light window and a very rich doorway with ogee hood-mould. The nave elevation here continues the Decorated scheme but in Perpendicular form, with panelled pillars.

Both west towers in medieval times rose only to the level of the nave eaves. They were lavishly completed in the 1870s under Sir George Gilbert Scott: perhaps giving some small compensation for the sixteenth-century losses. They were not made symmetrical. The north-west tower continues its late thirteenth-century style, and has a straight top. The south-west tower has become a tremendously rich and upthrusting Perpendicular-style structure, reaching a height of 150 feet.

The finest memorial is a carved Norman tomb slab of Tournai marble, thought to be that of the founder. Many fittings are good-quality Victorian work, including the stalls with carved misericords; there are also twentieth-century pieces by the well-known maker Thompson of Kilburn. Two short sections of fine late-Norman cloister arcade, recovered from excavation, were re-erected in about 1913 in the north aisle. The priory has a spacious churchyard and attractive green surroundings. To the south-west still stands the main gatehouse, known as the Bayle, now a museum.

Byland Abbey (Yorkshire, NR, now North Yorkshire)   Plate 28

After Fountains and Rievaulx, this is the third of Yorkshire's great ruined Cistercian abbeys. Its ruins are much less complete than those of the other two, but they convey a strong impression of the abbey's distinctive and beautiful quality. Its origins were in 1134, under the order of Savigny. A series of moves from place to place followed, during which in 1147 the Savignac order was absorbed into the Cistercian. Finally, in 1177, the community settled at the present site. Construction of the church, begun at that time, was completed with the west front in about 1225; there were no significant later alterations. When built it was the country's largest Cistercian church, and it is very different in character from those begun earlier. It is not austere: it is exquisite. The impression given is that it is Early English, yet other than in the west front all windows are round-arched. It is of beautiful yellow ashlar, for the most part little decayed. Workmanship is of very high quality, with beautiful rich mouldings.

The high chancel was of only three bays and straight-ended, with a range of five continuous chapels beyond the former east gable. However, the nave has twelve bays, and with the wide galilee west porch brings the total length to over 360 feet. The transepts have both east and west aisles (the former divided into chapels). All arcades have fallen, and only the west front and a fragment of the south transept stand tall. The front is the feature that most remains in the memory. Viewed externally, it has a lovely main doorway of four orders, in trefoil form; above it are three rich shafted lancets with blank arcading between, and then the lower half of a spectacular rose window, 26 feet in diameter. One of the big flanking pinnacles still points to the sky. This front is of full and perfect Early English design, with much dog-tooth. Internally, one can see that above the arcades were a triforium and clerestory, and sufficient details remain, together with excavated fragments, that their design is known accurately. This also applies to the former tracery of the rose window. The mouldings of the arcades were keeled. Still largely complete is the north aisle wall, with internal blank arcading and the shafting for rib vaults. The central spaces had timber wagon roofs. Much remains, too, of the outer walls of the transepts and chancel; in the south transept is a remarkable triple piscina, enriched with giant dog-tooth. In the chancel, the main vessel was flanked by stone screens with lovely trefoiled arcading, of which a section has been re-erected. Strikingly, large areas of the chancel and transepts retain their original tile floors: some have small, plain tiles, but many have rich and elaborate designs. There are also some tombs and matrices for brasses.

The ruins of the monastic buildings are extensive but mostly low; they too are beautiful. There is a very interesting museum, containing many large and excellently preserved architectural fragments, including capitals from the arcades. Many of the capitals have waterleaf. It also has fascinating artefacts such as an inkwell with holes for quill pens. Despite its ruination, this is one of the most lovely and evocative of monastic ruins.

Canterbury (Kent): St Augustine's Abbey

Founded in 598 in one of the first acts of Augustine's mission to evangelise England, this is an exceptionally historic place. It stands just east of the walled city. As with all monasteries founded early, it was Benedictine. Its income in 1535 was given as £1,413. A great new church was begun about 1071, and was one of England's earliest Norman churches. It was completed with its three towers perhaps in the 1120s. There were some later alterations, but it seems to have remained largely Norman until the dissolution in 1538. At the east end, a Lady Chapel was added in the fifteenth century and remodelled in the early sixteenth; curiously, its axis deviates markedly to the north. This brought the overall length to about 410 feet. The cloister stood on the north side.

Following the dissolution, the buildings on the west side of the cloister were incorporated in a new royal palace, and most of the rest was demolished. The main site is now beautifully laid out and in the care of English Heritage; it was largely excavated in the early twentieth century. It is especially interesting for its early remains. Three separate churches were built in the seventh century, approximately in axial alignment. The easternmost of these remains as a ruin, still probably partly of

the seventh century and constructed of Roman brick. Otherwise the Anglo-Saxon work is overlain by the Norman church, much of which remains as wall bases up to about 3 feet high. The Norman chancel was apsidal, with an ambulatory and originally three radiating chapels, all replicated in the crypt beneath. Much of the crypt remains and apart from its lack of vaulting is well preserved, with extensive ashlar facing in parts; the south-east radiating chapel is almost complete and still has its altar. A new vaulted roof was provided over the east chapel in 1937, allowing its use for small services. Both transepts had an apsidal east chapel. In place of the west side of the crossing, there are now exposed the considerable remains of an extraordinary rotunda constructed from about 1050 to join the two principal Anglo-Saxon churches, but perhaps never completed.

The Norman nave has eleven bays, plus another bay for the towers. On its north side towards the east, a low modern roof covers another section of excavated Anglo-Saxon work. Further west, however, six bays of the north aisle wall remain, in part to their impressive full height, the only section of the ruin to stand high. This was incorporated in the royal palace, involving alterations in brick. It is ashlar-faced and has one large window in each bay, internally shafted, with cushion capitals and a roll on the arch. The aisles were groin-vaulted. Above, there are windows at gallery level. The north-west tower stood until 1822; part of its south wall survives, showing some Perpendicular remodelling.

To the south, the English Heritage entrance building contains a fine display of artefacts. The area west of the cloister, once occupied by the palace, has buildings mainly of 1844–8 designed by William Butterfield, originally as St Augustine's College. They now belong to the King's School. Medieval parts are incorporated, and the whole is visually splendid and appropriate: an evocative sight here. Two impressive medieval gatehouses remain complete.

Downside Abbey (Somerset)

This Roman Catholic Benedictine monastery traces its origins to a foundation of 1605–7 for English and Welsh exile monks at Douai, now in northern France. This was sacked in 1793 during the French Revolution, and the community moved to England, settling at Downside in 1814. An existing house was used and new buildings and a chapel were added. In 1872, however, a plan was created by the architects A.M. Dunn and E.J. Hansom for a complete new church and monastic buildings on a larger scale. This has resulted in the most spectacular of all the churches of restored English monasticism. Though it is now the outcome of several constructional phases under different architects and in different styles, its character is consistent and entirely medieval in its inspiration, a remarkable re-creation of the Middle Ages. It is vaulted throughout and of cathedral scale and splendour.

The earliest work is by Dunn and Hansom. Surprisingly, this is the transepts, completed in 1882, each only two bays long but with both east and west aisles. They are in a lavish late thirteenth-century style, with a rose north window. There is a true crossing, but it carries no tower. Instead, the tower, of which the lower part was built at this time, is attached south of the south transept (and so stands within the cloister quadrangle, which here encompasses much of both nave and chancel). Next built and completed in 1890 was an apsidal ambulatory and part of a chevet of chapels at the east end, with a large and rich polygonal-ended Lady Chapel. The church thus stood as two unconnected sections until the chancel was built in 1901–5. This was designed by Thomas Garner, and has seven bays with a straight east wall, leaving a vaulted apsidal space between this and the earlier ambulatory. Its style is approximately Perpendicular, with no triforium but large transomed three-light clerestory windows and a quadripartite vault. The aisles are narrow, but the north side has a range of outer chapels, and at the south-east is an even more complex and extensive series of chapels, in Perpendicular style with tierceron and lierne vaults.

The nave is by Sir Giles Gilbert Scott, and was built in 1923–5. Its style is close to Decorated, with a triforium of twin two-light reticulated openings. Again, the vault is quadripartite. It has eight bays, bringing the present length of the church to about 330 feet; the west wall is temporary, however, with three further bays intended. Last

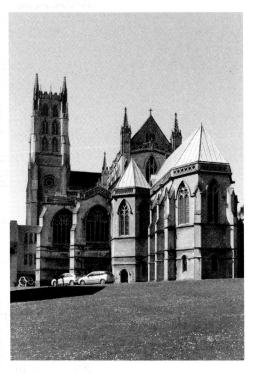

Downside Abbey

completed in 1938 was the upper part of the tower, also by Scott and
166 feet high. This is in Somerset Perpendicular style; the top three
stages each have paired two-light openings and the summit has battlements with many pinnacles.

There are many rich contents, all of medieval character. They include
memorials with recumbent effigies, some occupying tomb-recesses.
The rich canopied stalls were modelled on those of Chester Cathedral.
As well as the large attached monastic buildings, there are extensive
buildings belonging to the school.

Faversham Abbey (Kent)

This was a great royal foundation of 1147–8 by King Stephen and his
wife Matilda. Though colonised by Cluniac monks, it soon became
simply Benedictine. Construction initially proceeded rapidly. On Queen
Matilda's death in 1152, she was buried in the church; their elder son
Eustace followed in 1153, and Stephen himself in 1154. Stephen's reign
had been dominated by civil war with his cousin the Empress Matilda,
and it was to her son as Henry II that the crown went on Stephen's death.
Stephen's subsequent decline from his status as potential founder of a
dynasty was reflected in both financial and physical reductions in the scale
of his foundation. Its annual value in 1535 was only £286. Dissolution
came in 1538. Demolition followed rapidly, and in 1541 much of its stone
was being shipped to Calais for the construction of defence works.

The only survivals above ground are two large late-medieval barns and the timber-framed Arden's House, perhaps the guesthouse, with a fragment of the outer gatehouse attached to it. However, a major excavation in 1964–5 revealed a remarkably interesting story. The church was originally 361 feet long and was remarkable (especially as a Norman church) for having an eastern limb 20 feet longer than its nave. The east end was straight, but had an ambulatory with the unusual arrangement of three apsidal chapels all facing east. Uniquely, the six eastern bays of the high chancel were screened from the ritual choir to their west, and clearly formed a great royal chapel or mausoleum. Two deep pits were found which must have been the royal burial vaults; fragments were recovered probably of former monuments above. This royal chapel appears to represent a change of plan, perhaps ordered by the king after the death of his wife and son and as his own death approached. Very unusually, the cloister here abutted on the north transept rather than the nave, with the chapter-house and east range standing about 35 feet further east than the transept. A likely explanation is that during construction, in order to make the eastern limb longer, it was decided to build the transepts two bays further west than was first intended, but that by this time work on the cloister east range was too far advanced to be destroyed.

Further interesting changes took place probably in the early thirteenth century. Although foundations had been laid for the Norman west end, it may well not have been completed. A new front, probably with two towers, was constructed 18 feet further east. The central tower seems to have been reconstructed, perhaps after a collapse, and square chapels replaced the original twin apsidal east chapels of the transepts. Most remarkably, the east end was drastically reduced by the removal of the east chapels, ambulatory and two bays of the royal chapel. A straight east wall was constructed, with no ambulatory. A new west screen for the royal chapel was provided two bays further west than previously, so that it retained its original length. Even the cloister was made smaller, with new north and west ranges being constructed.

Hailes Abbey (Gloucestershire)

This Cistercian abbey was established in 1246 by Richard, Earl of Cornwall, brother of Henry III, in fulfilment of a vow made in 1242 on escaping a shipwreck. It was built remarkably quickly, being dedicated in 1251. In 1270, Richard's son Edmund gave a phial containing some drops of Christ's blood (their authenticity guaranteed by the Patriarch of Jerusalem). For this, in 1271–7 the east end was splendidly enlarged, and Hailes became a famous place of pilgrimage. The church was very large, and as a late Cistercian foundation was architecturally rich. It was vaulted throughout. The nave had eight bays; the transepts projected three bays beyond the aisles and had an east aisle divided into chapels.

Originally the chancel had four bays, with aisles; the enlargement added another bay and a polygonal apse surrounded by an ambulatory with a remarkable chevet of five polygonal chapels.

The site is now owned by the National Trust and cared for by English Heritage. It is most beautiful, but the ruins are low; the main survivals are the walls around the cloister, including that of the south aisle of the church. Otherwise the church is no more than wall bases or foundations marked in the grass: its upper form is largely conjectural. The foundations of the chevet are nevertheless impressive, and at the centre of the apse there remains something of the base of the shrine of the Holy Blood. The south aisle wall still preserves the doorway at its east end, with deeply undercut, filleted arch mouldings. West of this, no internal detail remains but the outside has five large recesses with pointed segmental arches. The triple arches of the rectangular chapter-house are fine. Some fragments remain of the cloister walks, which were rebuilt in about the late fifteenth century. Outstanding among the many relics in the excellent site museum are six large and perfect bosses from the chapter-house.

Lewes Priory (East Sussex)

This great Cluniac priory was founded in about 1081 by William de Warenne, an associate of William the Conqueror, with his wife Gundred or Gundrada. It was the most important house of the order. From about 1145, the first buildings were extensively reconstructed and a completely new church was begun. Work on the church continued into the thirteenth century, but it seems then to have remained to the end without major alteration. In 1535 the annual income was given as £920. Lewes was the first of the great monasteries to surrender, on

16 November 1537. By March 1538 demolition was in progress, as mentioned earlier, by a gang led by Giovanni Portinari; he describes features of what he was destroying, such as pillars 10 feet in diameter and 18 feet high. Further humiliation was visited on the priory in 1845 when the Brighton to Lewes railway was built, passing from south-west to north-east across the cloister and the eastern part of the church. This must have been an exceptionally splendid monastery, but it is a sad site to visit now.

Excavations began in the nineteenth century, and there were more in the 1970s. On the south-east side of the railway there remain substantial ruins of the buildings immediately east and south-east of the cloister. They are mainly Norman and have some interesting features, but they are confusing, and moreover are not normally accessible. The site of much of the church lies on the other side of the railway, in what at the time of writing is a meadow and also usually inaccessible. The church was elaborate in layout and over 430 feet long. It had a nave of eight bays plus a bay with west towers. There was a crossing and the transepts each had two apsidal east chapels. The chancel was of four aisled bays and then had a second crossing and pair of transepts, each in this case with one apsidal east chapel. Beyond was an apse and ambulatory, with five radiating chapels. Of all this, just a fragment of the south-west tower is exposed in an overgrown hollow, showing the shafts of internal blank arcading. The church was richly decorated, and fine architectural fragments can be seen both in Lewes and in the British Museum. Further north-west, a battered fragment of the gatehouse stands beside the parish church of St John the Baptist. This church started life as the hospitium of the priory, and contains some Norman work.

Remarkably, there is something more to be seen. In 1775 a splendidly decorated black marble tomb slab was found, with a long inscription identifying it as that of Gundred. It seems to be late Norman, so must date from long after her death. Moreover, during the cutting of the railway in 1845, two lead cists containing bones were found in the former chapter-house, with inscriptions identifying them as William and Gundred. The slab and cists are now in the church of St John the Baptist in a small richly Norman vaulted chapel built for them in 1847.

Reading Abbey (Berkshire)

This abbey was founded in 1121 by Henry I; he endowed it richly, and was buried before its high altar in 1136. It was consecrated in 1164 by Archbishop Thomas à Becket. As at Faversham, there was initially a Cluniac connection but it soon became Benedictine. This was one of the greatest of the abbeys; its annual income in 1535 was given as £1,938. Parliament quite often met here. Although the church was extended in the early fourteenth century by the addition of an eastern Lady Chapel, the Norman structure seems otherwise to have remained

*Reading Abbey:
the south transept,
looking south-west*

largely unaltered to the end. Dissolution came in 1539, brutally: the last abbot, refusing its voluntary surrender, was executed within the abbey precinct on a charge of treason. Much of the church seems to have stood into the seventeenth century, but it ended as a quarry: in the case of the nave, to provide stone for Civil War defences.

The church was about 450 feet in length and had an aisled nave of ten bays, probably with west towers. There was a crossing with transepts (each of which had two apsidal east chapels), an aisled chancel of four bays ending in an apse with an ambulatory, and a large straight-ended Lady Chapel. Although the site is close to the modern commercial centre of the town, much of it is green. Of the nave, virtually nothing survives: it mostly lies under a public garden, with a road along the site of the south aisle. Nor is anything to be seen of the chancel: the east end is now under the prison, of which the high brick wall runs immediately east of the ruins. Still standing are parts of the transepts and crossing. These are substantial and evocative ruins, but they are entirely of the rough flint cores of the walls; almost all of the ashlar facing with its architectural detail has been removed. Enough of the south transept remains to be impressive and to show the tremendous scale. Its west wall stands quite high and has ragged gaps for two large windows; of its apsidal east chapels the inner (which was longer than its partner) still has its two window openings arched across. Two pier bases are visible, one of which is a crossing pier. The area of the north transept is largely occupied by the Roman Catholic church of St James, with the adjacent school extending into the crossing; among these still stand a few crags of ancient masonry. Parts of the abbey church have been excavated at various times, most recently during alterations to the prison in 1971–2.

Also surviving is the shell of the east range of cloister buildings, running south from the transept, in a condition similar to that of the church. Most complete and impressive is the chapter-house, which is very large, with an apsidal east end. Standing further west is the late thirteenth-century inner gatehouse, which is intact though much restored. Important architectural fragments from the abbey can be seen in the excellent museum a short distance north-west of the site. They are mostly Norman, including carved capitals and other pieces from the cloister, of impressive quality. To see them is an especial pleasure after the ragged crags of the ruins.

Rievaulx Abbey (Yorkshire, NR, now North Yorkshire)

Monks settled here in 1132: this was the first of the famous Cistercian abbeys of northern England. Its early growth was spectacular, and under its third abbot, Aelred (1147–67), later canonised, it reportedly reached 140 monks and 500 lay brothers. The church and monastic buildings were constructed quickly. Its great days continued into the thirteenth century, when there was extensive reconstruction of both the buildings and the church. Later in that century, however, we hear of it being heavily in debt: the rebuilding probably contributed to its overreaching itself. It never recovered its previous greatness. By 1380 it had fallen to only fifteen monks and three lay brothers. Numbers subsequently recovered a little, but in the fifteenth century the dormitory and other buildings were reduced in size. Its annual income in 1535 was given as £278. Though less complete than Fountains, this is one of the most spectacular of monastic ruins, still showing impressive parts of both the church and buildings; and its setting is exquisite.

Unusually, as already remarked, the site forced the church to be laid out with the chancel aligned to almost due south. Ritual directions are used in this account. The nave, built perhaps in the 1140s, had nine bays. It has been reduced to low ruins. In accordance with early Cistercian ideals, it was austere. The surviving pillar bases are square; higher up they were chamfered. The aisles had transverse pointed tunnel vaults; there was no triforium. A low porch stands across the west end.

In contrast to the nave, the transepts and chancel stand to full height, and are spectacularly beautiful. Norman work remains in the west and end walls of the transepts, with plain round-arched windows in two tiers. The chancel is a glorious, lofty Early English work begun in about 1230; at the same time the transepts were raised in height to match and their east sides were rebuilt, with two chapels each. Construction is of beautiful creamy ashlar, contrasting with the darker stone used in the earlier work. Replacing a predecessor only two bays long, the chancel has seven aisled bays, and ends straight, bringing the total length to over 370 feet. This architecture has nothing of Cistercian austerity: it is exquisite and rich. The arcade pillars have sixteen shafts, and carry arches with very rich mouldings. There is a triforium, each bay having twin two-light openings with splendid mouldings. The openings have foiled circles, and the spandrels between them are also enriched with blank quatrefoils. The clerestory has twin lancets and a wall passage. The east wall has two tiers of three lancets. Enrichments including dog-tooth and shafts (mostly missing) are extensively employed. There were rib vaults throughout. Just one vault now remains, in a chapel of the north transept. Still standing is the east crossing arch, rising 75 feet from the ground and carrying a low section of tower. Curiously, though the main vessel stands virtually complete, the aisle walls have largely disappeared: just two narrow fragments have been left on the north side, carrying flying buttresses that were added in the fourteenth century. On the south side, by the cloister east doorway, a lovely ogee-trefoiled stoup recess remains intact.

Of the monastic buildings, the east and west ranges are low ruins, but other parts, especially the refectory, still stand as spectacular shells. Particularly remarkable was the late twelfth-century chapter-house, which had arcades and a clerestory and was apsidal with an ambulatory. There were two cloisters, in each of which a piece of the arcading has been re-erected. Much is known of the dismantling of Rievaulx under its purchaser, the Earl of Rutland, following the dissolution in 1538. Although the purpose here was primarily profit, a condition of purchase was the demolition of the east range, including the chapter-house. The Crown had also retained some materials including roofing lead, so the roofs had immediately to be stripped. Timber was also removed and sold. Though unintended, the nave collapsed during this process: four nine-hundredweight pigs of lead stamped with the crowned Tudor rose were found in it under masses of fallen masonry during clearance of the site in the 1920s.

Rievaulx Abbey: the south transept from the chancel

Tewkesbury Abbey (Gloucestershire)   Plates 29 and 30

This great Benedictine abbey had an annual income in 1535 of £1,598. It seems to have originated in the early eighth century, but in the tenth century, probably after damage in Danish raids, it became subordinate to the monastery of Cranborne (Dorset). It was re-founded by Robert Fitzhamon near the end of the eleventh century, when the relationship with Cranborne was reversed. The church was probably largely complete by its consecration in 1121. Its framework remains Norman, but equally important to the impression it now makes is the Decorated period, when the entire church was given new windows and splendid vaulting, and the chancel was almost completely rebuilt. It was dissolved in January 1540. Most of the nave had been used by the parishioners, so this might have survived, but remarkably, over two years they raised £453 to buy the rest too. It has a nave of eight bays plus a further bay at the west end, transepts originally each having an apsidal east chapel, and a chancel of two bays with a polygonal apse. The chancel has an ambulatory with a spectacular chevet of polygonal chapels. A long eastern Lady Chapel with a polygonal apse has been destroyed; its plan is marked in the grass. The Norman east chapel of the north transept was replaced in the thirteenth and fourteenth centuries by a complex of chapels, of which a section north of the transept has been lost since the dissolution. Otherwise the church is complete. It is excellently preserved.

Most of the Norman work is finely built and very perfect, but has little enrichment. Its most striking characteristic is the exceptionally tall cylindrical pillars of the nave, which are over 30 feet high (as mentioned earlier, this was a regional feature shared with Gloucester and Pershore). The pillars carry two-order arches with just a small roll on the outer order. Above is a small triforium of two twin openings per bay, and then a clerestory of small three-light Decorated windows. Inside, this clerestory is partly obscured by the vault, which is an exquisitely rich, complex lierne vault with a particularly fine series of large bosses, but seems to be set surprisingly low. Also Decorated are the aisle vaults. There is a tall two-storeyed Norman north porch with a barrel vault. It covers a very lofty doorway of four orders, with a plain tympanum. The west front is spectacular: it has a giant external arch of six orders, 65 feet high. Within it is now a Perpendicular-style window of seven lights, dating from 1686. Over the crossing is what is often considered the finest Norman tower in England. It is 148 feet high and dates perhaps from around 1150; it has three stages splendidly enriched with blank arcading and chevron. The battlements and corner pinnacles are seventeenth-century work, there having previously been a timber spire. In the south transept, the apsidal chapel has its Norman vault. Surprisingly, a second apsidal chapel is above the first, and a triforium above this. Fine lierne vaults now cover the transepts and crossing.

The eastern limb is the most exquisite part of the church. All that remains Norman is its relatively low cylindrical pillars. On the chancel side, these carry richly moulded Decorated arches and then a splendid Decorated clerestory of large five-light windows. Externally these windows have lavish enrichment including ballflower, and there are flying buttresses and an openwork parapet. Internally, they are surmounted by the most wonderful of all of the abbey's vaults, which is exceptionally complicated and has much enrichment of cusping and additional ornamental ribs. Modern colour has been applied. On the side facing the ambulatory, the chancel pillars carry lower Decorated arches. The four chapels of the chevet are spacious and splendid. Surprisingly, they are not entirely symmetrical: that to the north-east differs in plan from the rest and internally forms two smaller chapels. On the south side, there is also a sacristy, and this too is polygonal. Its door is internally reinforced by iron sheets said to be made from armour retrieved after the Battle of Tewkesbury in 1471.

The abbey is rich in fine contents. Especially notable are the memorials in the eastern limb, including several outstanding canopied tombs and three stone chantry chapels. Perhaps the most memorable of these chapels is that of Edward, Lord Despenser, who died in 1375. His chapel is fan-vaulted, and uniquely carries on its roof a canopied enclosure containing his kneeling, praying effigy, which faces towards the high altar. Remarkably, the seven windows of the chancel clerestory retain most of their original glazing, which is an outstanding survival. Some of the stalls are of the fourteenth century, with misericords. Another notable possession is what is called the 'Milton organ', originally built in the seventeenth century for Magdalen College, Oxford.

Nothing remains of the main monastic buildings. The cloister was on the south side, and its walks were rebuilt in the fifteenth century, with a fan vault: their panelling remains on the nave and transept, and one bay has been reconstructed. Until 1817 a detached bell tower survived near the north transept.

Thornton Abbey (Lincolnshire)

This Augustinian abbey was founded in 1139; it had a sixteenth-century annual value of £591. Following its dissolution in December 1539, it was maintained and (as we saw in chapter three) was re-founded in 1541 as a secular college. In October 1541 the king even spent three days here with his queen, Katherine Howard, during a progress through Lincolnshire and Yorkshire. It had a dean and four prebendaries. This new lease of life ended in dissolution in 1547, following which it was largely destroyed. What survives is now in the care of English Heritage.

The church and most of the buildings were rebuilt on a splendid scale from about 1264 to the mid-fourteenth century, beginning with the church. The remains are laid out in the grass but are generally no more than foundations or wall bases up to 3 feet high. In the church, there survive a few areas of tiles and many damaged coffin lids or ledgers, mostly with inscriptions. The nave was of eight bays, with aisles. Interestingly, the remains show that when begun, probably in about 1290, it was to have no south aisle. However, after three bays had been built in this form the plan was changed, which involved moving the whole cloister quadrangle to the south. The transepts had three bays, with an east aisle; the chancel was aisled and had seven bays, with the two east bays forming an ambulatory and chapels. In about 1400 a Lady Chapel 70 feet long was added at the east end, surprisingly only opening from the ambulatory by a doorway. Another addition was a large chapel north of the chancel.

Just one section stands up and gives an idea of the quality of the whole: part of the south transept and the immediately adjacent monastic buildings. The south wall of the transept has the fine arcade respond and in the aisle is lovely panelling of three-light geometrical tracery and a beautifully preserved piscina recess. Beyond are a narrow room retaining part of its vault, probably the parlour, and the chapter-house vestibule. Most memorable is the chapter-house itself, an octagon of which two sides remain, with exquisite detailing.

However, it is the gatehouse that has the greatest fame at Thornton. Still roofed, it is perhaps the largest and most splendid of all monastic gatehouses. Mostly built after licence to crenellate was granted in 1382, it has three storeys and makes extensive use of brick: a very early example. The walls contain numerous passages and small chambers, very like a castle. However, though defence was a factor, external display and internal comfort were equally important. Some of the large canopied niches on the external face contain medieval statuary.

Vale Royal Abbey (Cheshire)

This abbey originated in a vow made by Edward I during a storm at sea before he became king (a story resembling that of Hailes). His ambition was for it to be the greatest Cistercian house in England. It had a vexed history, however, and the huge church probably never stood complete. Initially a site was chosen at Darnhall, and monks arrived in 1274. However, owing to problems it was soon decided to move to a new site 4 miles away, named Vale Royal by the king. Construction began in 1277 on the most ambitious scale. The monks moved to temporary buildings at the site in 1281. However, mainly because of the king's wars in Wales and Scotland and the great campaign of castle building in Wales, his financial support for Vale Royal wavered and then in 1290 was withdrawn altogether. Construction ceased for ten years, and then resumed only at a slow rate. In 1330 the monks moved into the still incomplete main buildings. Matters improved when in 1353 the Black Prince resolved to complete the work begun by his great-grandfather. In 1359, a contract was signed for the construction of a great chevet at the east end. This may have been completed; but meanwhile, in 1360, a storm caused the collapse of much of the still-unfinished nave. Eventually the church was patched up to be usable, but on a reduced scale.

The annual value in 1535 was £518. After the dissolution in 1539, the church was almost immediately demolished. Its site was excavated in 1911–12 and again in 1958. The length was 421 feet. It had an aisled nave of nine bays with west towers and long transepts, each with three east chapels. The chancel had four straight bays and then the apse and ambulatory, uniquely surrounded by the extraordinary number of thirteen chapels. Alternate chapels were seven-sided; between them were smaller chapels of four sides. Nothing can be seen of all this. However, on or near the site of the high altar is a low mound with a decayed monument known as the Nun's Grave. This is mostly made up of column bases presumably from the abbey; its former centrepiece, the head of a churchyard cross, has been removed.

The west and south ranges of cloister buildings were retained at the dissolution, and are represented by the existing mansion. The west range is the main part and now seems to be mainly eighteenth-century; the south range was rebuilt in 1833. They probably incorporate some medieval walling, but only one feature is obviously visible.[5] The entrance porch on the west side covers a three-centred doorway apparently of Perpendicular work, which remarkably still contains its medieval door. The house and estate are well cared for as a wedding venue and golf course.

Wenlock Priory (Shropshire)

This beautiful ruined priory stands on the edge of the attractive small town of Much Wenlock; it is in the care of English Heritage. A monastery was first founded here in about 680: a double house for men and women. It was re-founded as a Cluniac priory by Earl Roger de Montgomery between 1079 and 1082. The Norman church then built was entirely replaced on a grand scale from the 1220s to about the 1250s. Dissolution took place in January 1540. As we have seen, Wenlock appears in the Henry VIII cathedral schemes but only as a supplier of endowments.

The church only just exceeds 350 feet; it had a nave of eight aisled bays, a crossing with transepts of four bays having east aisles, an aisled chancel of seven bays and an eastern Lady Chapel. There were major repairs to the eastern limb in the fifteenth century, including the rebuilding of the Lady Chapel; a small heptagonal sacristy was also added. Much is now represented only by the bases of walls and pillars, but three major sections stand up: part of the north transept, much ruined; the shell of the south transept, complete but for the wall of its east aisle; and the three western bays of the south side of the nave, to full height and complete with the aisle. The design is sophisticated and lovely; it was largely uniform, and there were quadripartite vaults throughout. The pillars have four major and four intermediate shafts, keeled or filleted, and moulded capitals carrying richly moulded arches. Above are a triforium of two large openings per bay and a clerestory with a wall passage. In the transepts the clerestory has one large lancet per bay, but in the nave it has two. Some capitals have stiff leaf, but there is no marble shafting, the

Wenlock Priory:
the nave and
south transept,
looking south-east

richness being mainly in the mouldings. The surviving nave bays retain their aisle vault: these bays represent an irregularity in the design, with the aisle being much lower than elsewhere to allow a vaulted room to exist above. This room (probably a chapel) survives, and has plate-tracery windows. Enough still stands to give an impression of the west front; the portal had six orders.

In an unusual position along the west side of the south transept is a tall, narrow chamber thought to have been the library; this, too, retains its vault. South of the transept is the rectangular chapter-house, which is late Norman and shows the richness and high quality characteristic of Cluniac building. The side walls have well-preserved lavish intersecting blank arcading in three tiers, with the springing of the rib vault above. Unusually, within the cloister garth there is an octagonal late-Norman lavatorium (washing place), retaining two fine carved panels (now represented by replicas). South-east of the cloister quadrangle is a second court, with the twelfth-century infirmary and late fifteenth-century prior's lodging surviving as a private house. The latter is a particularly fine example of the domestic architecture of its time.

Winchester (Hampshire): Hyde Abbey

This originated as a major church planned by King Alfred the Great but constructed after his death under his son Edward the Elder and dedicated in 903. Known as New Minster, as already mentioned it stood immediately beside Old Minster (the cathedral). It was served by secular canons, but in about 964, in the time of Dunstan, it became a Benedictine abbey. Part of its precinct was taken after the Conquest for the enlargement of the royal palace, and in 1110 it moved to a new site at Hyde on the north side of the city. The bodies of King Alfred, his wife Queen Ealhswith and their son Edward the Elder were reburied in front of the high altar of the new church. Its annual value in 1535 was £865. Following the dissolution, destruction was almost complete. The only substantial standing relic is the fifteenth-century gatehouse, much altered.

East of the gatehouse, across the Hyde Stream, the street called King Alfred Place, with Victorian houses, runs directly along the site of the nave and crossing of the church; the position of the west end is known approximately. Most of the chancel lay beyond the end of street and was excavated in 1997–9. It was apsidal with an ambulatory, flanked by two projecting chapels each also having an east apse. All this probably remained of unaltered early twelfth-century construction; a large square-ended eastern Lady Chapel was added later. The area has been made into a beautiful garden, with the plan marked on the ground and by yew hedges and holly bushes in frames. Three large ledgers indicate the lost royal burials. The finest survivals from the abbey are five superb carved Norman capitals, probably from the cloister, which are kept in the adjacent St Bartholomew's church.

York: St Mary's Abbey

Though it had antecedents, this Benedictine abbey was founded in 1088 by William II, who laid the foundation stone in 1089. It became the wealthiest monastery in the north of England, with an income given in the *Valor* as £1,650. It occupies a large

York: St Mary's Abbey, looking west

riverside precinct immediately outside the city walls, much of which is now a beautiful public park. The outlines of the Norman church are marked in the grass, but this was entirely replaced in 1270–94 by a new church on the same site. This then remained with little alteration until the dissolution in November 1539. It had a strikingly simple, large cruciform plan, without irregularities. There was an aisled nave of eight bays, a crossing with transepts of three bays with east aisles, and an aisled chancel of nine bays. The length was about 376 feet. Its design was almost uniform throughout. Could we see it complete, we might find it comparable in this uniformity to the cathedrals of Salisbury and Exeter, but stylistically somewhere between.

Most of the church is now little more than foundations and low wall bases, though in places these rise a few feet

and show good architectural detail. There has been some reassembly of fallen fragments. Still standing up are just the wall of the north nave aisle, much of the lower part of the west front, the north-west crossing pier with the arch from aisle to transept, and a little more of that transept. It is of fine cream-coloured ashlar, and was vaulted throughout. The aisle windows show remains of their fine geometrical tracery; though uniform in size, they were divided alternately into two or three lights. Rich blank arcading runs along the aisle wall and the inside of the west front; its marble shafting has gone. The springers of the arcade and triforium survive on the tower pillar, and above the arch from aisle to transept is a blank bay of triforium, with a geometrical design in four lights. Mouldings are rich and detailing is lavish; there are many decayed stiff-leaf capitals.

After the dissolution, the Abbot's House, south of the chancel, became the King's Manor, the headquarters of the Council of the North. This still stands today. Most of the rest of the site was bought by the Yorkshire Philosophical Society in 1827. The medieval remains were cleared and consolidated, and what is now the Yorkshire Museum was built on the site of the east range of the cloister buildings. Medieval parts can still be seen in the museum basement, notably the very rich late twelfth-century chapter-house entrance, partly in situ and partly reconstructed in 1987–8 from its fragments. Also displayed here are many other fine architectural pieces and a series of spectacular medieval statues, mostly from the chapter-house. Licence to crenellate was granted in 1318, and the precinct retains large sections of its fine walls, with impressive towers and two gatehouses.

Notes

1. Systems for measuring churches and other ancient buildings by area have been discussed by Francis Bond, E.S. Prior and John Harvey.
2. Strictly, a collegiate church served a parish as well its college. Where there was no parochial function, it is a collegiate chapel.
3. This estimate might be refined by a full statistical analysis.
4. See, for example, Baggs, T., 'Ramsey Abbey' in Coldstream and Draper (eds.) (1979).
5. But see Ramsay, N., 'Medieval Graffiti at Vale Royal Abbey, Cheshire' in Thacker (ed.) (2000).

GLOSSARY

Ambulatory: walkway, especially one behind the sanctuary at the east end of a church

Apse: semi-circular or part-polygonal termination to a chancel or chapel, usually facing east

Arcade: series of arches supported by pillars

Arts and Crafts: design philosophy inspired by William Morris, current in about 1880–1910

Ashlar: masonry of accurately squared blocks, with a smooth face

Baldacchino: freestanding canopy over an altar, resting on columns

Ballflower: small ornament resembling a ball within a three-petalled flower, usually applied in a series; characteristic of the Decorated period

Baluster: elegantly shaped small column, often turned

Balustrade: series of balusters, carrying a rail or coping

Baroque: florid and exuberant form of classical architecture, sometimes adopted in England in moderate form between about 1660 and 1720

Barrel vault: *see* tunnel vault

Basilica: church having a nave lit by a clerestory and flanked by lower aisles, perhaps also with transepts, apse, etc.

Bay: one of a series of repeating divisions of a building

Blank arcading: small arcade applied as ornament to a wall

Byzantine: architectural style with round arches, domes and mosaics developed from 330 in the Byzantine or eastern Roman Empire

Capital: crowning feature, often ornamented, of a pillar or shaft

Chamfer: narrow surface formed by cutting away a right-angled edge at forty-five degrees

Chancel: the principal part of the eastern limb of a church, normally containing the principal altar

Chantry: daily celebration of masses for the souls of persons specified

Chantry chapel: small chapel, often attached to or screened off inside a church, for the celebration of chantry masses

Chapter: the members of a cathedral or other religious house, considered as a body

Chapter-house: room for the meetings of the chapter; often architecturally splendid

Chevet: apsidal east end of a church with an ambulatory and radiating chapels

Chevron: bold three-dimensional zigzag ornament, characteristic of later Norman work

Choir: area, often part of the chancel, in which the services are sung

Church (with initial capital): institution uniting a particular group of Christians

Classical: architectural style derived from ancient Greek and Roman precedent

Clerestory: series of windows at an upper level, usually above an arcade

Compound pillar: one having multiple shafts, often attached

Continuous: of mouldings on an arch, continuing without capitals from responds to arch

Corinthian: classical column or pilaster having capital enriched with acanthus leaves

Credence: recess or shelf near an altar for bread and wine

Crocket: leafy knob forming a decorative feature, usually in a regular series

Crossing: in a cruciform church, the usually square space bounded by four arches at the intersection of the nave, chancel and transepts

Crown: ornate top to a tower; especially a crown spire, a small spire carried on four flying buttresses

Cupola: small classical domed circular or polygonal crowning feature

Cushion: simple rounded Norman form of capital

Cusp: point or ornamented projection between two arcs or foils

Decorated: style of architecture used approximately from 1280 to 1360

Denomination: group of Christians united by particular beliefs and practices

Diaper: surface decoration formed of a repeated square or lozenge pattern

Diocese: territory under the jurisdiction of a bishop

Dog-tooth: small cut-away ornamental pyramid, usually applied in a series; characteristic of the Early English period

Doric: classical column or pilaster with simply moulded capital

Double-chamfered: of an arch, one with two chamfered orders

Double respond: two responds back to back with an intervening thickness of masonry

Double-splayed: of a window, one widening both externally and internally from an opening midway through the wall; characteristic of Anglo-Saxon work

Easter Sepulchre: recess in the north wall of a sanctuary, usually with a tomb-chest, used in Easter celebrations

Early English: style of architecture used approximately from 1190 to 1280

Episcopal: of, relating to or governed by a bishop or bishops

Fan vault: rich late gothic form comprising large concave cones decorated with panelling

Feretory: chapel or enclosure behind a high altar to contain a shrine

Fillet: narrow raised flat band on a shaft or roll moulding, characteristic of Early English work

Flèche: slender spire, usually of timber, resting on the ridge of a roof

Fleuron: flower-like ornament, usually square; characteristic of the Perpendicular period

Flushwork: cut flint and dressed stone forming a design in a flat wall surface. Characteristic of East Anglia

Foil: lobe or arc between cusps

Four-centred: form of depressed pointed arch, mainly characteristic of the Perpendicular period

Galilee: entrance porch or chapel; narthex

Geometrical: of tracery: formed mainly of circles; characteristic of the period about 1260–1290, transitional between the Early English and Decorated styles

Giant order: arch order encompassing two or more storeys

Gothic: architectural style characterised by pointed arches. Principal subdivisions are Early English, Decorated and Perpendicular

Gothick: term for the rather superficial early gothic revival style of the eighteenth and early nineteenth centuries

Green man: human head with foliage issuing from the mouth: a motif probably of pagan origin

Groin vault: vault without ribs, effectively multiple intersecting tunnel vaults

Hammerbeam: in a roof, a horizontal bracket projecting from the wall at the base, carrying a post

Hatchment: lozenge-shaped framed canvas painted with armorial bearings of a deceased person

Herringbone: masonry with thin stones laid in successive courses sloping one way and then the other; characteristic of early Norman work

Hollow chamfer: chamfer with a concave surface

Hood-mould: projecting moulding above an opening in a wall

Hospitium: guest house attached to a monastery

Impost: horizontal slab or moulding from which an arch springs; often surmounts a capital

Ionic: classical column or pilaster with capital having two downward-curled scrolls or volutes

Jambs: the sides of a doorway or window

Keel: moulding with an obtuse point, resembling that of a ship, characteristic of Early English work

Lancet: long, narrow window with an acutely pointed arch, characteristic of the Early English period

Lantern: tower or other crowning structure with windows lighting the space below

Ledger: flat inscribed slab marking a grave

Lesene: narrow vertical strip of masonry projecting from a wall surface, characteristic of Anglo-Saxon architecture

Lierne: subsidiary vault rib of decorative purpose, unconnected with a springing point

Long-and-short: quoins or jambs in which long, narrow stones alternate with short, wide stones; characteristic of Anglo-Saxon work

Lucarne: window-like opening in a spire

Mark: two-thirds of a pound (13 shillings and 4 pence)

Metropolitan: relating to the principal see of a province or archbishopric

Minster: from *monasterium*, a monastery: came in Anglo-Saxon times to mean any important church

Misericord: hinged stall seat with a bracket beneath that can give some support to a standing occupant

Moulding: shaped outline on a feature. Mouldings vary by period: for example, deeply undercut mouldings are characteristic of the Early English style

Narthex: enclosed entrance hall of a church

Nave: main vessel of the west part of a church

Norman: Romanesque style of architecture brought to England by the Normans, prevalent approximately from 1066 to 1190

Ogee: of an arch, one with a convex curve at its top coming to an acute point; characteristic of the Decorated period

Order: of an arch or doorway, one of multiple successively recessed arches

Palladian: classical style inspired by Andrea Palladio

Parclose: screen separating a chapel from the rest of a church

Pediment: formalised low-pitched gable used in classical architecture as a decorative feature

Perpendicular: style of architecture used approximately from 1360 to the sixteenth century

Pilaster: representation of a column projecting slightly from a wall

Piscina: small basin with a drain, used for washing the vessels and hands in the mass; near an altar and often set in a recess

Plate tracery: earliest type of tracery formed by openings in a thin plate of stone in the head of a window

Portico: classical formalised open porch with columns

Porticus (singular and plural): projecting side chapel of an Anglo-Saxon church

Prebend: property assigned to support a canon of a collegiate church or secular cathedral

Prebendary: canon holding a prebend; since an Act of 1840, an honorary position

Pro-cathedral: provisional cathedral or *cathedral pro tempore*

Province: region under the jurisdiction of an archbishop, containing multiple dioceses

Pulpitum: the eastward of originally two adjacent screens separating the nave from the choir in a 'great church', containing a central doorway

Quadrant: quarter-circle

Quadripartite: vault divided by ribs into four compartments in each bay

Quatrefoil: applied to a circular opening or as a solid shape, four foils and four cusps

Quoins: dressed stones forming an angle of a building

Rere-arch: arch in the inner face of a wall above a window or doorway

Reredos: enriched screen behind an altar

Respond: half-pillar attached to a wall, supporting an arch

Reticulated: of tracery, net-like pattern with ogee shapes, characteristic of the Decorated period

Romanesque: heavy, round-arched architectural style

Rood: crucifix, often flanked by figures of St Mary and St John the Evangelist, set high at the east end of a nave

Rood screen: screen carrying the rood; in a 'great church' was the westward of two adjacent screens separating the nave from the choir, containing two doorways flanking the nave altar

Rood stair: stair, often in the thickness of a wall, for access to the rood on its screen

Royal free chapel: collegiate church under the control of the sovereign

Rustication: masonry with its joints emphasised by channels or chamfered block edges

Sacristy: chamber attached to a church for storing vessels, vestments, etc.

Sanctuary: area surrounding the principal altar

Sanctus bell: bell sounded at certain times in the mass

Scallops: decorative pattern in Norman architecture, formed of a series of truncated partial cones

Sedile (plural sedilia): seat on south side of a sanctuary; often three, for priest, deacon and sub-deacon

See: diocese, or the place within it where the cathedral is situated

Segmental: of an arch, one in which the curve represents only a small segment of a circle, because at its base it begins at an angle

Shaft: slender column, usually mainly ornamental in purpose

Slype: passage in a monastic cloister quadrangle between transept and chapter-house

Spandrel: the wall surface above the curve of an arch, often limited by surrounding straight mouldings

Spherical triangle: opening of three sides, each an arc of a circle

Stall: seat in the choir of a church for clergy or choir; normally mostly in rows facing north and south

Stiff-leaf: ornamental foliage with stiff stems and lobed leaves, characteristic of the Early English period

Stilted: semi-circular arch or apse that has a straight length before the curve begins

String-course: projecting moulded band running horizontally along a wall surface

Sunk quadrant: quadrant moulding recessed below the level at each side, characteristic of the Decorated period

Tierceron: additional rib from the springing point of a vault, contributing an appearance of richness

Tracery: pattern of ribs in the upper part of a gothic window, or sometimes decorating a surface

Transept: transverse arm of a cruciform church

Transom: horizontal member dividing a window

Trefoil: applied to a circular opening, three foils and three cusps; applied to an arch, three foils divided by two cusps

Triforium: passage opening by arches above the arcade and below the clerestory of a 'great church'

Tunnel vault: simplest type of vault, effectively a continuous arch, usually semi-circular

Tuscan: classical column or pilaster with simply moulded capital

Vault: arched ceiling of stone (or sometimes wood or plaster)

Venetian: classical window with an arched central opening flanked by smaller square-headed openings

Veranda: of a screen, one that is deep and carries a gallery

Vestibule: narthex

Volute: spiral scroll form, used in classical architecture and on Norman capitals

Wagon: of a roof, one with braces forming an arch shape

Waterleaf: leaf capital in which the tips turn inwards, characteristic of very late Norman work

SELECT BIBLIOGRAPHY

Ayers, T. and Tatton-Brown, T., (eds.) *Medieval Art, Architecture and Archaeology at Rochester* (British Archaeological Association Conference Transactions XXVIII, 2006)

Aylmer, G.E. and Tiller, J., (eds.) *Hereford Cathedral. A History* (The Hambledon Press, 2000)

Betjeman, J., (ed.) *Collins Guide to Parish Churches of England and Wales* (Collins, 1958; many subsequent editions)

Blair, J., *The Church in Anglo-Saxon Society* (Oxford University Press, 2005)

Blair, J., (ed.) *Minsters and Parish Churches: The Local Church in Transition, 950–1200* (Oxford University Committee for Archaeology, Monograph No. 17, 1988)

Blockley, K. and Bennett, P., *Canterbury Cathedral* (Canterbury's Archaeology 1992/1993. 17th Annual Report of Canterbury Archaeological Trust Ltd.)

Blockley, K., Sparks, M., and Tatton-Brown, T., *Canterbury Cathedral Nave. Archaeology, History and Architecture* (Dean and Chapter of Canterbury Cathedral and Canterbury Archaeological Trust, 1997)

Brown, S., *York Minster: An Architectural History c. 1220–1500* (English Heritage, 2003)

Butler, L. and Given-Wilson, C., *Medieval Monasteries of Great Britain* (Michael Joseph, 1979)

Campbell, J., *The Anglo-Saxon State* (Hambledon and London, 2000)

Cannon, J., *Cathedral: The English Cathedrals and the World That Made Them* (Constable, 2007)

Carrington, P., *Chester* (Batsford/English Heritage, 1994)

Clifton-Taylor, A., *The Cathedrals of England* (Thames and Hudson, 1967)

Cocke, T., *900 Years: the Restorations of Westminster Abbey* (Harvey Miller Publishers, 1995)

Coldstream, N. and Draper, P., (eds.) *Medieval Art and Architecture at Durham Cathedral* (British Archaeological Association Conference Transactions III, 1980)

Coldstream, N., and Draper, P., (eds.) *Medieval Art and Architecture at Ely Cathedral* (British Archaeological Association Conference Transactions II, 1979)

Collinson, P., Ramsay, N. and Sparks, M., (eds.) *A History of Canterbury Cathedral* (Oxford University Press, 1995)

Cook, G.H., *The English Cathedral Through the Centuries* (Phoenix House, 1957)

Coppack, G., *Abbeys and Priories* (Batsford/English Heritage, 1990)

Coppack, G., *Fountains Abbey* (Batsford/English Heritage, 1993)

Crook, J., (ed.) *Winchester Cathedral: Nine Hundred Years 1093–1993* (Phillimore, 1993)

Crossley, F.H., revised Little, B., *The English Abbey* (Batsford, 1962)

Curl, J.S., *Victorian Churches* (Batsford/English Heritage, 1995)

Deanesley, M., *The Pre-Conquest Church in England* (Adam & Charles Black, 2nd edn. 1963)

Demidowicz, G., (ed.) *Coventry's First Cathedral: The Cathedral and Priory of St Mary. Papers from the 1993 Anniversary Symposium* (Paul Watkins of Stamford, 1994)

Edwards, D.L., *The Cathedrals of Britain* (Pitkin, 1989)

Flegg, C.G., *Gathered Under Apostles. A Study of the Catholic Apostolic Church* (Clarendon Press, 1992)

Gem, R., 'The Episcopal Churches of Lindsey in the early 9th Century' in Vince, A. (ed.) *Pre-Viking Lindsey* (Lincoln Archaeological Studies, No. 1, 1993)

Gilyard-Beer, R., *Abbeys. An Introduction to the Religious Houses of England and Wales* (HMSO, 1959)

Green, L. and Bewley, D., 'Welbeck Abbey' in Marcombe, D. and Hamilton, J., (eds.) *Sanctity and Scandal: Medieval Religious Houses of Nottinghamshire* (University of Nottingham, 1998)

Hamilton Thompson, A., *The Premonstratensian Abbey of Welbeck* (Faber & Faber, 1938)

Harrison, S. and Norton, C., 'Reconstructing a lost cathedral: York Minster in the eleventh and twelfth centuries', *Ecclesiology Today* 40, July 2008

Harvey, J., *Cathedrals of England and Wales* (Batsford, 1974)

Heslop, T. A. and Sekules, V., (eds.) *Medieval Art and Architecture at Lincoln Cathedral* (British Archaeological Association Conference Transactions VIII, 1986)

Heywood, S., 'The Ruined Church at North Elmham', *Journal of the British Archaeological Association* 135, 1982

Hobbs, M., (ed.) *Chichester Cathedral: An Historical Survey* (Phillimore, 1994)

Jeffery, P., *The Collegiate Churches of England and Wales* (Robert Hale, 2004)

Jenkins, S., *England's Thousand Best Churches* (Penguin, 1999)

Johnson, P., *British Cathedrals* (Weidenfeld & Nicolson, 1980)

Keene, D., Burns, A. and Saint, A., (eds.) *St Paul's: The Cathedral Church of London 604–2004* (Yale University Press, 2004)

Kennedy, P., *The Catholic Church in England and Wales 1500–2000* (PBK Publishing, 2001)

Knowles, D. and Hadcock, R. N. *Medieval Religious Houses: England and Wales* (Longman, 2nd edn. 1971)

Knowles, D., *The Monastic Order in England* (Cambridge University Press, 2nd edn. 1963)

Knowles, D., *The Religious Orders in England. Volume III: The Tudor Age* (Cambridge University Press, 1959)

Leahy, K., *The Anglo-Saxon Kingdom of Lindsey: The Archaeology of an Anglo-Saxon Kingdom* (Tempus, 2007)

Meadows, P. and Ramsay, N., (eds.) *A History of Ely Cathedral* (The Boydell Press, 2003)

Midmer, R., *English Medieval Monasteries (1066–1540). A Summary* (Heinemann, 1979)

Morris, R., *Cathedrals and Abbeys of England and Wales: The Building Church, 600–1540* (Dent, 1979)

New, A., *A guide to the abbeys of England and Wales* (Constable, 1985)

New, A., *A guide to the cathedrals of England and Wales* (Constable, 1980)

Olson, L., and Preston-Jones, A., 'An ancient cathedral of Cornwall? Excavated remains east of St Germans Church', *Cornish Archaeology* 37–8, 1998-9

O'Sullivan, D., and Young, R., *Lindisfarne – Holy Island* (Batsford/English Heritage, 1995)

Pevsner, N. *et al.*, 'The Buildings of England' series (originally published 1951–74 by Penguin. For most counties there have now been one or more later editions.)

Pevsner, N. and Metcalf, P., *The Cathedrals of England*, 2 vols. (Viking, 1985)

Phillips, D., *Excavations at York Minster Volume II: The Cathedral of Archbishop Thomas of Bayeux* (Royal Commission on the Historical Monuments of England, 1985)

Philp, B., *Excavations at Faversham, 1965* (First research report of the Kent Archaeological Research Groups' Council, 1968)

Popper, G., (ed.) *Medieval Art and Architecture at Worcester Cathedral* (British Archaeological Association Conference Transactions I, 1978)

Rodwell, W., *Dorchester Abbey, Oxfordshire: The Archaeology and Architecture of a Cathedral, Monastery and Parish Church* (Oxbow, 2009)

Rodwell, W., *Revealing the History of the Cathedral: 4. Archaeology of the Nave Sanctuary* (Friends of Lichfield Cathedral 67th annual report, 2004)

Rodwell, W., Hawkes, J., Howe, E. and Cramp, R., 'The Lichfield Angel: A Spectacular Anglo-Saxon Painted Sculpture', *Antiquaries Journal* 88, 2008

Rodwell, W., *Wells Cathedral. Excavations and Structural Studies, 1978–93*, 2 vols, (English Heritage, 2001)

Royal Commission on the Historical Monuments of England (RCHME): *Inventories*. (1912 onwards; relatively few counties or towns are covered.)

Rylatt, M. and Mason, P., *The Archaeology of the Medieval Cathedral and Priory of St Mary, Coventry* (City Development Directorate, Coventry City Council, 2003)

Sawyer, P., *Anglo-Saxon Lincolnshire* (History of Lincolnshire Committee, 1998)

Scarisbrick, J.J. 'Henry VIII and the Dissolution of the Secular Colleges' in Cross, C., Loades, D. and
    Scarisbrick, J.J., (eds.) *Law and Government under the Tudors* (Cambridge University Press, 1988)
Sharpe, J., 'Oseney Abbey, Oxford: Archaeological Investigations, 1975–83', *Oxoniensia* 50, 1985, pp.95–130
Stocker, D., 'The Early Church in Lincolnshire' in Vince, A., (ed.) *Pre-Viking Lindsey* (Lincoln
    Archaeological Studies: No. 1, 1993)
Story, J., Bourne, J. and Buckley, R., *Leicester Abbey: Medieval History, Archaeology and Manuscript Studies*
    (Leicester Archaeological and Historical Society, 2006)
Swanton, M., (ed.) *Exeter Cathedral. A Celebration* (Dean and Chapter of Exeter, 1991)
Tatton-Brown, T., *Great Cathedrals of Britain: An Archaeological History* (BBC Books, 1989)
Tatton-Brown, T., *Lambeth Palace: A History of the Archbishops of Canterbury and their Houses* (SPCK, 2000)
Tatton-Brown, T. and Crook, J., *Abbeys and Priories of England* (New Holland Publishers, 2006)
Tatton-Brown, T. and Crook, J., *The English Cathedral* (New Holland Publishers, 2002)
Tatton-Brown, T. and Munby, J., (eds.) *The Archaeology of Cathedrals* (Oxford University Committee for
    Archaeology. Monograph No. 42, 1996)
Taylor, H.M. and Taylor, J., *Anglo-Saxon Architecture*, 3 vols (Cambridge University Press, 1965, 1965 and
    1978)
Thacker, A., (ed.) *Medieval Archaeology, Art and Architecture at Chester* (British Archaeological Association
    Conference Transactions XXII, 2000)
Victoria County History (VCH) of England (Multiple authors; no single publisher; began in 1899. For some
    counties this is complete; in some others new volumes continue to appear.)
Wade-Martins, P., *The Anglo-Saxon Dioceses in East Anglia* (East Anglian Archaeology, Report No. 9.
    Norfolk Museums Service, 1980)

INDEX

Page numbers in bold type indicate principal entries; those in italic type refer to illustrations.

Abingdon Abbey 13, **222**

Acton, Cardinal Charles 156

Adelphius, Bishop 16

Aelfgar, Earl 105

Aelred, Abbot 236

Aethelberht, King (later Saint) 32, 99

Aidan, Bishop 17, 34-5

Aldhelm, Bishop 44

Aldhun, Bishop 102

Alexander, Bishop 27, 106-7

Alfred the Great, King 114, 242

Alfriston church **199**

Altarnun church 198, **199**, *200*

Anselm, Archbishop 101

Aragon, Queen Catherine of 11, 78

archaeology 7, 14, 21-2, 33, 96, 98, 100, 112-3, 116, 219

Archer, Thomas 125-6

Arles, Council of 16

Arts and Crafts style 159, 170, 182, 197

Arundel Cathedral 154, 157, 159, **162-3**, *162, 163*, 176

Ashworth, Edward 104

Athelstan, King 40, 103, 104

Augustine, Archbishop 15-17, 99-100, 107-8, 111, 228

axially-aligned Anglo-Saxon churches 22, 35, 37, 58, 96, 101, 104-5, 112, 114-5, 228

Bailey, Arthur 124, 148-9

Bakewell, Robert 136

Baldwin, Abbot 63

Baldwin of Exeter, Archbishop 50, 56, 60-1

Bardney 37

Barking Abbey 218

Barton-upon-Humber church 97

Bath
  and Wells, diocese of 49, 51, 120
  Cathedral, now 'Abbey' 49-50, **51-3**, 56, 58, 74, 95, 97, **99**, 112, 213, *Plates 7, 8*

Battle Abbey 218

Bayeux, Archbishop Thomas of 117

Bayswater: Greek Orthodox Cathedral 187, **187-8**, *Plate 21*

Beauforest, Richard 28

Beaulieu Abbey 12, **222-4**, *223*

Becket, Archbishop Thomas à 98, 234

Bede, the Venerable 27

Bedfordshire 70, 78

Belcher, J. and J. 188

Belmont Abbey 51, **163-4**, *164*

Benson, Bishop E.W. 149-50

Bentley, J.F. 159, 184

Berkshire 39, 69-70, 73

Bernicia 29

Beverley
  Minster 71, 75, 82, 215, 220, **224-5**, *Plates 26, 27*
  RC diocese of 156-7, **164-5**

Birinus, Bishop 16, 27, 29, 113

Birmingham 15
  Cathedral 120-1, 123, **125-6**, *125*
  Greek Orthodox Cathedral 186, **188**
  RC Cathedral 156-9, 161, **165-6**, *Plate 19*

bishops 8-9, 16-20, 22, 38, 50-1, 68, 120, 155-6, 187

Bishops Tawton 20, 25

Blackburn Cathedral 120, 122, 124, **127-8**, *127*, 166

Black Prince, the 240

Blomfield, Sir Arthur 138, 192

Bloomsbury: Central Church of the Catholic Apostolic Church 154, **193-5**, *Plates 22, 23*

Blount, Gilbert 166

Blythburgh church 198

Bodley, G.F. 124, 141

Bodmin Priory 41, 71, 73, **82-3**

Bradford Cathedral 120, 122, 124, **128-9**, *128*

Bradwell-on-Sea 20-1, **22-3**, *Plate 1*

Brailes church **200-1**, *201*

Brandon, Raphael 139, 194

Brentwood Cathedral 154, 157, 159-60, **166-7**, *166, 167*

Bridlington Priory 219, **225-7**, *226*

Brighton: St Bartholomew 197, 216

Bristol 64, 156, 168
  Abbey, now Cathedral 9, 14, 64, 67, 71-3, 213, 219
  diocese of 73, 120
  St Mary Redcliffe **216**, *216*

Brixworth church 97

Buckinghamshire 70

Buckler, J.C. 101

Burges, William 89, 124

Burne-Jones, Edward 126

Burton upon Trent Abbey 75

Bury St Edmunds
  Abbey 10, 32, 53, 63, 69, 71, 74, **75-7**, 221, *Plate 10*
  Cathedral 74, 77, 120, 122-5, **129-31**, *130, Plate 16*
  St Mary 129

Butterfield, William 192, 229

Byland Abbey **227-8**, *Plate 28*

Caen: Abbey of St Étienne 101

Caistor 37

Camberwell: Greek Orthodox Cathedral **188**

Cambridge: King's College Chapel 52, 215

Camden Town: Greek Orthodox

Cathedral 187, **188-9**, *189*
Camden, William 43
Canterbury 16-19, 50, 60-1, 99, 111,
  157, 221
  Cathedral 8-10, 16, 48-9, 61, 68,
    74, 96-8, **99-101**, *100*, 117, 221
  St Augustine's Abbey **228-9**, *229*
Cardiff 163
Carlisle Cathedral 9, 19, 48, 50, 74,
  101-2, 103, 213
Caröe, W.D. 45
Carpenter, Bishop 64-5
Carpenter, R.H. 124, 142
cathedrals 6-16
  diocese with two 22, 49, 51
  monastic 13, 35, 49-51, 56, 64, 68,
    74, 163
  of the new foundation 74-5
  of the old foundation 75
  secular 13, 50-1, 56, 68, 74-5
Cathedral of Dartmoor *see*
  Widecombe-in-the-Moor church
Cathedral of Methodism *see*
  Finsbury: Wesley's Chapel
Cathedral of the Downs *see*
  Altarnun church
Cathedral of the Feldon *see* Brailes
  church
Cathedral of the Forest *see* Newland
  church
Cathedral of the Marsh (Kent) *see*
  Lydd church
Cathedral of the Marsh
  (Lincolnshire) *see*
  Theddlethorpe All Saints church
Cathedral of the Marshes (Norfolk)
  see Terrington St Clement
  church
Cathedral of the Moors *see*
  Altarnun church
Cathedral of the Peak *see* Tideswell
  church
Cathedral of Romney Marsh *see*
  Ivychurch church
Cathedral of the Weald *see*
  Cranbrook church
'cathedral synagogues' 193
Catholic Apostolic Church 154,
  188, 193-4
Catholic Emancipation Act 155
Catholic Relief Acts 155
Cedd, Bishop 15, 22-3
Cenwalh, King 113
Chad, Bishop 15, 20, 105, 118
Chatwin, J.A. 126, *188*
Chelmsford Cathedral 120, 122-4,
  131-2, *132*
Chester 15
  Abbey, now Cathedral 9, 53, 67,
    71-3, 80, 219, 231

St John the Baptist 13, 49, **53-5**,
  54, 55, 56, 106
Chester-le-Street church 18-19,
  23-5, *24*, 35, 102
Chetham's School 142
Chichester Cathedral 9, 43, 49, 86,
  97, **102**
Chiswick: Russian Orthodox
  Cathedral **189-90**, *189*
Christchurch Priory 218
Christian, Ewan 191
Christ the King, Gordon Square *see*
  Bloomsbury: Central Church of
  the Catholic Apostolic Church
Churches Conservation Trust 43,
  208
Church Norton 43
Church of England 13-14, 22, 119,
  153-6, 186, 216
Cirencester Abbey 219
Clifton Cathedral 154, 156-7, 160,
  168-9, *168*
Clinton, Bishop Roger de 56
Clutton, Henry 160, 183
Cnut, King 63, 114
Colchester
  Abbey 13, 71-2, **77**
  Priory 77
colleges 10-11, 13, 19, 50, 52, 68,
  70-2, 74-5, 121, 214, 221, 224
  academic 13, 215, 217
  chantry 13
  dissolution of 13, 75
collegiate churches *see* colleges
Colthurst, Edmund 52
Comper, Sir Ninian 124, 136, 149
Comper, Sebastian 136
Conrad, Prior 101
Constantine I, Emperor 16
Cornwall 16, 18, 25, 40-1, 66, 69, 71,
  74, 82, 104, 119, 149
Cornwall, Richard, Earl of 232
Coulby Newham *see*
  Middlesbrough
Coventry
  and Lichfield, diocese of 49, 53,
    56, 66, 73
  Cathedral of St Michael 7, 15,
    120-1, 124, **132-5**, 154, 160, 215,
    Plates 17, 18
  Cathedral of St Mary 49-50, 53,
    56-8, *57*, 74, 95, 97, **102**, 106
Cranborne Priory 237
Cranbrook church **202-3**, *202*
Cranmer, Archbishop 78
Crawley, John 179
Crayke 24
Craze, R.B. 182-3
Crediton church 18-20, 22, **25-6**, *25*,
  41, 44, 104, *Plate 2*

Cromwell, Thomas 67
Crowland Abbey 218
Croxden Abbey 222
Cuthbert, Bishop 24, 35, 102-3
Cyneberht, Bishop 37

Dance, George the Younger 195
Deerhurst church 97
Derby Cathedral 121-4, **135-6**, *135*, 161
Derbyshire 71-2
Despencer, Bishop 39
Despenser, Edward, Lord 239
de Warenne, William and Gundred
  233-4
Diuma, Bishop 20
Dommoc 16-18, 20-1, **26-7**, 38, 46
Dorchester Abbey 13, 16, 18-19,
  21-2, **27-9**, 33, 37, 49, 106, 113
  Plates 3, 4
Dorset 44, 66, 73, 120
Downpatrick Cathedral 49
Downside Abbey 217, **230-1**, *230,
  231*
Drury, Michael 147
Dugdale, Sir William 107
Dunn, A.M. 158, 175, 230
Dunstable Priory 13, 69-70, 74,
  77-80, *78*, 221
Dunstan, Archbishop 15, 49, 91,
  115, 242
Dunwich 22, 27, 46
Durham 18-19, 24, 35, 120
  Cathedral 9-10, 35-6, 50, 74, 81,
    89, 96-7, **102-3**, 117, 221
Dykes Bower, S.E. 124, 130-1

Eadmer 99
Ealhswith, Queen 243
East Anglia 16, 18, 20-1, 26-7, 32, 38,
  45-6, 53, 75-6, 110, 198
  RC diocese of 157, 169, 176
Eastern Orthodox Church *see*
  Orthodox Churches
Eastwood, J.H. 170
Eborius, Bishop 16
Ecclesiastical Titles Act 156
Edgar, King 60
Edinburgh: St Mary's Cathedral 124
Edmund, King 26, 32, 75
Edward the Confessor, King 91, 93
Edward the Elder, King 242-3
Edward I, King 240
Edward III, King 87
Edward VI, King 13, 74
Edwin, King 116
Elizabeth I, Queen 52, 74, 91, 216
Elmham 17-18, 20-2, 26-7, 32, 39,
  49, 63, 156
  North 20-1, **38-9**, *38*, 46, 64
  South 20-1, 39, **45-6**

Elstow Abbey 69-70, 78-9
Ely Cathedral 9, 48, 50, 74, 76, **103**, 142, 213, 220
English Heritage 38, 62, 76-7, 80, 170, 228-9, 233, 239, 241
Epstein, Jacob 135
Erkenwald, Bishop 23, 107, 109
Ernulf, Prior 101
Essex 22-3, 32, 70, 72, 77, 120
Etheldreda, Saint 103
Everton 160, 171
Evesham Abbey 218
Exeter Cathedral 9, 18, 25, 48, 95-7, **104**, 151, 213, 215, 243

Faversham Abbey 12, **231-2**, 234
Felix, Bishop 15-16, 21, 26
Felixstowe 27
Fenton, Peter 174
Finsbury: Wesley's Chapel **195-6**, *195*
Fitzhamon, Robert 237
Forsyth, W.A. 124, 127
Fountains Abbey 13, 71-2, 74, **80-1**, 91, 219, 221, 227, 236, *Plates 11, 12*
Free Churches *see* Nonconformist Churches
French architecture 92, 109, 149-50, 154, 162, 176, 185
French Revolution 155, 193, 230
Friaries 64, 214, 217
Frith Stool 31, *31*, 225

Gardiner, Bishop Stephen 68, 94
Garner, Thomas 230
Germanus, Saint 40
Gibberd, Sir Frederick 159, 173
Gibbs, James 136
Giffard, Bishop Godfrey 64-5
Gill, Eric 185
Gisborough Priory *see* Guisborough Priory
Glastonbury Abbey 10, 49, 51, **58-60**, *59*, 221, *Plate 9*
Gloucester Abbey, now Cathedral 9, 60, 67, 69, 71, 73, 120, 218-9, 238
Gloucestershire 71
Godiva, Lady 56
Golders Green: Greek Orthodox Cathedral **190**
Goldie, George 159, 165, 169, 173, 185
Goodridge, H.E. 168
Gorton: Franciscan friary 217
Grandisson, Bishop John de 215
Great Paxton church 97
Greenslade, S.K. 170
Gregory I, Pope 16-19, 99, 108
'great church' 14, 53, 151, 197, 213-7
Great Yarmouth: St Nicholas 215
Guildford Cathedral 120-1, 123-4, 129, **136-8**, *137*, 154

Guisborough Priory 71-2, 74, **81-2**, 221, *Plate 13*
Gundulf, Bishop 111
Guthred, King 24

Hackington 50, **60-1**
Hadfield, M.E. 158, 180-1
Hailes Abbey 217, 222, **232-3**, *233*, 240
Hallam, diocese of 157, 181
Hanley: Bethesda Methodist Chapel 198
Hansom, C.F. 158, 169, 179
Hansom, E.J. 158, 175, 230
Hansom, J.A. 158, 162, 164, 179, 217
Hansom, J.S. 158, 179
Hardman & Co. 163, 175, 182
Harold, King 88
Hawksmoor, Nicholas 92, 224
Heckington church 181
Hedda, Bishop 105
Hedon church 197
Henry I, King 77, 101, 234
Henry II, King 60-1, 88, 231
Henry III, King 92, 232
Henry V, King 220
Henry VII, King 92
Henry VIII, King 9, 11-13, 15, 48, 53, 66-8, 71, 74-5, 84-5, 90, 95, 119-21, 213, 224, 241
Herbert, A.S. 175
Hereford 17-18, 120
    Cathedral 9, 96, **105**, 213
Hereman, Bishop 39, 62
Herfast, Bishop 38, 63
Hertfordshire 70
Hexham 17-18
    Priory 14, 19, 21, **29-31**, *30*, *31*, 110, 214
    RC diocese of 156-7, 174
Hollar, Wenceslaus 85, 107-9
Holy Island *see* Lindisfarne
Honorius, Archbishop 16, 26
Honorius I, Pope 18, 27
Horncastle 37
Howard, Henry Fitzalan *see* Norfolk, fifteenth Duke of
Howard, Queen Katherine 239
Howden church 180
Hoxne 18-20, 22, **32-3**, 38
Hugh of Avalon, Bishop 106
Hull: Holy Trinity 215
Huntingdonshire 70, 73

iconostasis 186, 188, 190
Ine, King 58
Inwood, William and Henry 188
Ipswich 66, **169**
Ireland 16, 49, 124, 155
Irvingites *see* Catholic Apostolic Church
Ivychurch church **203-4**, *203*

Jocelyn, Bishop 58
John, King 222
John of York, Bishop 224
Johnson, R.J. 144
Johnson, Revd. J.N. 192
Jones, Inigo 109

Kensington
    Our Lady of Victories 185
    Russian Orthodox Cathedral **190**, *191*
Kentish Town: Greek Orthodox Cathedral **191**
Kilburn: St Augustine 217
King, Bishop Oliver 51-2
King, Laurence 124, 127
King's Weigh House Chapel *see* Mayfair: Ukrainian Catholic Cathedral
Kirby, Edmund 182
Kirkham Priory 218
Knights Hospitaller 215
Knights Templar 215

Lambeth 50, **61**
Lancashire 71, 80
Lancaster Cathedral 157, 159, 161, **169-70**, *170*
Lancing College 217
Lanfranc, Archbishop 48-50, 53, 101, 117
Launceston Priory 71, 73, **82-3**
Leeds Cathedral 157, 159, 164, **170-1**, *171*
Lee, J.T. 190
Leicester 15, 17-18, 22, 27, 120, 186
    Abbey 14, 70, **83-4**
    Anglo-Saxon Cathedral 19-20, **33-4**, *34*
    Cathedral 121, **139**, *139*
    Newarke College 83
Leicestershire 70
Leland, John 62
Leofric, Bishop 25, 104
Leofric of Mercia, Earl 53, 56
Lewes, Bishop Robert of 51, 112
Lewes Priory 12, **233-4**
Lichfield Cathedral 9, 96, **105-6**
Limesey, Robert de 56
Lincoln 22, 27, 37, 49, 66, 73
    Cathedral 9-10, 37, 97, **106-7**, 108, 180, 213, 221
Lindisfarne 17-19, 22-3, 29, **34-7**, *36*, 102, 156
    Gospels 24, 35
Lindsey 17-18, 20, 22, **37**, 106
Liturgical Movement 123, 160
Liverpool 7, 156-7
    Cathedral 10, 121, 123-4, 133, **140-1**, *141*, 154

RC Cathedral 154, 157, 159-60, 166, **171-3**, *172*, *Plate 20*
London 15-18, 22-3, 32, 73, 91, 120, 186, 221
  Council of 49, 62
  Franciscan Friary 214
  Priory of St Bartholomew the Great 218
  St Paul's Cathedral 6, 9-10, 14, 48, 59, 95-8, **107-10**, *108*, *109*, 126, 167, 213
Losinga, Bishop Herbert de 32, 38, 46, 63
Louth 37
Lower Brailes *see* Brailes
Ludlow church 198
Lumley Warriors 25
Lutyens, Sir Edwin 159-60, 172-3
Lydd church 203, **204-5**, *204*
Lyfing, Bishop 25, 41

Malmesbury Abbey 218
Malmesbury, William of 28, 114
Manchester 120, 156, 180
  Cathedral 121, 123-4, 134, **142-3**, *142*
Mary, Queen 74, 89, 91, 93, 119, 142
Mathew, Hugh 131
Matilda, Empress 56, 107, 231
Maufe, Sir Edward 124, 128-9, 136
Mayfair: Ukrainian Catholic Cathedral **196**
Mellitus, Bishop 22, 107
Mercia 17-18, 20, 27, 37, 53, 105
Merton Priory 218
Methodists 153, 192, 195, 198
Middlesbrough Cathedral 154, 157, 159-60, 164, **173-4**, *174*
Middlesex 70, 73, 91
monasteries 9-11, 13, 18-19, 49-52, 56, 66-70, 74-5, 155, 163, 214, 217-20, 233
  Augustinian 11, 13, 50, 214, 219, 221
  Benedictine 11, 13, 49-50, 214, 217, 219, 221, 228
  Bridgettine 220
  Cistercian 11, 80-1, 92, 214, 217, 219, 221-3, 236
  Cluniac 11, 214, 221, 242
  dissolution of 11-13, 49, 66-7, 72-3, 75, 98, 221
  Gilbertine 218
  Premonstratensian 11, 90
  Savignac 227
Monreale Cathedral 49
Montgomery, Earl Roger de 86, 241
Moore, Temple 31
Morris & Co. 126, 129
Much Wenlock Priory *see* Wenlock Priory

National Trust 80, 199, 210, 233
Newark church 180
Newcastle upon Tyne
  Cathedral 119-21, **144-5**, *144*
  RC Cathedral 156-8, **174-5**, *175*
Newland church **205-6**, *206*
Newnham Priory 69-70, 78-9
Newton, John 166-7
Nicholas IV, Pope 219
Nicholson, Sir Charles 124, 132, 139, 145, 147-8
Nonconformist Churches 153, 195
Norfolk, fifteenth Duke of 158, 162, 176, 178
Norham 35
Norman Conquest 10, 19, 48, 50, 95
Northampton Cathedral 156-7, 159, **175**, *176*
Northamptonshire 70, 73
Northumbria 16-17, 23-4, 29, 34-5
Norwich
  Cathedral 9, 32, 39, 50-1, 63, 74, 76, 97, **110**, 134, 213, 217
  RC Cathedral 154, 157, 159, **176-8**, *177*
Nottingham Cathedral 156, 158, **178**, *178*
Nottinghamshire 71-2

Offa, King 18, 106
Old Sarum Cathedral 39, 44, 49, *45*, **62-3**, *62*, 112
Orthodox Churches 15, 153, **186-7**
Osney Abbey *see* Oxford
Oswald, Bishop 115
Oswald, King 34
Othona *see* Bradwell-on-Sea
Ottery St Mary church 215
Oxford 73, 74, 84
  Cardinal College 66, 84, 86
  Christ Church 85
  Osney Abbey 67, 69-70, 73-5, **84-6**, *85*
  Priory of St Frideswide, now Cathedral 9, 73, 84-5, 219
Oxfordshire 69-70, 73

Paley, E.G. 159, 169
Palmer, John 127
Patrington church 197
Paulinus, Bishop 18, 34, 116
Pearson, J.L. 87-8, 123, 139, 149, 151-2, 217
Pearson, FL 149, 152
Pennethorne, James 191
Percy Thomas Partnership 168
Pershore Abbey 218, 238
Peterborough Abbey, now Cathedral 9, 67, 69-70, 73, 89, 219-20
Pilgrimage of Grace, the 12, 67

Piper, John 134, 173
Pius IX, Pope 156
Plymouth Cathedral 156, **179**
Plympton Priory 71, 83
Pont l'Evêque, Archbishop Roger of 117
Portinari, Giovanni 12, 234
Portsmouth 15
  Cathedral 120, 122-4, **145-7**, *146*
  RC Cathedral 157-8, 161, **179-80**, *179*
Pountney Smith, S. 87
Preston: St Walburge 217
pro-cathedrals 20, 51, 121, 138, 140, 145, 157, 163-5, 168-9, 172, 179, 182, 185
province 8, 17-19, 157
Pugin, A.W.N. 158-61, 165-6, 171, 174-5, 178, 182-3
Pugin, E.W. 158, 160, 163, 171, 175, 182
Pugin, P.P. 181

Ramsbury church 18-19, 22, **39-40**, *40*, 44, 62
Ramsey Abbey 220
Reading Abbey **234-6**, *235*
recusants 155
Regent's Park: Antiochan Orthodox Cathedral **191-2**
Regent's Park Mosque 160
Remigius, Bishop 27-8, 106
Repton church 20, 22
Restitutus, Bishop 16
Reyntiens, Patrick 173
Richard I, King 58, 61
Richard III, King 139
Richmond, Archdeaconry of 71, 80
Rievaulx Abbey 14, 221, 227, **236-7**, *237*
Ripon 102, 119-20
  Cathedral 10, 21, 30, 75, 95-6, **110-1**, 120-1, 215
Rochester 16-17, 120
  Cathedral 9, 50, 68-9, 74, 96-7, **111**, 213, 217
Roman Catholic Church 7, 14-15, 20, 51, 123, 153-4, **154-61**, 216-7
Rome: Basilica of St Peter 140, 172
Rope, Margaret 182
Rufus *see* William II, King
Rutland 70, 73
Russell, Lord John 156

St Albans Abbey, now Cathedral 10, 13, 69-70, 74, 120-1, 213, 219
St Edmundsbury *see* Bury St Edmunds
St Germans church 19, 22, 25, **40-2**, *41*, 71, 82-3

St Peter-on-the-Wall *see* Bradwell-on-Sea

Salford Cathedral 156, 158-9, **180-1**, *181*

Salisbury Cathedral 6, 8-9, 62-3, 97, **111-2**, 120, 134, 213, 217-8, 243

Sampson, Bishop 68

Savaric, Bishop 51, 58

Scotland 12, 16-17, 73, 75, 124, 240

Scott, Adrian Gilbert 172

Scott, Edmund 216

Scott, Sir George Gilbert 124, 130, 227

Scott, George Gilbert the Younger 159, 176

Scott, Sir Giles Gilbert 124, 133, 140-1, 170, 230-1

Scott, John Oldrid 124, 176-7, 187

Second Vatican Council *see* Vatican II

Selby Abbey 180, 218

Selsey 17, 19, **42-3**, *43*, 49, 102

Sempringham Abbey 218

Sheffield
 Cathedral 120, 122-4, **147-9**, *148*
 RC Cathedral 157-9, **181-2**

Shenouda III, Pope 192

Sherborne 17-18, 22, 25, 39, 62
 Abbey 13, 19, 21, **44-5**, 49, 96, 112, 214, *Plates 5, 6*

Shrewsbury 15
 Abbey 13-14, 71-4, **86-8**, *87*
 Cathedral 156-8, **182**
 sixteenth Earl of 158, 182

Shropshire 71, 93

Sidnacester 37

Simeon, Abbot 103

Soham 20-1

Sonning 39

Southwark
 Priory, now Cathedral 10, 120-1, 219
 RC Cathedral 156-8, 160, **182-3**, *183*

Southwell Minster (Cathedral) 10, 71-2, 74-5, 120-1, 215, 217

Spence, Sir Basil 124, 133

Staffordshire 71, 93

Stephen, King 56, 107, 231

Stevenage: Coptic Orthodox Cathedral **192**

Stigand, Archbishop 48

Stigand, Bishop 43, 102

Stow church 37

Street, G.E. 124, 139

Suffolk 27, 32-33, 39, 46, 66, 71, 74, 119, 129

suffragan bishopric 22, 27

suffragan diocese 156, 196

Supremacy, Royal 11-12, 67-8

Sutherland, Graham 134

Swainston, Frank 174

Swithun, Bishop 114

Syddensis civitas 37

synagogues 193

Syon Abbey 220

Talbot, John *see* Shrewsbury, sixteenth Earl of

Teddington: St Alban 198

Terrington St Clement church **207**, *Plates 24, 25*

Terry, Quinlan 167

Tewkesbury Abbey 13, 218, 220, **237-9**, *Plates 29, 30*

Thame Abbey 69-70, 84, 86

Theddlethorpe All Saints church **208**

Theodore of Tarsus, Archbishop 17, 105, 110, 115

Theodred, Bishop 32

Thetford 32, 38, 49, **63-4**, 75

Thornton Abbey 75, **239-40**

Thornton, William 224

Thurgarton Priory 71, 90-1

Tideswell church 198, **208-10**, *209*

Tijou, Jean 126

Trinitarians 215

Truro Cathedral 74, 121, 123-4, **149-51**, *150*, 153

Uffington church 198

Ullathorne, Bishop William 156

Vale Royal Abbey 13, 222, **240-1**

Valor Ecclesiasticus 11, 68, 219

Vatican II 160, 167-8, 172

Vaughan, Cardinal Herbert 51, 184

Vertue, Robert and William 52

Victoria, Queen 161

Villula, Bishop John de 51, 99

Vitalian, Pope 17

Vulliamy, L. 190

Wakefield Cathedral 120, 122-3, **151-2**, *152*

Wales 16, 156-7, 163, 240

Walpole St Peter church 207

Walter, Archbishop Hubert 50, 61

Waltham Abbey 11, 70-4, 77, **88-90**, *89, 90*, 221

Walton Castle *see* Felixstowe

Warelwast, Bishop 25, 104

Wastell, John 129

Waterhouse, Alfred 196

Weightman, J.G. 158

Welbeck Abbey 13, 71-2, **90-1**

Wells 18, 44, 120
 Cathedral 9-10, 37, 49, 51, 58, 96-7, **112-3**

Wenlock Priory 71-2, 86, **241-2**, *242*

Wesley, John 195-6

Wessex 18, 27, 40, 44, 113-4

Westbury-on-Trym church **64-5**, *65*

Westminster 50, 61, 119
 Abbey 10, 52, 58, 67, 69-70, 73-4, **91-3**, 221, 224, *Plates 14, 15*
 Cathedral 51, 154, 156-7, 159-60, **183-5**, *184, 185*

Whalley Abbey 128

Whitby Abbey 218

Whitby, Synod of 17, 23

Whitchurch Canonicorum church 198

White, William 206

Whiting, Abbot 58

Whithorn 24

Widecombe-in-the-Moor church **210-11**, *210*

Wilfrid, Bishop 15, 17, 29-31, 42, 110-11, 116

William I (the Conqueror), King 48, 91, 218

William II, King 101, 243

Willis, Professor Robert 98

Wilton 39

Winchester 16-17, 19, 44, 120, 221
 Cathedral 9, 21, 27, 44, 49-50, 74, 96, 98, **113-5**, *113*, 212-3
 Hyde Abbey 114, **242-3**
 New Minster *see* Hyde Abbey
 Old Minster *see* Cathedral

Windsor, Council of 49

Wiseman, Cardinal Nicholas 156

Wolsey, Cardinal Thomas 66, 83-4, 119

Wood Green: Greek Orthodox Cathedral **192**

Worcester 17-18, 41
 Cathedral 9, 49, 65, 74, 96-7, **115**

Worksop Priory 71, 90-1

Worth church 97

Wren, Sir Christopher 110, 160, 167

Wulfstan, Bishop 15, 115

York 16-19, 24, 29, 34-5, 42, 66, 72-3, 110, 120, 157, 164-5, 215, 218, 221, 224, 227
 Minster (Cathedral) 8-10, 96-8, **116-17**, *116*, 212-3
 St George 164
 St Mary's Abbey **243-4**, *243*
 St Wilfrid 165

Yorkshire 151, 218, 227, 244